Beginning Unreal Game Development

Foundation for Simple to Complex Games Using Unreal Engine 4

David Nixon

Apress®

Beginning Unreal Game Development: Foundation for Simple to Complex Games Using Unreal Engine 4

David Nixon
West Palm Beach, FL, USA

ISBN-13 (pbk): 978-1-4842-5638-1
https://doi.org/10.1007/978-1-4842-5639-8

ISBN-13 (electronic): 978-1-4842-5639-8

Managing Director, Apress Media LLC: Welmoed Spahr
Acquisitions Editor: Spandana Chatterjee
Development Editor: Rita Fernando
Coordinating Editor: Divya Modi

Cover designed by eStudioCalamar

Cover image designed by Freepik (www.freepik.com)

Distributed to the book trade worldwide by Springer Science+Business Media New York, 1 New York Plaza, New York, NY 10004. Phone 1-800-SPRINGER, fax (201) 348-4505, e-mail orders-ny@springer-sbm.com, or visit www.springeronline.com. Apress Media, LLC is a California LLC and the sole member (owner) is Springer Science + Business Media Finance Inc (SSBM Finance Inc). SSBM Finance Inc is a **Delaware** corporation.

For information on translations, please e-mail rights@apress.com, or visit http://www.apress.com/rights-permissions.

Apress titles may be purchased in bulk for academic, corporate, or promotional use. eBook versions and licenses are also available for most titles. For more information, reference our Print and eBook Bulk Sales web page at http://www.apress.com/bulk-sales.

Any source code or other supplementary material referenced by the author in this book is available to readers on GitHub via the book's product page, located at www.apress.com/978-1-4842-5638-1. For more detailed information, please visit http://www.apress.com/source-code.

Printed on acid-free paper

To Gi, for your love and patience during long nights of writing.

Table of Contents

About the Author xvii

About the Technical Reviewers xix

Acknowledgments xxi

Introduction xxiii

Chapter 1: Getting Started 1

Overview 1

Licensing...2

Registration..2

Download and Installation...4

Installing the C++ Source Code 5

Summary...6

Chapter 2: Basic Concepts 7

Projects...7

Unreal Project Browser..7

Levels..11

Creating, Opening, and Saving Levels 12

Playing a Level 14

Actors..14

Static Meshes...15

Geometry Brushes 16

Lights...18

Particle Systems..18

Components 19

Summary...19

Chapter 3: The Level Editor **21**

  Level Editor Overview 21

    Unreal Engine vs. the Unreal Editor 21

    Types of Editors 21

    Panels of the Level Editor 22

    Customizing the Interface 27

  Place Mode 28

    Place Mode Tabs 29

  Navigating Within the Viewport 30

    Mouse Navigation 30

    WASD Navigation 30

    Focusing 31

    Maya Navigation 31

    Camera Speed 32

  Moving, Rotating, and Scaling Actors 32

    Move Tool 33

    Rotate Tool 35

    Scale Tool 35

    World Space vs. Local Space 36

  Snapping 38

    End Key 38

    Surface Snapping 38

    Grid Snapping 41

    Rotation Snapping 42

    Scale Snapping 43

  Different Ways to View Your Level 43

    Immersive Mode 43

    View Modes 43

    Orthographic Views 47

    Show Flags 49

Game View 50

Piloting Actors Within the Viewport 50

Content Browser 51

Sources Panel and Asset Window 51

Back Button and Forward Button 52

Breadcrumbs 53

Add New Button 53

Import Button 54

Save All Button 54

View Options 55

Colored Folders 60

Content Browser Windows 60

Details Panel 61

Property Matrix 62

View Options 63

Transform Category 64

World Outliner 66

World Outliner Data 67

Grouping Actors 68

Organizing and Finding Actors 70

Summary 71

Chapter 4: Actors 73

Static Meshes 73

Replacing the Mesh of a Static Mesh Actor 74

Physics 75

Brushes 76

Brushes vs. Meshes 76

Brush Settings 78

Stair Brushes 80

Materials 84

    Apply Material to All Surfaces 85

    Surface Materials Category 85

    Elements 86

    Textures 86

    Surface Properties Category 87

Lights 88

    Overview of Light Types 89

    Building the Lighting 90

    Mobility 90

    Directional Light 91

    Point Light 95

    Spot Light 97

    Rect Light 98

    Sky Light 99

Fog 100

    Atmospheric Fog 100

    Exponential Height Fog 103

Player Start Actor 104

Components 106

    Adding Components 106

    Component Structure 107

    Rotating Movement Component 108

Volumes 109

    Blocking Volumes 110

    Trigger Volumes 110

    Pain Causing Volumes 111

    Kill ZVolume 112

    Physics Volume 112

Summary 113

Chapter 5: Blueprints..**115**

Introduction to Blueprints 115

    Level Blueprint vs. Blueprint Classes 115

    Level Blueprint Editor 116

    Event Graph 116

    Nodes 117

    Pins and Wires 118

    Adding Nodes 119

    Compiling 120

    Simple Blueprint Example 120

Variables 121

    Data Types 121

    Get Node 124

    Set Node 124

    Default Value 125

    Updated Blueprint Example 125

    Variable Properties 126

Arrays... 128

    ForEachLoop Node... 128

    Add Node 129

    Insert Node 130

    Set Array Element Node.. 130

    Removing Elements from an Array 131

    Retrieving Elements from an Array.. 132

    Contains Item Node 132

    Find Item Node 133

    Length Node and Last Index Node.. 133

Functions 134

    Function I/O 135

    Function Example 136

    Advantages of Using Functions 137

Function Properties 137

Local Variables 139

Flow Control 139

Branch Node... 139

Do N Node... 140

DoOnce Node.. 140

DoOnce MultiInput Node... 141

FlipFlop Node.. 142

ForLoop Node 142

ForLoopWithBreak Node... 143

Gate Node.. 143

MultiGate Node.. 144

Retriggerable Delay Node... 145

Sequence Node 145

WhileLoop Node... 146

Switches... 146

Accessing Actors Within Blueprints 147

Getting a Reference to an Actor.. 148

Creating an Event from an Actor... 149

Blueprint Classes 151

Blueprint Class Example... 152

Instances... 153

Instance Editable Variables 153

Timelines... 155

Tracks and Keys.. 155

Timeline Example 156

Other Types of Tracks 158

Add an Existing Curve to a Track 158

Timeline Options... 159

Timeline Node Pins.. 159

Debugging Blueprints 160

   Breakpoints 163

Summary.. 164

Chapter 6: Players and Input 165

   Game Modes 165

      Game State... 165

      Create a New Game Mode Blueprint 166

      Game Mode Properties.. 167

      Assigning Game Modes 169

   Pawns 170

      Adding a Static Mesh Component to a Pawn 171

      Adding a Camera Component to a Pawn 172

      Adding a Spring Arm Component to a Pawn 172

   Characters... 174

      Character Components.. 174

      Creating a Jump Input 176

   Controllers.. 177

      Advantages of Using a Controller 178

      Adding Input to a Player Controller.............................. 178

   Input Mapping... 179

      Action Mappings vs. Axis Mappings 179

      Creating New Input Mappings 180

   Setting Up Basic Character Movement 182

      Setting Up the Input Mapping....................................... 182

      Using Input Mappings in Blueprints............................. 184

   Summary.. 189

Chapter 7: Collisions...**191**

   Collisions Overview...191

      Hit Events and Overlap Events..191

      Collision Presets...192

      Can Character Step Up On Property.......................................195

   Block vs. Overlap Example..195

   Causing Damage Due to Collisions..202

      Event Hit Node...202

      Apply Damage Node..203

      Damage Example...204

   Summary..207

Chapter 8: User Interfaces...**209**

   Unreal Motion Graphics (UMG) Overview..................................209

      History of Unreal Interfaces..209

      Widget Blueprints..210

      Widget Blueprint Editor...211

   Root Widget...214

      Color and Opacity...215

      Foreground Color...216

      Padding..217

      Is Focusable..217

   Canvas Panel...217

      Canvas Panel Slot Properties...218

   Common Widget Properties...222

      Behavior Category...222

      Render Transform Category...223

      Performance Category...227

      Clipping Category..228

      Navigation Category..228

      Localization Category..229

Visual Designer 230

Text Widget 233

Button Widget 236

Border Widget and Image Widget 239

Progress Bar Widget 241

Horizontal Box and Vertical Box 243

Summary 245

Chapter 9: Audio 247

Audio Overview and Sound Waves 247

    Ambient Sound Actor 248

    Sound Wave Properties 250

    Play Sound Nodes 254

Sound Cues 256

    Audio Nodes 257

Attenuation 264

    Attenuation Curves 266

    Attenuation Hierarchy 267

Importing and Converting Audio 269

    Audacity 269

Summary 270

Chapter 10: Additional Topics 271

Migrating Content Between Projects 271

Downloading Content from the Epic Games Launcher 272

    Learn Tab 272

    Marketplace Tab 274

    Vault 274

Importing 3D Objects from the Internet 275

    www.free3d.com 275

    www.cgtrader.com 277

    Importing .fbx Files 279

Packaging 280

    Selecting a Default Map 280

    Packaging the Game.. 281

    Advanced Packaging Settings 282

    Pak Files 283

Summary... 284

Chapter 11: Tutorials 285

Tutorial 1 – Creating the Sky... 286

    Creating a New Project and Empty Level 286

    Creating the Atmosphere, Sun, and Clouds 286

    Setting the Game Default Map 288

Tutorial 2 – Creating the Playing Area... 289

    Creating the Ground 289

    Adding a Player Start Actor.. 290

    Adding the Wall Enclosure... 291

Tutorial 3 – Building the Inner Structures 292

    Adding the Inner Walls... 292

    Adding a Platform of Blocks 294

    Adding a Fire Obstacle 296

    Adding the House Structures.. 297

Tutorial 4 – Building the Elevator Platform 302

Tutorial 5 – Creating the Enemies... 308

Tutorial 6 – Creating a Rotating Door.. 316

Tutorial 7 – Creating a Playable Character... 322

    Creating a Game Mode 323

    Creating the Character 323

    Adding Pause Functionality 331

    Making the Door Open with a Button Press.. 332

Tutorial 8 – Adding a Damage System 333

Tutorial 9 – Creating the Orb Item 339

    Creating the Orbs 340

    Modifying the Door Behavior 342

Tutorial 10 – Creating the HUD 345

Tutorial 11 – Damage Tint and Collect Item Tint 350

Tutorial 12 – Restricting the Opening of the Door 355

Tutorial 13 – Adding a Pause Menu 358

Tutorial 14 – Game Over and Win Screen Menus 362

    Adding a Game Over Menu 362

    Adding a Win Screen Menu 369

Tutorial 15 – Adding Audio to the Game 372

Tutorial 16 – Packaging the Game 376

Summary 379

Index **381**

About the Author

 **David Nixon** is a professional software developer with a
degree in computer science from Florida Atlantic University.
He is a lifelong video game aficionado who started with the
Atari 2600 and never looked back. He enjoys music, reading,
and sports in his spare time.

About the Technical Reviewers

 **Wojciech Jakóbczyk** is a senior software professional with experience in various industries. For the last few years, he has been engaged in virtual reality development, mostly technologies for content creation. He has experience working with Unreal Engine 4 on VR platforms ranging from mobile and stand-alone to high-end desktop headsets.

Pranav Paharia is a game developer who has worked on game technologies like Cocos2d-x, Unity3D, Unreal Engine 4, and more. He has a degree in information technology and a postgraduate degree in game development. After realizing his die-hard interest in games, he started his career in game development by working in Indie Game Studios making mobile games of many genres. One of the projects he has worked on, *Song of Swords*, has won NASSCOM 2013 "People's Choice of the Year Award." During all the development years, he has worked on a variety of systems in games, like gameplay, multiplayer, data pipelines, cinematics, and so on. He is proficient in C++ and C# and can work on any game technology to create mind-boggling simulations. He is a self-taught programmer and designer. Since 2013, he has created simulations for single-player games, multiplayer games, card games, VR games, AR simulations, serious games, training simulations, and learning games. He has also worked on a few game development books. With his vast experience in creating simulations, he is now involved in solving real-life problems using latest technologies like creating architectural visualizations, VR training systems, medical data imaging, and so on for clients such as DRDO India, Zaha Hadid, and Line Creative.

Apart from developing graphical software, he has an interest in learning virtual production techniques and new ways to make technology interact with people. He is an avid gamer who loves *Dota 2* and also has keen interest in photography. He is into reading books with philosophical context and loves riding his bike on long road trips. He is grateful to Krsna for guiding him through the purpose of his life. You can contact him at pranavpaharia@gmail.com and also check out his web site at www.pranavpaharia.com.

Acknowledgments

I'd like to thank Spandana Chatterjee for bringing this opportunity to me, Divya Modi and Rita Fernando for their editorial work, and Wojciech Jakóbczyk and Pranav Paharia for their contributions as technical editors. Thank you to the rest of the staff at Apress and, most importantly, thank you to my parents for their continued love and support.

Introduction

For years, the world of 3D game development was largely closed off to the average amateur and enthusiast. The hurdle of developing a working 3D game engine was just too large of an obstacle for most to overcome. Thankfully, those days are over, and there are now free, state-of-the-art, open source 3D game engines available to everyone. The most popular of these engines is Unreal Engine, now in its 4th version.

This book will give you a solid foundation in 3D game development using Unreal Engine. You will first get an overview of the engine and learn the fundamentals of game development. You will learn how to construct breathtaking environments for your game, limited only by your imagination. You will learn how to script logic and define rules for your game. The book will teach you key gaming concepts, such as players, input, collisions, and damage. You will learn how to craft user interfaces, so you can create menus, HUDs, and loading screens for your game. Finally, you will learn about the audio system Unreal uses so you can work with music and sound effects.

This book was designed with the non-programmer in mind, meaning anyone can jump right in and start learning game development today! It is also useful for experienced programmers who are curious about learning a visual scripting system.

Topics include

- Levels

- Actors

- Meshes

- Brushes

- Materials

- Lighting

- Characters

- Input
- Collisions
- Blueprints
- User interfaces
- Audio

CHAPTER 1

Getting Started

In this book, you will be learning how to use what many consider to be the best game engine in the industry, Unreal Engine 4. This chapter will give you a brief overview of the engine, explain its licensing model, show you how to register an account with Epic Games, and show you how to download and install the engine.

Overview

The Unreal Engine is a game development engine created by Epic Games. The first game to use it was *Unreal*, released in 1998, which is the origin of its name. It was originally designed to develop first-person shooter games but has since been upgraded to support any genre of game. It has been used to create several blockbuster games and game franchises, including *BioShock*, *Gears of Wars*, *Splinter Cell*, *Rainbow 6*, *Borderlands*, *Dishonored*, *Mass Effect*, and many more.

There have been a few generations of the software released since the original version in 1998. Unreal Engine 2 was released in 2002, UE3 in 2006, and the current generation, UE4, in 2014. As of the time of this writing, the latest version is 4.23, which is the version used throughout this book. Versions are made to be backward compatible, however, so all examples in this book should continue to work with newer versions.

Today, the Unreal Engine is the most widely used open source engine in the world and is known for its robust graphics and high performance.

1

© David Nixon 2020
D. Nixon, *Beginning Unreal Game Development*, https://doi.org/10.1007/978-1-4842-5639-8_1

Licensing

While Unreal Engine is open source, meaning it is free to download and use, this comes with some stipulations. In order to download and use the engine, you must agree to Epic Games' licensing terms, which requires you to share a small portion of your profits with them. If you create something using the engine that makes more than $3,000 in a single quarter (meaning a quarter of a year), then you have to pay a 5% royalty to Epic Games for any sales above the $3,000.

Registration

You will need to register an account with Epic Games, the creators of the Unreal Engine, in order to download and install it. To register an account, perform the following steps:

1. Open a web browser and go to `www.unrealengine.com`.

2. Click the blue button in the middle of the page that says "Get Started Now." You will be taken to a screen where you can register for an account with Epic Games (Figure 1-1).

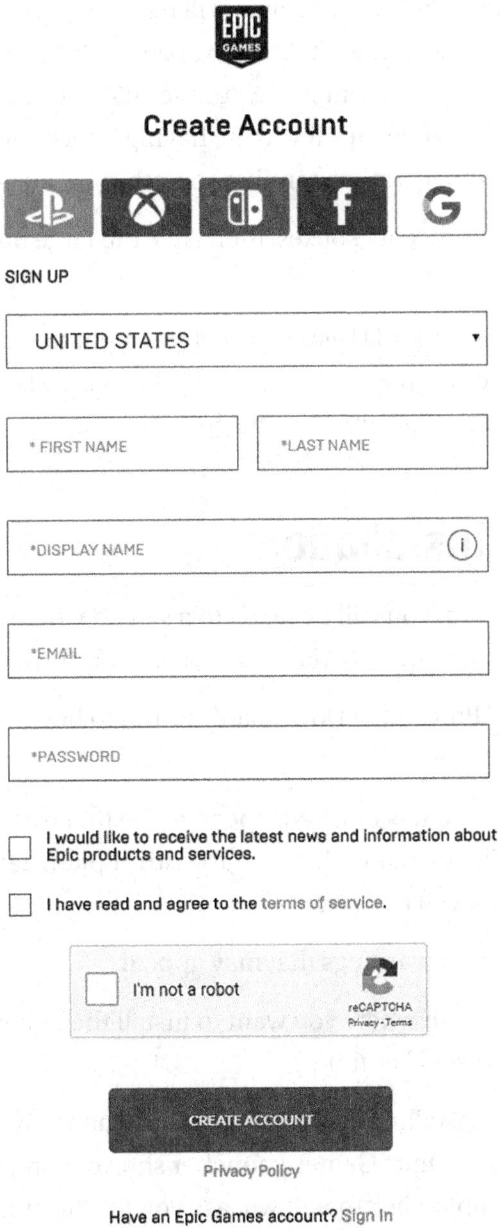

Create Account

SIGN UP

UNITED STATES ▾

* FIRST NAME   *LAST NAME

*DISPLAY NAME   ⓘ

*EMAIL

*PASSWORD

☐ I would like to receive the latest news and information about Epic products and services.

☐ I have read and agree to the terms of service.

☐ I'm not a robot

reCAPTCHA
Privacy · Terms

CREATE ACCOUNT

Privacy Policy

Have an Epic Games account? Sign In

Figure 1-1. *The form to register an account with Epic Games*

3. Fill out the fields. The Display Name will be used as your handle
    on the Unreal Engine forums (https://forums.unrealengine.com/)
    which are a great place to interact with the UE4 community and
    to get answers and feedback if you are having issues with the
    software or need help understanding something.

4. Check the necessary checkboxes, then click the large button that
    says "Create Account."

5. You will be given an End User License Agreement to read. Once
    you have read and agree to it, check the checkbox indicating you
    have done so, then click the "Accept" button.

Download and Installation

After completing registration, you will be taken to a screen where you can download the
installer for something called the *Epic Games Launcher*. Perform the following steps:

1. Click the large "Proceed to Download" button to begin the
    download.

2. Once the download has finished, open the file that was
    downloaded. The filename should start with "EpicInstaller" and
    the file extension will be *.msi*.

3. Accept any security warnings that may appear.

4. Choose a folder path where you want to install the launcher and
    then click the "Install" button.

5. Once it finishes installing, it should open automatically. If it
    doesn't, look for an Epic Games Launcher shortcut on your
    desktop and double-click that. It will ask you for the email and
    password you provided during registration. Enter that information
    and click "Sign In."

6. Now you will be on the home screen of the Epic Games Launcher.
    From here, click the "Unreal Engine" tab. In that tab, click the
    yellow button that says "Install Engine" (Figure 1-2).

Figure 1-2. *The Install Engine button*

    7.   Choose the folder path where you want to install the engine, then click "Install." The Launcher will now begin to download the latest version of the Engine. Once the download completes, the Launcher will automatically install it.

Once the installation is complete, the yellow button will now say "Launch," and if you click it, that will launch the Engine.

Installing the C++ Source Code

If you are an experienced software developer, you may want to download and install the C++ source code for the engine. This gives you access to daily updates to the source code and gives you an opportunity to make your own improvements to Unreal which you can then submit back to Epic Games. Note that you should only do this if you have extensive programming experience and are familiar with using GitHub. This step is NOT required to follow along with anything in the book.

To access the Unreal Engine source code

    1.   Go to www.github.com and register for an account.

    2.   Go to www.unrealengine.com and sign in with your Epic Games account you created earlier.

    3.   Go to your account dashboard by hovering over your username and clicking the "Personal" button.

    4.   Click the "Connected Accounts" tab.

    5.   Click the "Connect" button below the GitHub logo.

    6.   If you haven't already agreed to the Unreal Engine EULA, you must do so here.

    7.   Click the "Link your Account" button.

8. Click the "Authorize EpicGames" button. The two accounts should now be linked, and you should receive a confirmation email.

9. Fork and clone the Unreal Engine repository at `www.github.com/epicgames`.

10. Install Visual Studio 2017 or higher (Community, Pro, or Enterprise).

11. Open the source folder containing the repository and run "Setup.bat."

12. Run "GenerateProjectFiles.bat."

13. Double-click the "UE4.sln" file to open the project in Visual Studio.

14. Set the solution configuration to "Development Editor" and the solution platform to whichever platform you are using.

15. Right-click the UE4 target and select "Build." Compilation will take anywhere from 10 to 40 minutes depending on the speed of your computer.

16. Once the build is complete, set your startup project to UE4 and press F5 to debug.

Summary

In this chapter, you learned about the history of the Unreal Engine and how its licensing model works. You also registered an account with Epic Games and downloaded and installed the engine. In the next chapter, you will learn the most fundamental concepts of the engine, in order to create a solid foundation for you to build upon.

CHAPTER 2

Basic Concepts

Before diving deep into any topic, you must learn the fundamentals. In this chapter, you will learn about three basic concepts in Unreal Engine – Projects, Levels, and Actors.

Projects

In the context of the Unreal Engine, a *project* is the unit that stores all the information for an individual game. Meaning each game you create will be stored in its own project.

For example, for a first-person shooter game, you might have a project called "ShooterProject." If you wanted to work on another game, a puzzle game, you would create a new project and perhaps call it "PuzzleProject." So if you are working on five different games, you should have five different projects, one for each game.

Unreal Project Browser

To launch the Unreal Project Browser

1. Go to your desktop and double-click the Epic Games Launcher shortcut that you created during installation.

2. Make sure you are on the *Unreal Engine* tab.

3. Click the yellow "Launch" button in the upper-right corner.

The *Unreal Project Browser* is where you can open your existing projects or create new ones. It is divided into two tabs.

© David Nixon 2020
D. Nixon, *Beginning Unreal Game Development*, https://doi.org/10.1007/978-1-4842-5639-8_2

Projects Tab

The first tab is simply called *Projects* and will be selected by default whenever the Project Browser first opens (Figure 2-1). This tab is for existing projects. It contains thumbnail images of all existing projects that the Project Browser was able to find, which would include any projects within the installation directory, and any projects you previously created or opened using this installation of Unreal.

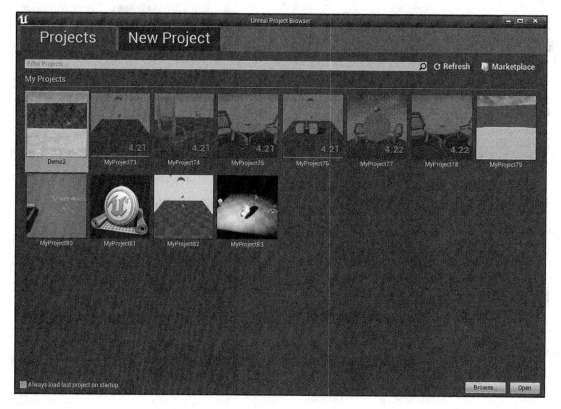

Figure 2-1. *The Projects tab of the Unreal Project Browser*

To open a project, simply double-click it, or select it and click the "Open" button in the bottom-right corner, and it will open the Unreal Editor and load that project into it.

If you have lots of projects and need help finding one, you can enter all or part of the name of the project in the search bar at the top and it will narrow down the results based on what you entered.

As previously mentioned, the Projects tab will only list the projects that the Project Browser could find. For example, if you were to download an existing project from the Internet onto your desktop, then the Project Browser won't know about it until you open that project. This is what the "Browse" button in the bottom-right corner is for. In this situation, you would need to click the Browse button and browse to that project file on your desktop and open it from there. Once you open it, from then on, the Project Browser will know about it and it will appear in the list.

In the upper-right corner of the Project Browser, there are two buttons – *Refresh* and *Marketplace*. The Refresh button is used to refresh the list of project thumbnails. Again, let's say that you download a project from the Internet, but instead of saving it to the desktop, you saved it in the installation directory instead. In that scenario, the Project Browser will be able to find it. However, it won't appear in the list until you click the Refresh button.

If you click the Marketplace button, this will take you to the Marketplace tab of the Epic Games Launcher where you can download existing environments, objects, characters, and so on either for free or for a price.

In the bottom-left corner is a checkbox labeled "Always load last project on startup." If you check this, the next time you hit the Launch button in the Games Launcher, it will skip the Project Browser altogether and automatically open the last project you worked on. This is useful if you plan to be working on only one project for several days, weeks, or months at a time. It will allow you to skip this step every time.

If you do this and then want to open a new or different project, you can still do that through the File menu of the Unreal Editor. If you later decide you *do* want the Project Browser to open on launch, you can change this setting in the Editor Preferences.

New Project Tab

The second tab is the *New Project* tab (Figure 2-2). This tab has two tabs itself – a *Blueprint* tab and a *C++* tab. On the Blueprint tab, there are several options to choose from – a blank project and several template projects.

Figure 2-2. *The New Project tab of the Unreal Project Browser*

The templates are all based around common game types. For example, the *First Person* template will load with several features common to first-person games already hooked up and ready to go. For a racing game, the *Vehicle* template would make a good choice. If you don't choose these features here, you still have the option to add them in later if you want. You could choose a blank project to start with and then add in "First Person" features later, within the Editor.

Toward the bottom of the tab, there are three different settings available to configure (Figure 2-3). You also have the option to change any of these settings later within the Editor.

Figure 2-3. *Settings available on the New Project tab*

First, you can choose the overall class of hardware that you are planning to develop your game for. You can choose between *Desktop/Console* for developing computer and console games and *Mobile/Tablet* for developing phone and tablet games.

Next, you have the option of choosing between *Maximum Quality* and *Scalable 3D or 2D*. In general, you would pair the Desktop/Console setting with Maximum Quality, and Mobile/Tablet with Scalable 3D or 2D, which makes this setting somewhat redundant. However, if you wanted to, for example, create a desktop game that could operate using minimal resources, you could pair the "Desktop" and "Scalable" settings together.

Lastly, you have the option of choosing between *With Starter Content* and *No Starter Content*. Choosing the blank template will start you off with no code, but if you wanted to start with a truly empty project, you would choose the blank template along with the No Starter Content setting. However, the With Starter Content setting is useful as it will load into your project, from the start, a lot of basic content you can use to get you going such as materials, basic shapes, and so on.

Finally, when you have selected the template you want to use and have chosen your settings, you just need to go to the bottom of the window and choose where you want the project to be saved, give it a name, and click the *Create Project* button in the bottom-right. This will open the Unreal Editor and load a new project into it based on the settings you chose.

Levels

A *Level*, in the context of the Unreal Engine, can be defined as a collection of objects and their properties that together define an area of gameplay.

That's the technical definition, but an easy way to visualize this is, if you've ever played a fighting game such as *Super Smash Bros*, or *SoulCalibur*, or *Mortal Kombat*, you know that each match takes place in a different location. The first match might take place in a palace and the next one in a forest, and so on. Each of these different locations would be its own Level within the Unreal Editor.

Also, think of first-person shooter (FPS) games such as *Call of Duty* or *Battlefield*. When you're playing multiplayer, you might get asked to choose a map for the match to take place in. Each of those maps is it's own Level.

Levels are loaded and unloaded into memory one at a time. So if you're playing a game where you're in a town, and you can walk around the town, and every time you enter or exit one of the buildings in the town, the game has to load, then that means that the outside of the town is a single Level, and each building interior is its own Level.

A single game may consist of only one Level, but often will consist of many Levels. Major releases often contain hundreds of Levels.

Creating, Opening, and Saving Levels

To create a new Level, go to File ➤ New Level (Figure 2-4), or use the shortcut *Ctrl+N*.

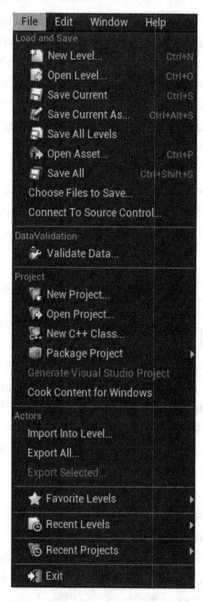

Figure 2-4. *The File Menu*

You have the option of choosing between "Default," "VR-Basic," and "Empty Level" (Figure 2-5). "Default" will start you off with some basic stuff already added, including a platform, an atmosphere, some lighting, and so on. "VR-Basic" will give you a basic level that can be viewed inside of a VR headset. The "Empty Level" option will start you off with a completely empty Level.

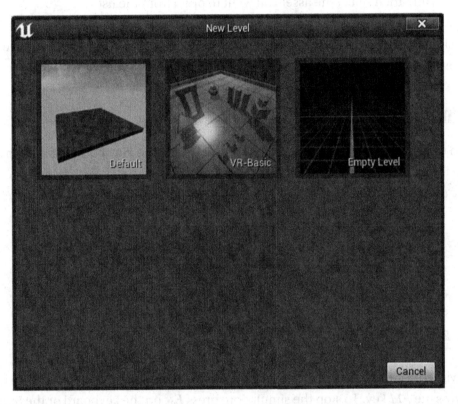

Figure 2-5. *You can choose between Default, VR-Basic, and Empty Level when creating a new Level*

To open an already existing Level, go to File ➤ Open Level, or use the shortcut *Ctrl+O*. From there, navigate through the Content folder to find the Level you want, then double-click to open it.

There are multiple options available for saving. You can go to File ➤ Save Current to save it with its current name. Or you can select "Save Current As" and save it under a different name. If you have multiple Levels that are unsaved, and want to save them all, you can select "Save All Levels."

In addition to Levels, it is possible to open and save other assets as well. An *asset* is anything that can be used to help develop your game that can be saved and opened. For example, anything you can open or add to your game within the Content Browser is an asset.

If you want to open an existing asset for editing, you would select "Open Asset," or use *Ctrl+P*, and then select the asset you want to open from the list.

To save everything you have open, including all Levels and other assets, select "Save All," or simply press *Ctrl+Shift+S*. To save only some of the files you have open, select "Choose Files to Save..." and select which of the unsaved files you want to save.

Playing a Level

You can test your Levels directly in the Editor by clicking the Play button at the top of the screen (Figure 2-6). This will simulate the Level immediately, without having to do a full build of the game, so you can quickly test things as you develop them.

Figure 2-6. *The Play button*

To view the Level fullscreen, or to exit fullscreen, make sure the Viewport is in focus, then press the *F11* key. To stop the simulation, press *Esc* on the keyboard or the Stop button at the top of the screen.

Actors

An *Actor* is any object that can be added to a Level. Consider the objects on the left side of the Unreal Editor when you first start a project. If you click the cube, for example, and drag it into the Level, it will become an Actor within the Level (Figure 2-7).

Figure 2-7. *This cube is an Actor within the Level*

Actors can be physical, visible objects within the Level, such as the cube, but they don't have to be. For example, there is something called the *Player Start Actor*. Wherever this Actor is placed within the Level is where the player will start when the Level begins. Even though the Player Start Actor isn't a physical object within the Level, it is still considered to be an Actor.

Static Meshes

The *Static Mesh Actor* is one of the most common types of Actors used to construct Levels in the Unreal Editor. If you're not familiar, "mesh" is a 3D modeling term and simply refers to a 3D object. When you're playing a game, pretty much every object you see in the game will be a mesh. For example, you may see tree meshes, bird meshes, table meshes, chair meshes, and so on.

Static Meshes refer to meshes with no moving parts, for example, the cube and the other geometric shapes in that list.

There is another type of mesh, a *Skeletal Mesh*, which is simply a mesh that *does* have moving parts. Skeletal Meshes have polygons that are combined to form the appearance of the mesh, just like Static Meshes, but they also have a set of bones which are connected together and used to animate the vertices of the polygons. Skeletal Meshes are an intermediate to advanced topic and won't be covered in detail.

15

In the Starter Content that comes with the Unreal Engine, you have some Static Meshes in the form of furniture and some basic architectural objects (Figure 2-8).

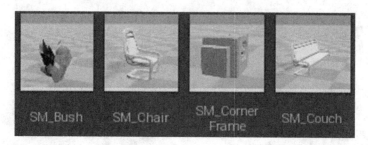

Figure 2-8. *Some Static Meshes are included in the Starter Content*

So you have some Meshes to start with, but the vast majority of meshes used in games are created in external 3D modeling applications, such as Maya, 3D Studio Max, Blender, and so on, and then imported into the Unreal Editor. If you're not a 3D modeling artist, don't despair; there are lots of great content available on the Internet for you to use, for free or for a price, and the final chapter of this book will show you where you can find some of that content.

Geometry Brushes

A *Geometry Brush*, or simply "Brush" for short, is an Actor used to represent 3D space (Figure 2-9). There is a Box Brush, a Cone Brush, and so on. This is very similar to a Mesh, but there are a few key differences. These differences will be discussed in greater detail in Chapter 4, so, for now, just know the following:

- Brushes are only used for basic geometric shapes, while Meshes can be crafted into objects with a high level of detail.

- Brushes are useful for quick level design but are less memory efficient than Meshes. Therefore, Brushes are generally used to prototype Levels early on and are then replaced with better-looking and better-performing Meshes for the final project.

Figure 2-9. *A Box Brush*

Materials

Before moving on to the next Actor, you should know about a property that is common to both Meshes and Brushes – the Material of the Actor. A *Material* in Unreal Engine is an asset you can apply to a surface to make that surface, and thus the geometry behind that surface, look like it's made out of a certain substance. For example, if you apply a wood Material to a Cube Mesh, it will look like a wooden cube (Figure 2-10).

Figure 2-10. *A wood Material has been applied to this Cube Mesh*

Meshes that are imported into the Unreal Editor may already have one or more Materials applied to them that get imported in alongside them. But you can replace these Materials if you wish.

Lights

A *Light Actor* in the Unreal Engine is used to represent visible light in the real world. Thanks to a lot of complex, mathematical algorithms that the Unreal Engine uses, it will behave much like light does in the real world. It will make objects that it hits more visible, depending on the intensity of the Light and the Material of the object. It will reflect off the surface of objects and light up other objects indirectly. It will cast a shadow if a visible, opaque object is in its path, and so on.

Lights will be discussed in greater detail in Chapter 4, but for now, just know that Light Actors are used to represent only the light itself, and not any of the objects from which the light emanates from. For example, if you wanted a working flashlight in your Level, you would need to combine a Light Actor with a Static Mesh Actor that looked like a flashlight. You would place the Light Actor at one end of the flashlight to make it look like the light was coming out of the flashlight.

Particle Systems

A *Particle System* is an Actor used to represent objects made of many tiny particles, such as smoke, fire, sparks, lasers, and so on. A Particle System is comprised of one or more Particle Emitters, which can be combined in a variety of ways to create different-looking particle effects.

The Starter Content contains a number of pre-made particle systems, but you also have the option of creating your own using *Cascade*, the particle effects editor within Unreal.

Components

Components are a type of object in Unreal that are attached to Actors. In fact, Actors can be thought of as simply containers that are used to hold Components. For example, a Static Mesh Actor is just an Actor that has a Static Mesh Component.

Components will be covered in detail in Chapter 4.

Summary

In this chapter, you learned the basics of the Unreal Engine. Specifically, you learned about Projects, Levels, and Actors. In the next chapter, you will learn about the Level Editor, the main editor of the Unreal Engine.

CHAPTER 3

The Level Editor

This chapter will cover the Level Editor. You will start by getting an overview of the editor before learning about each of its panels in detail. You will learn how to move, rotate, and scale Actors, the concept of snapping, and how to view your Level in different ways.

Level Editor Overview

This section will give a basic overview of the Level Editor without going into too much detail. First, we will spend a few moments discussing some terminology which can be confusing.

Unreal Engine vs. the Unreal Editor

The Unreal Engine is an application that is used to run games. It's a program that has algorithms for determining how objects are rendered frame by frame, how lighting should affect them, and so on. The Unreal Editor is an application for *creating* games that can run on the Unreal Engine. So that's what you're learning in this book – how to create games with the Unreal Editor that can be played using the Unreal Engine.

When you hit the Play button to play your game, the Unreal Editor is using the Unreal Engine to run the game. To summarize, the Unreal Editor is used for *creating* games, while the Unreal Engine is used for *running* those games.

Types of Editors

The Unreal Editor has several sub-editors within it, including the Blueprint Editor, the UMG Editor, the Sound Cue Editor, the Level Editor, and many more.

The *Blueprint Editor* is used to define the logic and gameplay of your game. It is covered in detail in Chapter 5.

© David Nixon 2020
D. Nixon, *Beginning Unreal Game Development*, https://doi.org/10.1007/978-1-4842-5639-8_3

The *UMG Editor* is used to create menus, HUDs, and other 2D overlays for your game. It is covered in Chapter 8.

The *Sound Cue Editor* is used to combine and modify existing sound waves to create custom audio for your game. It is covered in Chapter 9.

The *Level Editor* is used to design the Levels for your game. What can be confusing about the Level Editor is that it essentially acts as the home screen for the Unreal Editor. So the main window of the Unreal Editor is the Level Editor itself. All of the other sub-editors will open in their own separate windows. For example, if you double-click a Blueprint, it will open the Blueprint Editor in a separate window.

Panels of the Level Editor

Figure 3-1 shows an example of a Level Editor window. The large rectangle in the middle is the *Viewport*. The thin strip above that is the *Toolbar*. At the bottom of the screen is the *Content Browser*. On the left side of the screen is the *Modes Panel*. On the right side of the screen is the *World Outliner* at the top, and below that, the *Details Panel*.

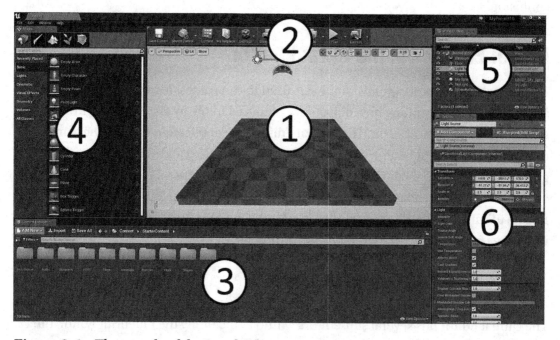

Figure 3-1. *The panels of the Level Editor – 1. Viewport 2. Toolbar 3. Content Browser 4. Modes Panel 5. World Outliner 6. Details Panel*

Keep in mind that these panels can be moved and resized and also that this is just the default layout of the current release and could change in future releases.

The *Viewport* is used to give you a visual representation of your game. You will see a representation of the environment you create, along with characters and objects that players will see in the game. You will also be able to see certain objects in the Viewport that won't be visible when playing the game, such as cameras, event triggers, and invisible barriers. You can also manipulate objects directly through the Viewport (Figure 3-2).

Figure 3-2. *The Viewport*

The *Toolbar*, shown in Figure 3-3, is a strip of buttons meant to give you quick access to common and/or important functions, such as saving, changing settings, or playing your game.

Figure 3-3. *The Toolbar*

The *Content Browser* is for storing and organizing content that you can add to your game (Figure 3-4). This includes content such as Meshes, Materials, music, sound effects, visual effects, and more. Some types of content can be created directly within the Unreal Editor. But you can also create content outside of the Unreal Editor and then import it in. For example, you could create a motorcycle using third-party 3D modeling software and then use the Content Browser to import the motorcycle into your project. There is also a lot of already made content available on the Internet, for free or for a price, that you can download and then import into the Content Browser.

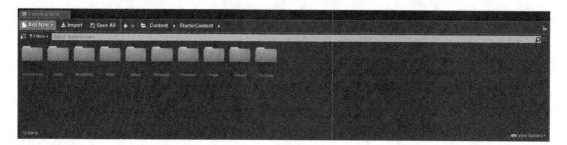

Figure 3-4. *The Content Browser*

The *Modes Panel* allows you to change the mode of the Level Editor to various modes that make it easier to perform certain tasks (Figure 3-5). These tasks include dragging and dropping objects into your Level, adding color and texture to those objects, modifying the geometry of those objects, editing the Landscape of your Level, and adding foliage, meaning plant life, to your Level.

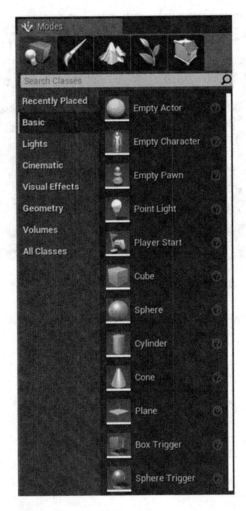

Figure 3-5. *The Modes Panel*

The *World Outliner* is used to list and group the objects in your Level in a way that makes them easy to find when you want to select and edit them (Figure 3-6).

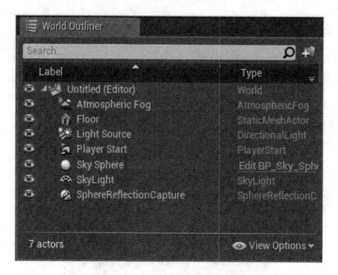

Figure 3-6. *The World Outliner*

The *Details Panel* allows you to view and edit the details of whatever object is currently selected, such as the object's size and location (Figure 3-7).

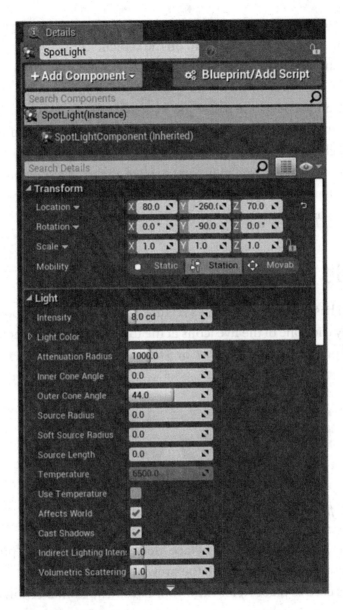

Figure 3-7. *The Details Panel*

Customizing the Interface

The Unreal Editor gives you a great deal of control over how the interface looks. One thing you can do is resize the individual panels. To do this, simply click the edge between two panels and drag, and you can make them any size you wish.

You also have the option to move panels around. If you click the tab of the panel and drag, you can drag it to wherever you want on the screen.

You can also choose which panels are open at any given time. To close a panel, simply click the "X" on the right side of the panel's tab. To open a panel, go to the menu bar, and under Window, select the panel you wish to open.

Finally, you can choose to show or hide the tabs of each panel. To hide the tab, right-click it, and choose *Hide Tab*. To show the tab, click the yellow triangle in the upper-left corner of the panel. You may want to have all the tabs showing while you are still learning the names of the panels, and then once you have them memorized, close the tabs in order to have a little more screen room to work with.

Place Mode

The Modes Panel has five different modes (Figure 3-8). To select the mode you want to work in, simply click one of the five icons at the top of the Modes Panel, or hold down the *Shift* key and press either the *1*, *2*, *3*, *4*, or *5* key depending on which mode you want to select.

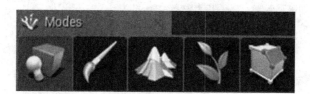

Figure 3-8.   *The five modes of the Modes Panel*

The first mode is called *Place Mode*. Place Mode can be selected by pressing *Shift+1* or by clicking the first icon, the one with the brown box and light bulb.

Place Mode is used to place Actors into your Level. The Content Browser is also used for placing Actors but there are a few key differences. Place Mode is used for simple, common, generic Actors, while the Actors in the Content Browser tend to be more complex. Also, the list of Actors in Place Mode remains static. You cannot add new Actors to the Place Mode panel, while in the Content Browser, you can import content created outside of the Unreal Editor into your project or create new ones.

To use Place Mode to place an Actor into a Level, simply click the Actor and drag it into the Viewport. To delete an Actor from the Level, press the *Delete* key when that Actor is selected.

Place Mode Tabs

Place Mode is divided into tabs of different groupings of Actors (Figure 3-9). Starting with the *Basic* tab, the Basic tab simply contains the most commonly used Actors.

Figure 3-9. *The tabs of Place Mode*

Above the Basic tab is the *Recently Placed* tab. This will be a list of Actors that you have recently placed into your Level. This is useful when you are going to be working with a small set of the same types of Actors for a while. In that scenario you would be able to just keep the Recently Placed tab open and drag and drop everything from there, without having to switch between all of the other tabs.

Below the Basic tab is the *Lights* tab. As mentioned earlier in the book, a Light in the Unreal Engine is an Actor that is meant to represent the light projecting from some source.

Below the Lights tab is the *Cinematic* tab. This has Actors used for creating Cinematics, which is basically a rendered 3D video. So, in the context of gaming, these would be used for the cut scenes in your games.

Then we have *Visual Effects*, which, as its name suggests, contains Actors that add a variety of effects to your Level.

The *Geometry* tab contains the Geometry Brushes that were briefly introduced earlier.

The *Volumes* tab is used to define gameplay volumes. A Volume is a 3D area of space that is invisible to the player and serves a specific purpose depending on its type. For example, a Blocking Volume will prevent Actors from being able to enter that Volume, a Pain Causing Volume will cause damage to an Actor who enters that volume, and so on.

Last is the *All Classes* tab, which contains all the Actors from the other tabs, plus some additional Actors not found in any of the other tabs, either because they are less common or just didn't fit nicely into one of the other groups. The list is somewhat long, so you may want to use the search bar above. By typing into the search bar, you can quickly narrow down the results to what you are looking for.

Navigating Within the Viewport

There are three main ways to navigate in the Viewport.

Mouse Navigation

The first way to navigate the Viewport is by *mouse navigation*. Try holding down the left mouse button (LMB) and dragging the mouse. This allows you to move the camera forward or backward and to rotate it left and right. There is no way to move up and down with this movement. It is only for traveling along the X and Y axes. Also, you cannot move directly left or right with this movement, you can only rotate left and right.

Now hold the LMB and the right mouse button (RMB) at the same time and drag the mouse. This will allow you to move directly left and right and up and down. Also, if you have a middle mouse button, you can hold that down instead of the left and right mouse buttons, to achieve the same effect.

Finally, try holding down just the RMB and dragging the mouse. This won't move the camera along any axes but what it does do is allow you to rotate the camera in any direction so you can look at the scene from whatever angle you wish.

WASD Navigation

The second way to navigate the Viewport is to use *WASD navigation*. This is used to move around the Viewport in a way that more closely mimics the controls commonly used when playing a standard first-person game using the mouse and keyboard. It's called WASD because it uses the *W*, *A*, *S,* and *D* keys on the keyboard and a few of the keys surrounding those keys.

To use WASD navigation, you will need to keep the RMB clicked the whole time. This will allow you to rotate the camera in any direction using the mouse, as discussed before, but also, when the RMB is clicked, the WASD keys will cause movement. Use the *W*, *A*, *S,* and *D* keys themselves to move the camera forward, backward, left, and right. Use the keys *Q* and *E* to move the camera up and down. Use the keys *Z* and *C* to zoom the camera in and out. Note that zooming is only temporary. Once you let go of the RMB, the zoom will go back to default.

Focusing

Before learning the third way of navigating the Viewport, you should know about *focusing* – a very simple yet powerful feature of the Viewport window. Focusing is useful in conjunction with the third navigation method and on its own.

To focus, press the *F* key, and it will focus the camera on whatever object is selected. This is useful in large Levels and Levels with many Actors. In these cases, it is often much easier to find the Actor in the World Outliner list and then press *F* to go straight to it in the Viewport, rather than trying to hunt for the Actor visually in the Viewport.

Maya Navigation

The third way to navigate the Viewport is to use *Maya navigation*. Maya refers to a popular 3D modeling program in which these controls are used. The three controls in Maya navigation are performed by holding down the *Alt* key.

The first Maya control is done by holding the *Alt* key, along with the LMB, and dragging the mouse. This will "tumble" or "orbit" the camera around a single point of interest. However, even if an Actor is selected, it won't actually use that Actor as the point of interest. To do that, you must press *F* to focus on the Actor.

The second Maya control is performed by holding the *Alt* key and the RMB and dragging the mouse. This will "dolly" or "zoom" the camera toward, and away from, a single point of interest. Again, press *F* to focus on an object first, in order to dolly directly toward and away from it.

The final Maya control is performed by holding down the *Alt* key and the MMB and dragging the mouse. This will cause the camera to "track," or "pan," up, down, left, and right.

Camera Speed

To adjust the speed at which the camera moves about the Level, adjust the camera speed slider in the upper-right corner of the Viewport (Figure 3-10). If you have a very large Level and want to be able to move about it quickly, you can set the camera speed up to an 8, and your camera will move very quickly. Conversely, if you need a fine level of control over the camera speed, you can set it down as low as a 1, and it will move very slowly. A setting of 4 is the default speed.

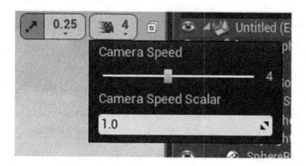

Figure 3-10. *Setting the Camera Speed*

Moving, Rotating, and Scaling Actors

Moving, rotating, and scaling Actors within the Viewport are performed by using the Move, Rotate, and Scale tools. When you select an Actor, you will automatically be ready to use one of the tools, depending on which of the three are selected at that moment. To see which tool is selected, look at the first three icons in the upper-right of the Viewport. From left to right, these three icons represent the Move, Rotate, and Scale tools (Figure 3-11). Whichever tool is currently selected will have an orange background.

Figure 3-11. *The Move, Rotate, and Scale tools*

To change between the tools, click their icons, or use the shortcut keys *W*, *E*, and *R* to switch between them. The *W*, *E*, and *R* keys are in a row on the keyboard and activate the Move, Rotate, and Scale tools in the same order as those icons appear on the screen. So the *W* key will activate the Move Tool, the *E* key will activate the Rotate Tool, and the

R key will activate the Scale Tool. If you forget what the shortcut keys are, just hover over the icon and it will tell you in parentheses at the end of the description.

Move Tool

When the Move Tool is active and an Actor is selected, three different-colored arrows will appear on the Actor, as seen in Figure 3-12. These three arrows are aligned with the X, Y, and Z axes of the Level. To move an Actor in just the X direction, left-click the red arrow, and use the mouse to move the Actor back and forth in that direction. No matter what direction you drag the mouse, the Actor will only move along the X-axis when the red arrow is held. To move an Actor along the Y-axis, select the green arrow instead. To move an Actor up and down, along the Z-axis, use the blue arrow.

Figure 3-12. *A Static Mesh being moved with the Move Tool*

To move an Actor in two dimensions, click the connector between those axes. For example, let's say you already have a chair Mesh perfectly aligned with a floor, and you don't want to mess that up, but you do want to change where the chair is located otherwise. In that case, you would click the connector between the X and Y axes, and then you could move the chair forward, backward, left, and right, but not vertical in any direction, so that it remains perfectly aligned with the floor.

To move an Actor in all three dimensions at once, select the white sphere in the middle of the arrows and drag the mouse.

If multiple Actors are selected, they will all move at once. To select multiple Actors, once the first Actor is selected, hold down the *Ctrl* button and continue to left-click each additional Actor you wish to select. Note that the Move Tool will only be visible on the last Actor selected, but in the World Outliner all the selected Actors will be highlighted.

If the *Shift* key is held while using the Move Tool, the camera will move in tandem with the Actor. This is useful if you want to move your Actor while keeping the camera focused on it in the exact same way or if you want to move the Actor some distance off screen and don't want to have to keep moving back and forth between moving the Actor and camera. Note that this only works when moving in one or two dimensions.

To make a copy of an Actor, you can select that Actor and press *Ctrl+W*. Alternatively, when you are using the Move Tool, if you hold down the *Alt* key, when you hold and drag along an axis, instead of moving the Actor, it will make a copy of that Actor which you will now be moving along that axis (Figure 3-13). You can hold down the *Alt* key to drag out several copies of an Actor.

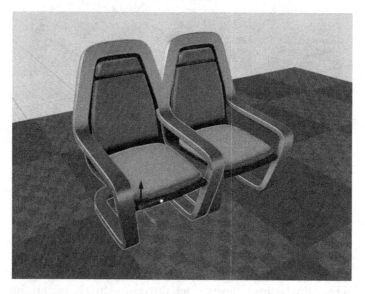

Figure 3-13. *An Actor being copied using the Move Tool*

Rotate Tool

Pressing the *E* key will activate the Rotate Tool, as seen in Figure 3-14. Using the Rotate Tool, you can rotate an Actor around any of the three axes. Clicking the red arc and dragging the mouse will rotate an Actor around the X-axis. The green arc rotates around the Y-axis. The blue arc rotates around the Z-axis.

Figure 3-14. *The Rotate Tool*

Similar to the Move Tool, if the *Alt* key is held when dragging the mouse, it will instead make a copy of the Actor which will then rotate out of the original Actor.

Scale Tool

Pressing the *R* key will activate the Scale Tool, as seen in Figure 3-15. The Scale Tool allows you to make your Actors bigger or smaller.

Figure 3-15. *The Scale Tool*

Using the same concept as the Move Tool, you can increase or decrease the size along just one axis at a time, or adjust the size two dimensions at a time by clicking and dragging one of the connectors between the axes. You can change the overall size of the Actor uniformly by clicking the white square in the middle and dragging the mouse.

World Space vs. Local Space

An important concept you should understand is that of "world space vs. local space." Look at the box to the right of the Move, Rotate, and Scale tools. If that box displays an icon of the Earth, it means that the axes of an Actor will be oriented to *world space* (Figure 3-16). If it displays an icon of a gray cube, Actors will be oriented to *local space*. Clicking the icon or using the shortcut *Ctrl+~* will toggle between the two settings.

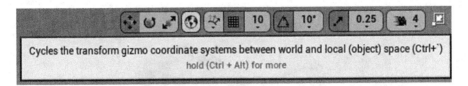

Figure 3-16. *An icon of the Earth means that Actors will be oriented to world space*

Let's say the Move Tool is active and Actors are currently oriented to world space. That means that no matter which way an Actor has been previously rotated, the arrows of the Move Tool will still point in the same direction, and thus the Move Tool will still move the Actor in the same direction relative to the world, as seen in Figure 3-17.

Figure 3-17. *Actor oriented to world space*

In local space, however, the direction of the arrows depends on the rotation of that particular Actor, as seen in Figure 3-18. In other words, world space makes the axes point relative to the world, while local space makes the axes point relative to the Actor.

Figure 3-18. *Actor oriented to local space*

The same concept applies to the Rotate Tool. In local space, an Actor will rotate around the locally oriented axes. This setting does not apply, however, to the Scale Tool. The Scale Tool will always be in local space, and it won't allow you to toggle when the Scale Tool is selected.

Snapping

Snapping is a technique used to perfectly align Actors with one another. There are several different ways of using snapping.

End Key

The first method involves using the *End* key. When the *End* key is pressed while an Actor is selected, it will snap that Actor directly onto the nearest surface. This is useful for quickly aligning objects, such as getting Actors to sit directly on a floor.

Surface Snapping

Another way of using snapping is called *Surface Snapping*. Clicking the icon to the right of the world space icon will bring up a small pop-up where you can turn on Surface Snapping (Figure 3-19). With Surface Snapping on, when the Move Tool is used to move an Actor around in three dimensions, any time it gets close to the surface of another Actor, it will snap the selected Actor to the surface of the nearby Actor.

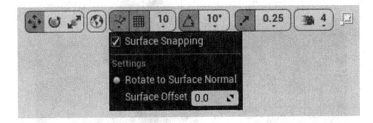

Figure 3-19. *Surface Snapping turned on*

Note that this only works when moving the object in three dimensions. It doesn't work when moving Actors around in just one or two dimensions at a time. In other words, you need to be dragging the Actor around by the white sphere in the middle for Surface Snapping to work.

Surface Snapping has a couple of settings you can adjust to change how it behaves. The first setting is called *Rotate to Surface Normal,* and it is set to "On" by default. The following example will illustrate how this works.

Imagine there is an Actor that was rotated such that its bottom surface was no longer in alignment with the surface of the floor. With Surface Snapping on and Rotate to Surface Normal off, when the Actor gets close to the floor, it will snap to the floor, but it will keep the Actor at the same rotation it was without attempting to rotate it to align with the floor, as seen in Figure 3-20.

Figure 3-20. *Rotate to Surface Normal was off when this chair was snapped to the floor*

However, with Rotate to Surface Normal on, when the Actor snaps to the floor, it will also be rotated so that its bottom surface is perfectly aligned with the surface of the floor, as seen in Figure 3-21.

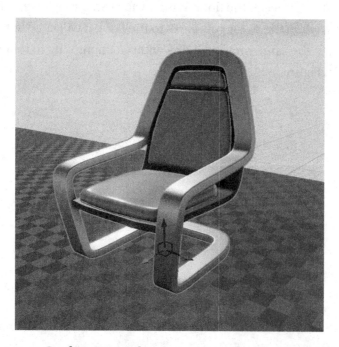

Figure 3-21. *Rotate to Surface Normal was on when this chair was snapped to the floor*

The second setting of Surface Snapping that you can adjust is the *Surface Offset*. This tells the Editor how far away the surfaces of the two Actors should be when they snap together. A value of 0 will cause Actors to be directly touching when they snap. A value of 20 would cause Actors to be 20 centimeters apart after snapping.

Grid Snapping

You can also align objects by using *Grid Snapping*. While Surface Snapping is useful for aligning objects that are close to one another, Grid Snapping is useful for aligning objects across distances.

Clicking the icon to the right of the Surface Snapping icon will toggle Grid Snapping on and off. With Grid Snapping on, when an Actor is moved, it will only be able to move it in the increments that the grid is divided into. The Actor will "snap" to each line of the grid and can't move a smaller amount than that (Figure 3-22). With Grid Snapping off, an Actor can be moved any distance.

Figure 3-22. *With Grid Snapping on, this chair will snap to each line of the grid when moved*

Snap Size

To the right of the Grid Snapping icon is a box where you can adjust the *Snap Size* (Figure 3-23). This will change the number of units that the Actor can move at a time. Set at 10, the Actor will move in increments of 10 units at a time.

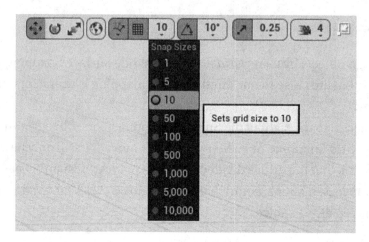

Figure 3-23. *Setting the Snap Size*

Note that the number of lines visible on the grid at any given time is dependent on the Snap Size that is set. Set at 10, the grid is actually only displaying one out of every ten lines it contains. At a Snap Size of 1, every line on the grid will become visible.

Grid Units

In the Unreal Editor, 1 grid unit represents 1 centimeter in your game. So whenever you see a number in the Unreal Editor meant to represent a unit of distance, you can think of that number in centimeters. For example, with Snap Size set to 10, an Actor moved within the Viewport will move 10 "in-game" centimeters at a time.

Rotation Snapping

Just like with the Move Tool, snapping can be turned on or off for the Rotate Tool. To toggle *Rotation Snapping*, click the icon to the right of the Snap Size icon. With Rotation Snapping on, an Actor can be rotated in specific increments along a *Rotation Grid*, with those increments being measured in degrees. So the Unreal Editor measures distances in centimeters, and it measures rotation in degrees.

You can choose how many degrees the Actor should rotate each time, by clicking the icon to the right of the Rotation Snapping icon. Set to 10, an Actor will rotate in increments of 10 degrees.

Scale Snapping

Just like with Move and Rotate, you can toggle *Scale Snapping* on or off. To do so, click the icon to the right of the rotation degrees icon.

To change the increment that is scaled by, click the icon to the right of the Scale Snapping icon. With the Scale Tool, the increment is a multiplier. For example, if 0.25 is selected, and you increment an Actor one size larger, its size will increase by 0.25 times its current size. In other words, its size will increase by 25%. If you make it smaller, it will decrease by 25% at a time. With a setting of 0.5, it would increase or decrease in increments of 50%, and so on.

Different Ways to View Your Level

This section will show you different ways you can view your Level, that can make level design easier, depending on the situation.

Immersive Mode

Pressing *F11* will fullscreen the Viewport. This is what Unreal calls *Immersive Mode*. Pressing *F11* again will exit fullscreen.

View Modes

Another way you can view your Level differently is by changing the *View Mode*. To change the View Mode, hover over the second-to-last box in the upper-left corner of the Viewport and click one of the selections from the menu that appears (Figure 3-24).

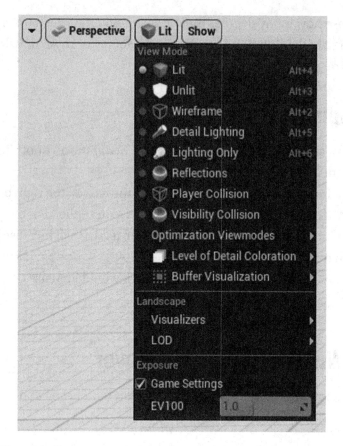

Figure 3-24. *View Modes*

Lit Mode

Lit is the default View Mode of the Level Editor and is for viewing the Level with full lighting and rendering, similar to what the player will see in-game.

Unlit Mode

Unlit is for viewing the Level without the lighting having any impact on what you see, as shown in Figure 3-25. In essence, this allows you to see the base colors of all objects without the amount of light or shadow affecting that color. Unlit is also useful for working in Levels or areas of Levels where the lighting would otherwise be too dark to easily see what you're doing.

Figure 3-25. *A Level in Unlit Mode*

Wireframe Mode

Wireframe allows you to see just the edges of the polygons of the objects in your Level, as shown in Figure 3-26. This can be helpful for aligning objects, visualizing the overall structure of something, and, in general, just giving you a more architectural view of your Level.

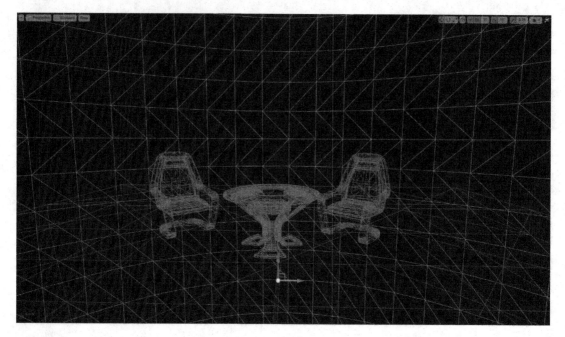

Figure 3-26. *A Level in Wireframe Mode*

Detail Lighting Mode

Detail Lighting will display the Level with a neutral Material applied to every surface. This can be used to determine how the color of a surface is affecting the lighting.

Lighting Only Mode

Like Detail Lighting, *Lighting Only* will display the Level with a neutral Material applied to every surface. However, unlike Detail Lighting, it will not display the texture of surfaces, so that the only thing affecting the appearance of the surfaces is the lighting.

Reflections Mode

Reflections will display the Level with the roughness of all surfaces set to the minimum. This causes all surfaces to multiply the amount of light they reflect, which makes it easier to determine the amount of reflection occurring at any given spot.

Player Collision Mode

Player Collision will display the complexity of the simple geometry used to construct the Landscape of the Level.

Visibility Collision Mode

Visibility Collision will display the complexity of the complex geometry used to construct the Landscape of the Level.

Orthographic Views

To the left of the View Modes menu is a menu that allows you to change from the default 3D perspective view of the Level to an orthographic view of the Level. There are several different orthographic views to choose from, but they all share two common traits. The first is that they default to a wireframe view mode, although you can still change the View Mode if you want.

The main thing about orthographic views is that they are meant to be a two-dimensional view of your Level, rather than a three-dimensional view. For example, in the "Top" view, shown in Figure 3-27, your vision is directly parallel with the Z-axis, so it is as if you are looking directly down at your Level and only seeing the X and Y axes. Conversely, in "Bottom" view, you are looking directly up at the Level.

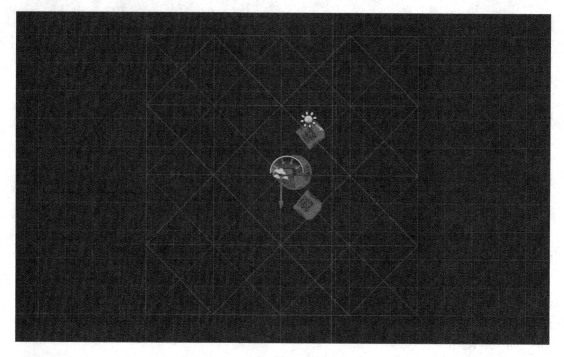

Figure 3-27. *A Level in Orthographic Top view*

In the "Left" and "Right" views, you are looking down the X-axis and only seeing the Y and Z axes. In the "Front" and "Back" views, you are looking down the Y-axis and only seeing the X and Z axes.

So each of the orthographic views has the point of vision coming from a different place, but it will always be directly along an axis, giving you a two-dimensional view.

Orthographic views are useful for aligning the objects in your Level in just two dimensions at a time. When paired with the wireframe view mode, the idea is to get a 2D architectural view of your Level.

When working in orthographic views, the navigation is a bit different than the perspective view. When in an orthographic view, holding down the LMB and dragging is used for drawing a selection box that you can use to select one or more objects. To navigate, hold down the RMB and drag to pan the Viewport camera, or hold the left and right mouse buttons down and drag in order to zoom the camera in and out. So LMB to select, RMB to pan, and both mouse buttons to zoom.

Show Flags

Another way to change the view of your Level is by toggling the various *Show Flags* on and off. Show Flags can be toggled using the checkboxes found in the icon to the right of the View Modes icon (Figure 3-28). Show Flags tell the Editor whether or not to show various types of Actors or effects in the Viewport.

Figure 3-28. *Show Flags*

For example, if you uncheck the "Static Meshes" Show Flag, all of the Static Meshes in the Level will disappear from the Viewport. This doesn't delete the Static Meshes from the Viewport, it only makes them invisible for the time being. It also doesn't make them invisible in the game, only in the Viewport.

Show Flags are useful for temporarily removing some of the clutter from view, once your Levels start to get complex. Even when they're not complex, sometimes you may have one type of object blocking another type, and it's just easier to temporarily get the one out of the way.

Game View

If you press the *G* key, you can toggle the Viewport in and out of *Game View*. When the Viewport is in Game View, it will hide all Actors and icons that are invisible in-game. So the Player Start Actor, for example, will be hidden, along with the icons for your Light Actors, and so on. Game View is meant to show you in the Viewport, exactly what the player would see from that perspective in the game.

Piloting Actors Within the Viewport

Sometimes it is useful when placing Actors, especially Camera and Light Actors, to see from the perspective of the Actor itself. This makes it easier to have the Actor point at the exact location you want it to point at.

For example, if you place a Light Actor in a Level, and want it to shine directly on a table Mesh, you can pilot the Light in order to more easily aim it directly at the table.

To pilot an Actor, right-click it, then look for an airplane icon and the text "Pilot [Actor]" (a Spot Light Actor will say "Pilot Spot Light" as shown in Figure 3-29). Alternatively, select the Actor and use the shortcut *Ctrl+Shift+P*.

Figure 3-29. *Piloting an Actor in the Viewport*

Content Browser

The *Content Browser*, just like Place Mode of the Modes Panel, can be used to drag and drop Actors into a Level. However, while Place Mode contains a list of generic, built-in Actors for you to use, the Content Browser can be used to create Actors or to import in Actors created outside of the Unreal Editor.

Sources Panel and Asset Window

Most of the space of the Content Browser is taken up by the *Asset Window*. The Asset Window contains the folders and assets for the current project.

In the upper-left corner of the Asset Window is a button which, when clicked, will toggle the visibility of the *Sources Panel*, which is hidden by default. The Sources Panel contains the folder directory for the Content Browser.

When a folder is selected in the Sources Panel, that folder will open in the Asset Window. The Asset Window will contain both the subfolders of that folder, and, unlike the Sources Panel, it will also contain the files, or assets, within that folder.

The Sources Panel is useful for navigating through the folders without the clutter of the files themselves, but, if you just want to work with the Asset Window alone, you can hide the Sources Panel by clicking the button in the upper-left again.

The Sources Panel contains a search box that can be used to find specific folders. The Asset Window contains a search box that can be used to find specific assets. For example, you could type "lamp" to search for all assets with "lamp" in their name, as shown in Figure 3-30.

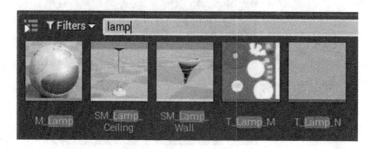

Figure 3-30. *Searching the Asset Window*

The Asset Window also has a Filters menu that can be used to find content of a certain type. For example, clicking "Static Mesh" will show all the Static Meshes, and only the Static Meshes, within the current folder and its subfolders. Clicking the "Reset Filters" button will clear out any filters currently being applied.

The search and filter functions can be combined. Let's say you were specifically looking for Static Meshes of lamps. By typing "lamp" into the search box and applying the Static Mesh filter, it will narrow down the results to only Static Mesh files with "lamp" in the name.

Back Button and Forward Button

Above the Sources Panel and Asset Window, there is a back button and a forward button. These work just like the back and forward buttons in Windows or in a web browser. You can use them to go back to the last so many folders you were in and then forward again if you wish. So if you go to a "FirstPerson" folder, and then a "MyImports" folder, and then a "StarterContent" folder, and then hit the back button, it will take you back to the MyImports folder. If you hit the back button again, it will take you back to the FirstPerson folder. Now if you hit forward, it will go to the MyImports folder, and then to the StarterContent folder again.

Breadcrumbs

To the right of the back and forward buttons are the breadcrumbs (Figure 3-31). You've probably seen this kind of navigation layout before even if you've never heard the term, but the basic idea is to show you the direct path from the root folder down to the folder you're in.

Figure 3-31. *Breadcrumbs*

Each folder in the folder path will have its own button. Clicking a button will take you directly to that folder. Clicking the arrow icon to the right of the folder name will bring up a list of all the subfolders, which can also be navigated to directly by clicking.

Add New Button

In the upper-left corner of the Content Browser is a green *Add New* button which can be used to add a variety of assets to the Content Browser (Figure 3-32). For example, clicking *New Folder* will add a new folder within the current folder.

Figure 3-32. *Add New button*

At the very top of the Add New menu is *Add Feature or Content Pack*. This gives you the chance to add in some of the content that is available when you first create a project (Figure 3-33). For example, selecting "First Person" and then clicking the "Add to Project" button will add folders containing some basic content for creating a first-person game. Note, however, that unlike when you choose the First-Person template when starting a project, this method doesn't automatically add and hook up any content into your Level, it just adds it to the Content Browser. From there you can drag and drop the content into your Level as you choose.

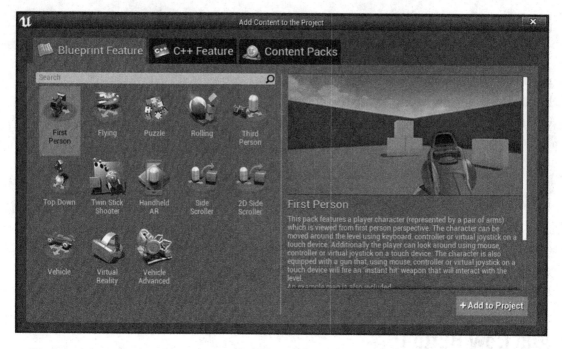

Figure 3-33. *Add Feature or Content Pack*

The Content Packs tab gives you the option to add the Starter Content into the Content Browser if you hadn't already done so when creating the project. There is also an option for Starter Content specifically for mobile devices.

Import Button

To the right of the Add New button is the *Import* button. If you have a file on your computer that you want to import into the current project, all you need to do is click the Import button and select the file, and it will import that file directly into whatever folder you're currently in, in the Content Browser. Alternatively, you can simply drag and drop files from your computer directly into the Content Browser.

Save All Button

To the right of the Import button is the *Save All* button. When the icon of an image in the Content Browser has an asterisk in its lower-left, this means that this asset hasn't been saved. By clicking the Save All button, it will bring up a window that lists all the unsaved assets in the Content Browser and allows you to unselect any if you don't want to save

them. Once "Save Selected" is clicked, the asterisk will go away, indicating that the asset
has been saved and has no new modifications.

View Options

In the bottom-right of the Content Browser is the View Options button. As the name
implies, if you click this button, you will get a menu of options related to viewing the
content in the Content Browser, as shown in Figure 3-34.

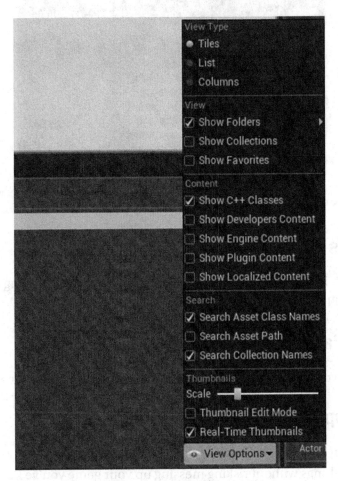

Figure 3-34. *View Options in the Content Browser*

Tiles vs. List vs. Columns

For example, you can change the way the files are displayed. By default, it is set to *Tiles*, which will display the files with large icons in a grid formation. *List* will make the files display using smaller icons and larger text and will be positioned one per row. *Columns* will display additional information for each asset, as seen in Figure 3-35.

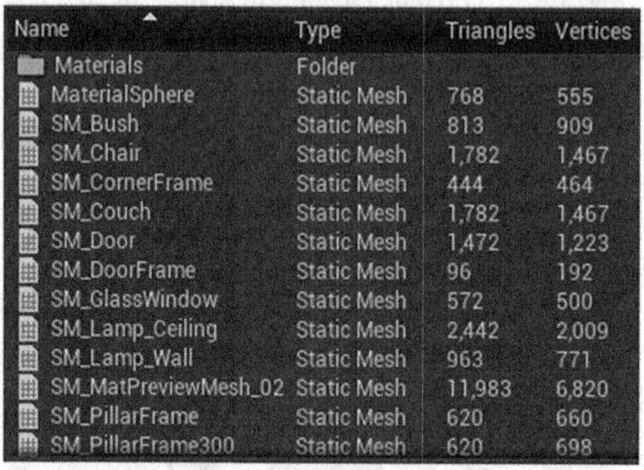

Name ▲	Type	Triangles	Vertices
Materials	Folder		
MaterialSphere	Static Mesh	768	555
SM_Bush	Static Mesh	813	909
SM_Chair	Static Mesh	1,782	1,467
SM_CornerFrame	Static Mesh	444	464
SM_Couch	Static Mesh	1,782	1,467
SM_Door	Static Mesh	1,472	1,223
SM_DoorFrame	Static Mesh	96	192
SM_GlassWindow	Static Mesh	572	500
SM_Lamp_Ceiling	Static Mesh	2,442	2,009
SM_Lamp_Wall	Static Mesh	963	771
SM_MatPreviewMesh_02	Static Mesh	11,983	6,820
SM_PillarFrame	Static Mesh	620	660
SM_PillarFrame300	Static Mesh	620	698

Figure 3-35. *Assets in Columns view*

Show Folders

By default, folders in the Asset Window are displayed, but by unchecking *Show Folders*, only the assets will show, and not the folders.

Show C++ Classes

A few options down is *Show C++ Classes*. This allows you to see files that contain C++ code.

Show Developers Content

The next option in the menu is *Show Developers Content*. Sometimes you might want to experiment with things without risking messing up your game you've been working on, or you may just prefer to keep unfinished assets separate from your game until they've been completed. In these situations, you want a sandbox environment you can work in that's separate from the rest of your content. This is what the Developers Folders are for.

If you click Show Developers Content, you will see an additional entry in the Sources Panel labeled "Developers." If you expand that, you should see another folder with your name on it that you can use to store your test assets. If there were multiple people working on a project, each person would have their own folder. This is so everyone's test assets are not only kept separate from the game but also separate from each other, to reduce unnecessary clutter.

Show Engine Content

The next checkbox is *Show Engine Content*. This will allow you to see and thus modify the source code for the Unreal Engine itself. Even if you know how to code, you shouldn't try modifying any of this content unless you really know what you're doing.

Show Plugins Content

The same goes for *Show Plugins Content*. Checking this will allow you to see the content used by the third-party plugins that have been added onto the Unreal Engine. For the most part, this content is just the source code for these plugins, so, you're probably not ever going to have a need to access it. So you can go ahead and leave these two options unchecked.

Show Localized Content

The next option is *Show Localized Content*. This is used when you are adapting your game to other regions and cultures. Checking this option will allow you to see these kinds of assets, such as Dialog Waves for each different language used or image files that each contain a particular currency symbol.

Show Collections

Under Show Folders is the *Show Collections* option. If enabled, a Collections panel will appear over in the bottom-half of the Sources Panel. *Collections* are a way to help you organize your assets by placing them into groups. Often, organizing your assets into a logical folder structure is enough, but that can only go so far.

For example, let's say you wanted to have a grouping of all your chair assets. You could make a folder called "Chairs" and move all the chairs into it. But what if you also wanted to group all of the yellow objects? You could make a folder called "Yellow," but then you would have to choose whether to put the yellow chair in the Chairs folder or the Yellow folder. And you don't want to have to try and track and maintain multiple copies of your assets either.

The solution is to use Collections, because when you add an asset to a Collection, you are really only adding a shortcut to that asset in the Collection and not the asset itself. So you can add an asset to multiple Collections without having to move or make a copy of the asset itself. You can make a Collection called "Chairs" and add a chair to it, and make a Collection called "Yellow" and add the chair to that as well.

To make a new Collection, click the "Add" button, and you'll be given a list of three types of Collections to choose from, as seen in Figure 3-36. The first two only apply when you are working with other people on the same project and will be grayed out otherwise. The only other option is *Local Collection*.

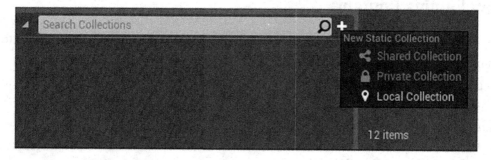

***Figure 3-36.** Adding a new Collection*

Directly to the left of the name of a Collection is an icon indicating what type of Collection it is. There is also a small box that will be gray when the Collection is empty and green when the Collection has content. To add an asset to a Collection, simply click the asset and drag it onto the name of the Collection.

That's how to create *Static Collections*, but there's also a way to create what's called *Dynamic Collections*. For example, if you searched for "lamp" again in the Assets Window, and then clicked the save icon to the right, you can save the search results as a Dynamic Collection. This doesn't save the assets as the Collection, it saves the search query itself as the Collection. Meaning, every time you click the "lamps" Collection, it will be performing that search and returning the results. So if a new asset with the word "lamp" is added, that asset would be automatically added to this Collection.

You can see which of your Collections are Static and which are Dynamic by looking at the icon to the right. A rectangular icon indicates a Static Collection, while a lightning icon indicates a Dynamic Collection (Figure 3-37).

Figure 3-37. *The icons to the right indicate if the Collection is Static or Dynamic*

Search Asset Class Names

The next group of options concern where to look for search terms that you enter in the Asset Window search box. With all these unchecked, it will only look at the name of the asset itself.

For example, if you type the term "blueprint," the only assets that appear are those with "blueprint" in the name. But if *Search Asset Class Names* is checked, you will get a lot more results, because now it will return assets that are of the *type* Blueprint, even if that word isn't in their name.

Search Asset Path

If you click *Search Asset Path*, even more results will appear because now it will also return any assets that have the word "blueprint" in their folder path.

Search Collection Names

Search Collection Names will return assets contained in a Collection with that search term. So the search term "chairs" will bring up the assets added to the Chairs collection.

CHAPTER 3   THE LEVEL EDITOR

Thumbnail Options

The last group of options in the View Options menu concern the thumbnail images of the assets. The slider is used to scale the size of the thumbnails larger or smaller.

The next option is *Thumbnail Edit Mode*. Clicking this gives you the ability to change the perspective on the thumbnails. When you're in Thumbnail Edit Mode, there will be a yellow banner across the bottom, and when you click a thumbnail and drag, instead of dragging that asset, it will rotate the image of the asset within the thumbnail. After you are finished, you can click "Done Editing" to exit Thumbnail Edit Mode.

The final option is *Real-Time Thumbnails*. Some Materials, such as a water Material, have an associated animation. Unchecking Real-Time Thumbnails will turn the animation off in the Content Browser. Note that the Material will still have that animation, the preview of that animation will simply be turned off in the thumbnail.

Colored Folders

Another way to help organize your content is to use a color-coded system for your folders. To change the color of a folder, simply right-click it, in either the Sources Panel or Asset Window, and choose "Set Color" from the menu that appears. You can then set the color in a variety of ways using the Color Picker tool.

Content Browser Windows

If you ever close the Content Browser, you can quickly reopen it by going up to the Toolbar and clicking the Content button (Figure 3-38). This is useful if you want to keep the Content Browser closed while you are editing existing items in your Level, giving you a large Viewport to work with, but still have a way to quickly reopen it.

Figure 3-38. *The Content button will reopen the Content Browser*

Also, the Unreal Editor allows you to have up to four Content Browsers open at once. If you go up to the file menu and go to Window ➤ Content Browser, you can open up to three additional Content Browsers. If you have multiple monitors, you can drag these additional Content Browsers over to those monitors and work on them from there.

Another piece of functionality relating to multiple Content Browsers is the lock button in the upper-right. To understand the lock button, we must temporarily jump ahead a bit and introduce the Find button within the Details Panel.

For example, let's say a Static Mesh Actor is selected. Clicking the Find button in the Static Mesh category of the Details Panel will navigate the Content Browser directly to the Static Mesh asset being used by that Actor (Figure 3-39). Clicking the Find button in the Materials category will navigate to the Material being used by that Actor.

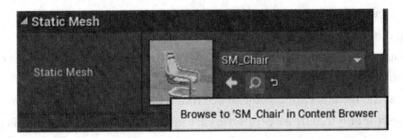

Figure 3-39. *Clicking the Find button will navigate the Content Browser directly to that asset*

However, if you are in a certain folder in the Content Browser and want to remain in that folder, you can click the lock button to lock that Content Browser down, and now when you click one of the Find buttons, it will open that asset in a *new* Content Browser, instead of changing the location in the current one.

Details Panel

When you select an Actor, the Details Panel will display lots of information about that Actor, most of which is editable. At the top of the Details Panel is the name of the Actor, which can be changed (Figure 3-40).

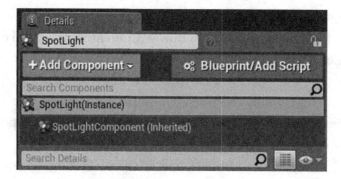

Figure 3-40. *The top of the Details Panel*

To the right of that box you will see a Lock icon. By toggling the Lock icon to the locked setting, this will keep the details of the currently selected Actor locked in the Details Panel, even if other Actors are selected.

Below that is a button for adding a component to the Actor and a button for creating a Blueprint out of the Actor. Below that, you will see the component structure of the Actor. Components and Blueprints will be covered in detail in Chapter 5.

Looking at the Details Panel, you will see that it is mostly comprised of properties of the selected Actor and that those properties are grouped into Categories. This can be a long list, so there is a search box available to quickly find a property or category.

Property Matrix

To the right of the search box is a button that will launch the *Property Matrix*, shown in Figure 3-41. The Property Matrix is for bulk comparison and editing of properties. Meaning it is used to compare and edit the values of properties of multiple Actors at once.

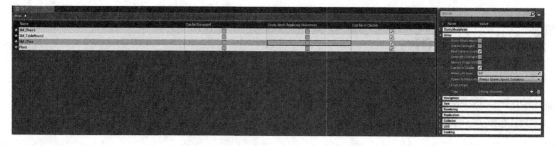

Figure 3-41. *The Property Matrix*

Whichever Actors are selected when the button is clicked will be opened in the Property Matrix. By default, the grid will start with just the Name column, which will display the name of the Actors that have been selected.

To the right of the grid is a menu of properties that are common to all the selected Actors. This menu can be used to select which properties should be displayed as columns in the grid. Just like with the Details Panel itself, there is a search bar you can use to search for a category or property.

To "pin" a property to the grid, click the pin icon to the left of the name. This can be used to quickly compare lots of properties between Actors and quickly edit their values. You can sort by a column by clicking the column label. You can edit the values by clicking any of the cells and making changes. You can copy and paste values between cells, and so on.

View Options

To the right of the Property Matrix button is the View Options menu for the Details Panel (Figure 3-42).

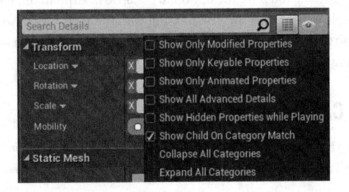

Figure 3-42. *View Options in the Details Panel*

First on the list is *Show Only Modified Properties*. This will hide any properties that still have their default values and only show you those properties which have been modified since this Actor was created.

The next two options on the list are *Show Only Keyable Properties* and *Show Only Animated Properties*. These options will only show properties relating to cinematics and animations.

Next is *Show All Advanced Details*. At the bottom of some of the categories in the Details Panel, there is a little strip with a downward facing triangle in it. This means that the category has "Advanced Details." Advanced Details are properties that are less commonly used and are thus hidden by default to reduce clutter. To view Advanced Details for a category, you can simply click the strip with the triangle to expand the menu, and then click it again to collapse it. But if you want to expand all of the Advanced Details menus at once, you could do so by checking Advanced Details in this menu here.

The next option is *Show Hidden Properties While Playing*. This allows you to see every property on the selected object while the game is being simulated – even properties that aren't normally visible or editable. This option is very useful for debugging purposes, but you have to be careful when changing values for properties that weren't meant to be changed at runtime as this could cause your game to crash or could even cause data to get corrupted.

Next is *Show Child on Category Match*. This is checked by default, but when it is unchecked, the search bar will no longer try to match the text with Category names, it will only search the property names.

By default, all the categories in the Details Panel are expanded. However, they can be collapsed if you wish. You have the option to collapse or expand them individually by clicking the triangle to the left of their names. But with the View Menu, you also have the option to collapse them all at once by clicking *Collapse All Categories* or expand them all at once by clicking *Expand All Categories*.

Transform Category

The Details Panel has a lot of functionality in it that is specific to the type of Actor selected, but the Transform category, shown in Figure 3-43, is common to all Actors.

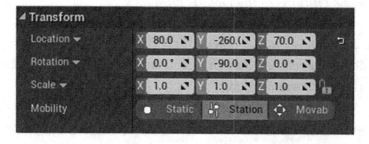

Figure 3-43. *The Transform Category of the Details Panel*

Earlier, you learned how to transform Actors using the Move, Rotate, and Scale tools. But another way to move, rotate, and scale Actors is to use the Transform category of the Details Panel. The tools are useful when placement and scale don't need to be exact and you want to transform things quickly. But for finer precision or when exact values are needed, you can use the Details Panel to insert exact values manually.

The location of an Actor can be changed by changing the X, Y, and Z coordinates in the Location row. For Rotation, you can enter the number of degrees manually or left-click the arrows and drag left and right to adjust the value.

With Scale, you can directly enter a multiplier to scale by. For example, if the Z scale for a chair is currently 1.0, and you change it to 0.5, it will make the chair half as tall. But if you change it from 1.0 to 2.0 instead, it will double the height of the chair.

To the right of the Scale numbers, there is a little lock icon. When it is unlocked, and one of the numbers is changed, it affects that axis only. But let's say you want to scale an Actor uniformly, you can click the lock icon to toggle it to locked, and now any change made to one of the axes will apply to them all equally.

Unless they are already set to their default values, each group of numbers will have a yellow arrow icon to their right. Clicking this icon will reset those numbers to their default values, which for Location and Rotation are all zeroes and for Scale are all ones.

When multiple Actors are selected, any values that happen to be common to all the Actors selected will be displayed, but in all other cases, the text "Multiple Values" will be displayed in the box instead. Entering a value in the box will apply that value to all Actors selected.

Relative vs. World

By clicking their labels, you can change the Location, Rotation, or Scale "type" to either *Relative* or *World* (Figure 3-44). So far, all the Actors we've worked with have had the world itself as its parent, so in those cases there is no difference between the two settings.

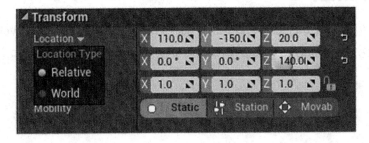

Figure 3-44. *Setting the Location Type to Relative*

In Unreal, Actors can have parent Actors and/or child Actors. This concept will be discussed in more detail in the next section, but for now, just imagine that there is a cone Actor that is set to be the child of a chair Actor. Put another way, the chair is the parent of the cone.

If Location is set to Relative, and the coordinates of the cone are set to 0-0-0, the cone will be located directly in the center of the chair, its parent. But if Location is set to World, the cone will now be located at the center of the world, instead of at the center of its parent.

Mobility

Mobility is a setting that applies mainly to Static Mesh Actors and Light Actors.

For Static Meshes, there are two options – *Static* and *Moveable*. Static means that the Actor will remain stationary the entire time, while Moveable means that it is possible for the Actor's location to change. To clarify, the "static" in "Static Mesh" refers to the fact that the Mesh doesn't have any moving parts relative to itself, while the Static mobility setting means that the Actor's location will never change.

With Light Actors, there is a third option – *Stationary*. This is used for Lights that don't move, but can change in other ways such as being turned on or off or having its color change.

So what's the point of the Mobility setting? Why not just make all Actors moveable even if they are just meant to be decorative? The answer is that moveable Actors require more processing power than static Actors because of things like light and shadow rendering. If an Actor is static, the Engine can predetermine how these things should look. So you should always make an Actor static if you can, and only increase the Mobility if you need it.

World Outliner

The *World Outliner* is used as an organized list of all the Actors in your Level (Figure 3-45). By default, it is located in the upper-right of the Level Editor.

Figure 3-45. *The World Outliner*

Clicking one of the Actors in the World Outliner will select that Actor in the Viewport. Double-clicking will focus on that Actor in the Viewport. This is useful if you have a Level you've been working on for a long time and it has hundreds or even thousands of Actors and you want to go to a specific one. Instead of hunting for it visually throughout your Level, you can just find it in the World Outliner list, double-click, and it will take you straight to it.

World Outliner Data

The World Outliner is comprised of several individual columns. The main column contains the name of the Actor, which can be changed to whatever you like. There are a few ways you can do this. Just like with a file in Windows, if the Actor is already selected and is left-clicked again, it will allow you to rename it. You can also select the Actor and press *F2* to achieve the same result. Or, you can select the Actor, then come down to the box in the Details Panel and rename it from there.

In the left-most column is an icon of an eye for each row. This is a button that will toggle the visibility of the Actor on and off in the Viewport. This is useful when you are working on your Level and you have, for example, a large wall or some other Actor that is getting in the way and making it hard to see what you're doing; you can just toggle its visibility off temporarily to make things easier.

The right-most column lists the type of the Actor. The icon directly to the left of the name of the Actor also gives this information. A small gray house icon is used for Static Mesh Actors and a blue box is used for Brush Actors, and so on. Each type of Actor will have their own special icon. This icon also displays other information. If an Actor's mobility is set to Moveable, an orange dot will appear on the icon. If it is set to Stationary, a yellow dot will appear. If it is set to Static, no dot will appear.

The Actors in the World Outliner can be listed alphabetically. Clicking at the top of the column with the Actors' names will sort the list alphabetically by name. Clicking again will sort the list in reverse alphabetical order. Clicking at the top of the Type column will sort the list alphabetically by type.

Grouping Actors

Another feature of the World Outliner is that you can use it to attach Actors to one another. Dragging the listing of one Actor onto the listing of another will make the first Actor a child of the second Actor. Children will be listed under their parents and indented to the right.

When you move a Parent, it will automatically move all of the Children of that Parent the same amount. But this doesn't work in reverse. Moving a Child will not affect its Parent.

If you want to manipulate a group of Actors all at once, but it doesn't make sense to make any parent-child relationships out of them, you just want them all grouped as equals, you can do that too. First, you need to select all the Actors you wish to be part of the Group. If you want to quickly select a long list of sequential Actors, you can select the first Actor then hold down the *Shift* key and press the down key to continually select the Actors below it. Or you can hold down the *Ctrl* key and left-click each of the Actors you wish to select, or click them again to deselect them.

If you have multiple Actors selected, you will still only see the Move/Rotate/Scale tool on one of them – the last one that was selected. But if you use the tool, it will still apply the same effect to all the Actors in the grouping.

To make a grouping "permanent," you can formally define a selection of Actors as a *Group* by pressing *Ctrl+G*. You will see green brackets around the Actors, letting you know that they are a Group (Figure 3-46). To ungroup Actors, press *Shift+G*. Alternatively, with your Actors selected, you can right-click them and select "Group" or "Ungroup" from the pop-up menu.

Figure 3-46. *Actors that have been defined as a Group will have green brackets around them*

When you create a Group, this will also create a "Group Actor" in the World Outliner, which you can rename to your liking. To select the Group in the World Outliner, you can either select any of the Actors in the Group or just select the Group Actor itself.

So what if you've just done a lot of work grouping several Actors together and then decide you want to adjust one of the individual Actors within the Group? Luckily, there is a way to do this without having to ungroup the Actors and then selecting and grouping them all again. In this situation, you can temporarily "unlock" the Group, which will allow you to move, rotate, or scale the individual Actors without affecting the others, and then "lock" the Group again once you're finished.

All Groups are locked by default upon creation. A locked Group is indicated by the green brackets around them. To unlock a Group, right-click within the Group, scroll down to "Groups" in the menu, and select "Unlock." The brackets around the Group will turn to red, indicating that the Group is unlocked. Adjustments to the individual Actors within the Group can now be made. When you are done, right-click again, go down to "Groups," and select "Lock" to lock the Group once more (Figure 3-47).

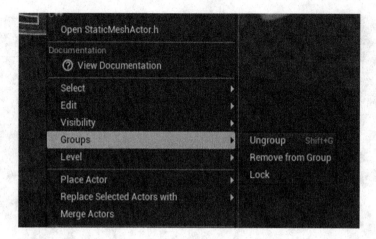

Figure 3-47. *Locking and unlocking Groups*

Unlocking a Group does one other thing. It also allows you to remove individual Actors from a Group. With a Group unlocked, if you right-click one of the individual Actors in the Group, and go down to Groups, there will be an option to "Remove from Group." If you click that, it will remove the Actor from the Group while still keeping all the other Actors grouped together.

Organizing and Finding Actors

As mentioned before, the main purpose of the World Outliner is to be able to organize and find your Actors. One way to help organize your Actors is by grouping them into folders. To create a new folder in the World Outliner, click the New Folder icon, and it will create a new folder which can then be named. If you click the New Folder icon while an Actor is selected, it will create the folder and then automatically add the Actor to that folder.

The World Outliner also has its own search bar. If you know the name of the Actor you're looking for, you can type it in the search bar and it will return all matches, even partial matches (Figure 3-48). For an exact match, meaning the query has to match the name exactly, put a plus sign in front of the search term. To exclude something from the search results, type the word preceded by a negative sign.

Figure 3-48. *Using the World Outliner to search for Actors*

Summary

In this chapter, you learned about the Level Editor. You learned about the various panels of the Level Editor; how to move, rotate, and scale Actors; the concept of snapping; and how to view your Level in different ways. In the next chapter, you will learn about Actors in detail.

CHAPTER 4

Actors

An *Actor* is any object that can be added to a Level. In Chapter 2, you were briefly introduced to some of the various types of Actors in Unreal Engine, including Static Meshes, Brushes, Lights, Volumes, and more. In this chapter, you will get a more in-depth look at those Actor types.

Static Meshes

A *mesh* is a 3D model of an object. There are two specific types of meshes that you can use as Actors in the Unreal Engine. These are the *Static Mesh* and the *Skeletal Mesh*.

A Static Mesh is a Mesh that doesn't bend, deform, or change shape in any way. A Static Mesh can still move around on the screen, it just can't animate. For example, you could use a Static Mesh in the shape of a cube to represent a cardboard box, and you could have that box slide across a surface, or fall off a table, or fly across the room, but you couldn't have flaps that open and close. For objects with moving parts, you would use a Skeletal Mesh.

There are a few different Static Mesh Actors in Place Mode of the Modes Panel. Under the Basic tab, there are Static Meshes in the shape of a cube, sphere, cylinder, and cone, as seen in Figure 4-1. These can be dragged into the Level and then positioned, rotated, and scaled as desired.

© David Nixon 2020
D. Nixon, *Beginning Unreal Game Development*, https://doi.org/10.1007/978-1-4842-5639-8_4

Figure 4-1. *The Modes Panel contains Static Meshes in the form of some basic shapes*

While there are some basic Static Meshes in the Modes Panel, more often than not you will be dragging and dropping Static Meshes from the Content Browser that you import in. The Starter Content comes with some Static Meshes, but this is a small supply. You will want to import in meshes that you download or create yourself in a 3D modeling application. Chapter 10 will show you where you can download collections of meshes and other content for you to use in your games and how to import them into UE4.

Replacing the Mesh of a Static Mesh Actor

In Unreal, the Static Mesh itself is actually a property of the Static Mesh Actor. For example, if you drag a mesh of a chair into the Level, Unreal will create a Static Mesh Actor and assign the chair mesh as the mesh to use for that Actor. You could then tell Unreal to use a mesh of a couch for that Actor, and you would have a couch at the same location, rotation, and scale as the chair was.

One way to replace the mesh of an Actor is to use the dropdown in the Static Mesh category of the Details Panel, as shown in Figure 4-2. The dropdown will contain a search box you can use to find the mesh you want to use.

Figure 4-2. *You can use the dropdown in the Static Mesh category to replace the mesh asset that is used*

Another way is to browse to the replacement mesh in the Content Browser, select it, and then click the arrow in the Static Mesh category of the Details Panel. The arrow will replace the current mesh with whatever is selected in the Content Browser when you click it.

Physics

If you drag a Cube Mesh into a Level, and then click Play, the cube won't fall to the ground, it will just sit suspended in the air. If you press up against it, it won't move.

There are two reasons for this. The first reason is that the default Mobility of a Static Mesh Actor is Static. When the Mobility is Static, we are telling the engine that this Actor will never change its position or rotation for any reason. The Mobility will need to be set to Moveable before the cube will be able to move.

The second reason is that Static Meshes have physics turned off by default. To turn on physics for an Actor, with the Actor selected, go to the Physics category (Figure 4-3) in the Details Panel and check the box next to *Simulate Physics*.

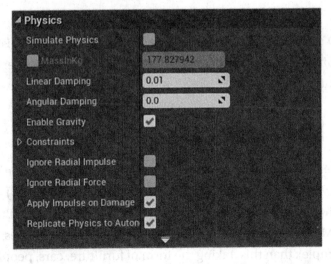

Figure 4-3. *The Physics category in the Details Panel*

If you were to click Play after changing these two settings, the cube would now fall to the ground, and you would be able to push it along the ground.

The Physics category has several other properties. One of them is the mass of the Actor, measured in kilograms. Objects with more mass require more force applied against them in order to be affected.

The next two properties are *Linear Damping* and *Angular Damping*. Damping refers to the amount of drag that is applied to the movement of the object. Similar to having more mass, the more drag an Actor has, the harder it is to move. But in this case, drag is meant to represent friction on the object. For example, if a cube were a smooth block of ice, it would have less drag on it than a rough block of stone, even if the two had the same mass.

The *Linear Damping* property affects translational movement of the object, meaning a change in location, while the *Angular Damping* property affects rotational movement of the object, meaning a change in rotation. By increasing Linear Damping, an Actor won't travel as far when pushed, but will still spin just as easily. Decreasing the Linear Damping to a negative value will cause the Actor to travel farther when pushed and still doesn't affect the spin. Increasing or decreasing the Angular Damping won't affect how far the Actor travels in response to force, but will make it easier or harder to spin the object.

Below the Angular Damping property is the *Enable Gravity* setting. If this is turned off, but Simulate Physics is on, an Actor will still react to force, but gravity will not affect it. This can replicate zero-gravity environments such as outer space.

Brushes

In the world of 3D modeling, a Brush is simply a 3D area of space. This is nearly identical to our understanding of what a Mesh is, but there are several key differences between Brushes and Meshes.

Brushes vs. Meshes

The first difference is that Brushes are used for more basic shapes. In the Modes Panel, in the *Geometry* tab, you can see the Brushes that are available (Figure 4-4). There are some basic geometric shapes and some Brushes in the shape of stairs. In the Basic tab, we also have some Static Meshes available in the form of basic geometric shapes, but Meshes can be much more complex than this, taking the form of furniture, cars, people, and so on.

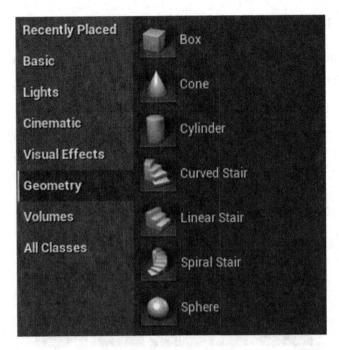

Figure 4-4. *The Brushes available in the Geometry tab of Place Mode*

The second key difference is in how the Unreal Engine handles Brushes and Meshes in memory. For example, let's say you make several copies of a Brush Actor. Each copy made gets stored in memory, and thus each copy made increases the memory demands of the game. However, no matter how many copies of a Mesh you make, it will not increase the memory needed at all. This is because a single Mesh only gets stored in memory once, no matter how many instances of it there are in your Level.

So Meshes look better and they perform better, but the advantage of Brushes is that they are easier to edit than the more complex Meshes. This makes Brushes better suited for making a prototype, or a rough draft, of a Level. So you can use Brushes to sculpt the basic layout of your Level and then replace those Brushes with Meshes once the layout is finalized. In theory, once you have the basic layout sculpted in Brushes, you won't need to keep making minor changes over and over to the more difficult to edit Meshes. While the final version of most games will have very little or no Brushes in it at all, chances are each of its Levels started out made almost exclusively as Brushes.

Brush Settings

Brushes have several different properties available for you to edit under the Brush Settings category of the Details Panel (Figure 4-5).

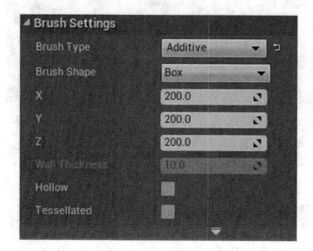

Figure 4-5. *Brush Settings for a Box Brush*

Brush Type

Some of these properties are different, depending on the base shape of the Actor, but one property that is common to all Brushes is *Brush Type*. The Brush Type for any Brush can either be Additive or Subtractive. You can choose what type you want your Brush to be, before you drag it in, by choosing the type in the Modes Panel. Or you can change the type of an existing Brush, by changing it in the Details Panel.

The Additive type is pretty straightforward. An "additive" Brush will add geometry to the Level. A subtractive Brush, on the other hand, will subtract from existing geometry in the Level. For example, if a subtractive Cylinder Brush is dragged onto an additive Box Brush, wherever the subtractive Cylinder Brush is overlapping is causing the geometry that was there to be removed. You can think of subtractive Brushes as "holes" in the shape of the Brush.

This feature is one of the main reasons why Brushes are so well suited to sculpting overall Level design. By adding and subtracting geometry in this way, you can sculpt the layout of a Level much faster than you could trying to use Meshes.

Brush Shape

The next property under Brush Settings is *Brush Shape*. Brush Shape simply refers to if the Brush is in the shape of a box, a cylinder, a cone, and so on. You can choose which Brush Shape to use by choosing which Actor to drag into the Level, but you can also change the shape of an existing Brush Actor in the Brush Settings category.

Size Properties

Some of the properties in Brush Settings are dependent on the shape of the Brush being used. For example, a Box Brush will have X, Y, and Z properties denoting the length of the Box in those dimensions. Adjusting these values will adjust the size of the Box. This is similar to using the Scale property in the Transform category, with one key difference when it comes to Materials that I will talk about in the section on Materials.

The Cylinder and Cone Brushes have their size determined by just a Z length and an *Outer Radius* property. The Z is how tall the cone or cylinder is, and the Outer Radius is how wide around it is. For the Cone, this is the radius as measured at the base. For the Sphere Brush, radius is the only property used to determine its size.

Sides Properties

The Cylinder and Cone Brushes also have a property called *Sides*. As you might have noticed already with these Brush shapes, their "curved" edges, so to speak, aren't actually curves, but are made up of a series of flat sides. The Sides property determines how many of these flat sides the Brush has. The more sides it has, the smoother around it will appear.

The Sphere Brush has a property similar to this, which is the *Tessellation* factor. The higher this number is, the more sides the sphere will have, and the smoother it will appear.

The Cylinder and Cone Brushes also have the property *Align to Side*. If this is checked, it will align the sides of the Brush with the grid.

Hollow Property

Another property of Brushes that is common to the Box, Cone, and Cylinder Brushes is whether or not the Brush is *Hollow*. This is just what it sounds like. If this property is checked, instead of the Brush being solid all the way through, it will be hollow inside, and the Brush will essentially be a shell, with walls of some thickness. For Box Brushes, this is set with the *Wall Thickness* property. For Cylinder Brushes, this is set by the *Inner Radius* property. The Inner Radius is the radius of the hollow part. For Cone Brushes, this is set by both the Inner Radius property and the *Cap Z* property. The Cap Z property determines how tall the hollow area is within the cone. For each of these, the property is grayed out unless the Hollow property is checked.

One thing the Hollow feature is particularly useful for is for quickly creating rooms or buildings. This can be done by making a large Box Brush, setting it to Hollow, and then using a smaller, subtractive Box Brush to make a doorway.

Stair Brushes

The *Linear Stair*, shown in Figure 4-6, is the simplest of the three Stair Brushes. It has Length, Height, and Width properties to determine the size of each individual step (Figure 4-7). You can also choose the number of steps for the staircase. The default is 10 but you can make this larger or smaller as you wish.

Figure 4-6. *A Linear Stair Brush*

The *Add to First Step* property is essentially a Step Height property for the first step only. While the Step Height property increases or decreases the height of all of the steps, the Add to First Step property will only affect the height of the first step.

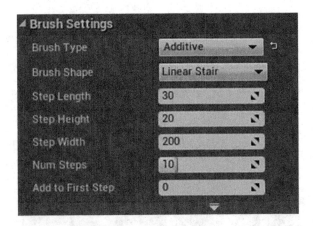

Figure 4-7. *Brush Settings for a Linear Stair*

The *Curved Stair* (Figure 4-8) has some of the same properties as the Linear Stair, such as Step Height, Step Width, Number of Steps, and Add to First Step. But it also has some other properties that pertain to its curve (Figure 4-9).

Figure 4-8. *A Curved Stair Brush*

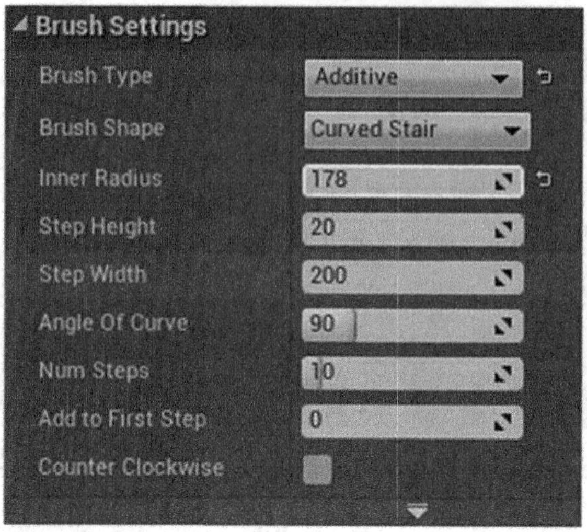

Figure 4-9. *Brush Settings for a Curved Stair*

The first of these properties is the *Inner Radius*. Imagine the Curved Stair wrapping around an invisible column. When the Curved Stair is selected, you will see the Transform tool at the center of this invisible column. The Inner Radius property sets the length between the center of this invisible column and the edge of the staircase. In other words, it affects the width of this "invisible column."

Next is the *Angle of Curve* property. This will set the angle that is made between the two vectors pointing from the center of the invisible column to each end of the staircase. The default is 90 degrees.

Last is the *Counter Clockwise* property. This one is pretty straightforward. With this unchecked, the staircase will curve in a clockwise direction. With it checked, the staircase will instead curve in a counterclockwise direction.

The final staircase is the *Spiral Stair* (Figure 4-10), whose Brush Settings category can be seen in Figure 4-11. With the Spiral Stair, the Step Height property is a little different than it is on the other two stairs. With the Spiral Stair, the Step Height won't affect how tall each step is, it will affect how much each step overlaps the step above and below it.

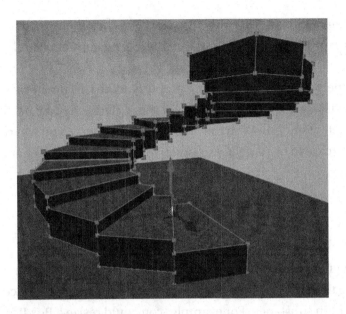

Figure 4-10. *A Spiral Stair Brush*

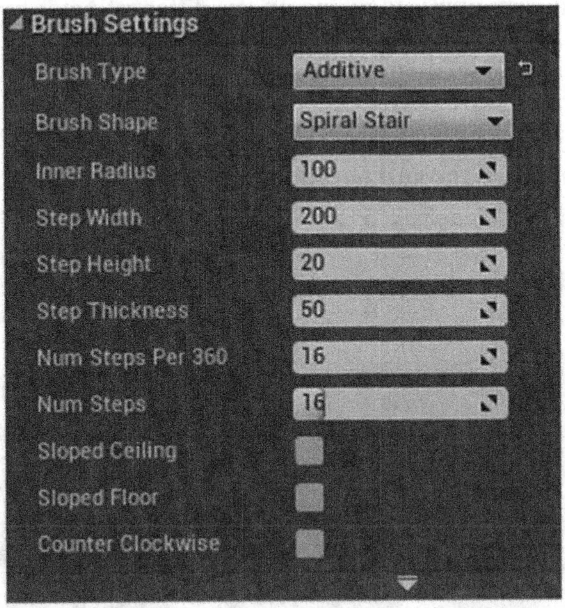

Figure 4-11. *Brush Settings for a Spiral Stair*

At the Default Value, each step overlaps its adjacent steps by about 50%. But if the value is increased, the amount of overlap will begin to decrease, and eventually the steps will no longer overlap and begin to have some distance from each other. If you want to make each step actually taller, you need to use the *Step Thickness*.

83

The Spiral Staircase has a *Num Steps* property like the other two, but it also has a *Num Steps Per 360* property. This defines the number of steps in one full spiral of the staircase.

The next property is the *Sloped Ceiling* property. With this unchecked, the underside of the staircase will just resemble upside down stairs. If it is checked, it will make the underside completely smooth. With the *Sloped Floor* property, you can change the top surface of the staircase to be perfectly smooth. You can, in essence, change a staircase into a curved ramp.

Materials

In the Unreal Engine, a *Material* is an asset that you can apply to the surface of a Brush or Mesh, to make that surface, and thus the geometry behind that surface, look like it's made out of a certain substance. For example, you could resize a Box Brush and use it as a wall. Then, if you apply a wood Material to the wall, it will look like a wooden wall.

Note that, while this chapter is focusing on the different Actor types, Materials aren't Actors themselves. They are simply an important property of Mesh and Brush Actors which is why they are being discussed here.

To apply a Material to a surface, select the Material in the Content Browser and drag it into the Viewport and onto the surface you wish to apply it to, as shown in Figure 4-12.

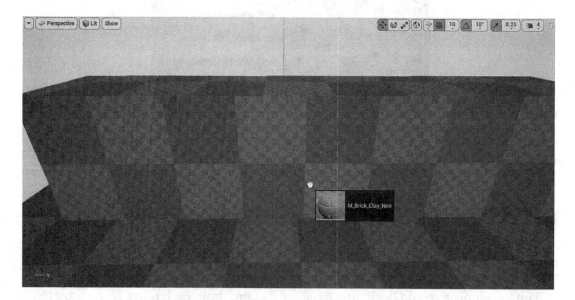

Figure 4-12. *Drag a Material onto a surface to apply it to the surface*

Apply Material to All Surfaces

If you want a Material to be applied to all the surfaces of a Brush, one way to do this is to select the Material first, and with that Material selected in the Content Browser, drag the Brush Actor into the Level, and it will get created with that Material applied to all the surfaces of the Brush.

If you want to apply a Material to all the surfaces of a Brush that is already existing in your Level, perform the following steps:

1. Make sure you don't already have the Brush selected. If you do, just click one of the other Actors in the World Outliner.

2. With the Brush unselected, click one of the surfaces of the Brush to select just that surface. When only a surface or surfaces of the Brush are selected, and not the Brush itself, the *Surface Materials*, *Geometry*, and *Surface Properties* categories will appear in the Details Panel.

3. Go down to the Geometry category and click "Select," then "Select All Adjacent Surfaces," or use the shortcut *Shift+J*, and now all the surfaces of the Brush will be selected.

4. Drag a Material onto the Brush and it will apply that Material to all the surfaces.

Surface Materials Category

In addition to dragging and dropping, another way you can apply a Material to a surface is to use the *Surface Materials* category of the Details Panel (Figure 4-13). This works just like replacing the Static Mesh did in the earlier section.

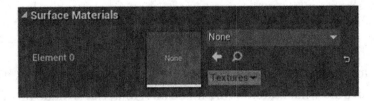

Figure 4-13. *The Surface Materials category*

You can use the dropdown box to select the Material you want to use. Or you can select the Material you want to use in the Content Browser and then click the arrow to apply it. Or, if you want to find the Material that is currently applied in the Content Browser, click the magnifying glass to go straight to it.

Elements

A single Mesh can have different Materials applied to different parts of it. When a mesh gets created in a 3D modeling program, such as Maya or 3D Studio Max, if it has different materials applied to different parts of its surface, once that mesh gets imported into the Unreal Editor, each of those sections of surface becomes known as Elements, and you will have the ability to apply a different Material to each Element, as seen in Figure 4-14.

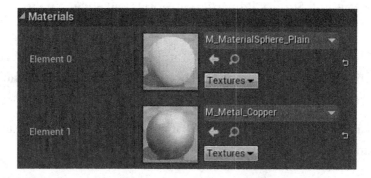

Figure 4-14. *Each Element of a Mesh can have a different Material*

If you drag a Material onto the Mesh through the Viewport, the Material will only be applied to the specific Element it was dragged onto. In the Details Panel, in the Materials category, there will be one Element for each Material, and you can set them each individually.

Textures

I won't go into too much detail about *Textures* in this beginner-level book, but just know that Textures are what Materials are made of. A Material is made up of one or more Textures, and each Texture is just an image file that defines one of the properties of the Material. So one Texture may be the actual colors of the Material, while another Texture maps its smoothness or roughness, and so on. This data is combined to form the composite Material.

Textures should be square image files with dimensions that are powers of two. For example, images whose dimensions, in pixels, are 64 x 64, 1024 x 1024, 2048 x 2048, and so on. UE4 supports importing the following formats for use as textures – .bmp, .png, .jpg, .float, .pcx, .psd, .tga, .exr, .dds, and .hdr.

The Textures dropdown in the Materials category of the Details Panel will show you the Textures that make up the currently applied Material. If you select one, it will take you to that Texture in the Content Browser.

Surface Properties Category

When a Material is applied to the surface of a Brush, and you select that surface, there will be a *Surface Properties* category in the Details Panel (Figure 4-15). Before we discuss that, however, you need to understand how the axes of a Material are labeled. A Material is a two-dimensional object, and normally you would use X and Y as the names of the axes of a 2D object. However, X and Y are already being used to describe two of the axes of our Levels. To avoid confusion, the letters U and V are used for the axes of a Material.

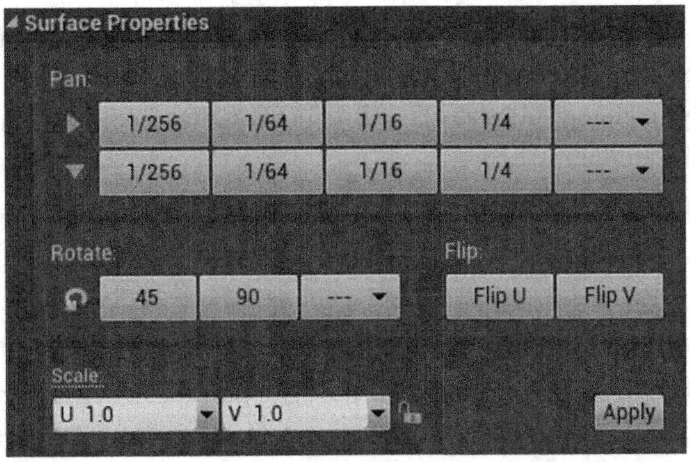

Figure 4-15.   The Surface Properties category

At the top of the Surface Properties category is a section where you can pan the Material across the surface of the object. The first row of buttons is used to pan the Material along its U-axis. The different values represent how much to pan with each click. The last column can be used to enter a custom amount. The second row of buttons is used to pan the Material along the V-axis.

Below that is a section where you can rotate the Material relative to the surface it's on. You can toggle which direction the Material will rotate, either clockwise or counterclockwise, and then there are buttons to rotate it 45 degrees, 90 degrees, or a custom amount.

To the right of that is a section where you can flip the Material, either along the U-axis or the V-axis.

Material Scaling

When you scale an Actor, the Material that is applied to it will get scaled as well, meaning it will get stretched or compressed. Even if you scale the Actor first, and then apply the Material, the effect will be the same.

With Static Meshes, there's no way around this. Brushes, however, are a bit more flexible. If the Material on a Brush surface gets scaled, you can see it in the Details Panel, in the Scale section of the Surface Properties category. To reset the scaling, you simply need to set the Scale property back to a 1:1 ratio and then click the Apply button.

With Brushes, you can edit the dimensions directly, instead of having to rely on scaling. When you change the size of a Brush in this way, it doesn't change the scale ratio of the Material. So if you use the X, Y, and Z properties of the Brush, under the Brush Settings category, to change the size of the Brush, no matter what size you make the Brush, the ratio will remain 1:1.

Lights

In Unreal Engine, a *Light* is simply an Actor that will generate light for your Level. They are not meant to represent the object producing the light, only the light itself. You would use a Mesh for, say, a lamp or a flashlight and then use a Light Actor to produce the light itself.

Wherever you place the Light Actor in the Level is where the light will emanate from. If an object gets in the path of some light, the engine will generate shadows. Lighting and shadows take a relatively long time to render, so there are various settings meant to help you save on performance cost, such as the Mobility setting, discussed later on in the section. There are also different types of Light Actors in UE4, depending on the type of light source you are trying to mimic. These are discussed in the following section.

Overview of Light Types

There are five types of Light Actors in Unreal, as seen in Figure 4-16.

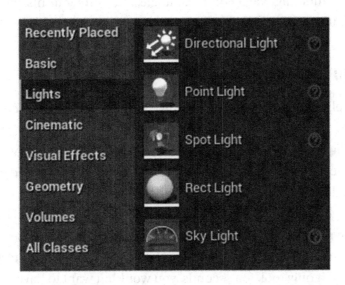

Figure 4-16. *The five Light Actors available in Unreal*

The first of these is the *Directional Light Actor*. The Directional Light Actor is used to emulate light coming from an extremely long distance away, such as outer space. All the light will hit the level at the same angle, meaning all shadows produced by this light will be parallel. This Actor is used primarily for sunlight and moonlight.

Next is the *Point Light*. The Point Light will produce light that emanates in all directions. This is useful for mimicking the light coming from a light bulb, or fire, for example.

The *Spot Light*, on the other hand, will emit light in the shape of a cone. This is like the light coming from a flashlight, or, as the name suggests, a spot light, like they use at the theater.

The *Rect Light*, or Rectangular Light, projects lights out of a rectangular plane. This is useful for representing any light sources that are rectangular in shape, such as televisions, monitors, smartphones, overhead lights, and so on.

The *Sky Light Actor* is used to emulate the light that gets reflected off of the atmosphere and other distant objects. When light comes from the sun or moon, a lot of it comes through as direct sunlight or moonlight. That's what the Directional Light Actor mentioned earlier represents. But some of that sunlight or moonlight hits particles in the atmosphere, or clouds, or distant mountaintops, and then gets reflected off of those objects at a different angle. The Sky Light Actor represents that light that gets scattered in the atmosphere, or reflected off of other objects, and that comes through as weaker, indirect sunlight or moonlight at all different angles. In simpler terms, you could say it represents the faint glow of the atmosphere.

Building the Lighting

Changes to a Level will not affect the lighting like they should until the Editor is told to *build* the lighting.

Building the lighting just means that the Engine runs a lot of calculations to determine how the light and shadows should now look on objects based on the changes that have occurred since the last time the lighting was built.

To build the lighting, simply go up to the Toolbar and click the Build button (Figure 4-17). The reason the Editor has you do this manually is because when you start to have many Actors and/or Lights in your Level, the build can take quite a while to perform. So, even if it only took ten seconds, you wouldn't want to have to wait those ten seconds every time you moved an Actor in your Level. This allows you to build only when you're ready.

Figure 4-17. *The Build button*

Mobility

In the Transform category of a Light Actor or Static Mesh Actor is the *Mobility* property (Figure 4-18). If an Actor is Static, that means it can't move or change any other property while the game is running. If an Actor is Stationary, it still can't move, but it *can* change its other properties during the game; a Light could change its color or brightness, for example. If an Actor is Moveable, it can move and change its other properties during the game.

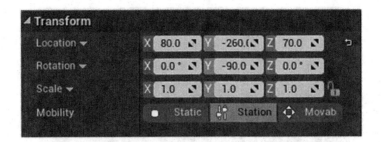

Figure 4-18. *The Mobility property in the Transform category*

As you move to the right along these three settings, they get more flexible in terms of what the Actor can do, but they also demand more resources from the processor. Actors set to Static have low performance cost, Actors set to Stationary have medium performance cost, and Actors set to Moveable have high performance cost.

The Mobility settings of two or more Actors when they interact also affect performance. For example, when a Light Actor shines light on a Static Mesh Actor, the way that the light and shadows are rendered depends on the combination of Mobility settings. A Light set to Static shining on a Static Mesh set to Static, for instance, will use mostly precomputed lighting and shadows and have a low performance cost. On the other hand, a Light set to Moveable shining on a Static Mesh set to Moveable will use all dynamic lighting and shadows and have a very high performance cost.

Directional Light

The *Directional Light*, shown in Figure 4-19, is used to represent sunlight or moonlight. It has several properties that can be viewed and edited in the Details Panel.

Figure 4-19. *A Directional Light Actor*

Intensity

In the *Light* category of the Details Panel, shown in Figure 4-20, the first of these properties is *Intensity*. This controls the brightness of the Light. Increasing the Intensity makes the Light get brighter and decreasing the Intensity makes the Light get dimmer.

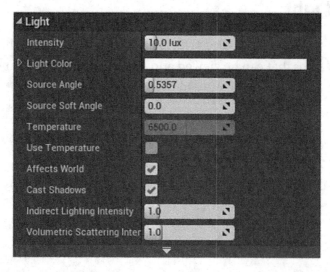

Figure 4-20. *The Light category properties of a Directional Light*

Light Color

The next property is the *Light Color*. By default, the color of a Light is white, but this can be changed. There are two ways to change the Light Color property. One way is to click the triangle to the left of the property name and expand the RGB menu. With the RGB menu, you can adjust the amount of red, green, and blue in the Light to determine its overall color.

The second way to edit the Light Color is to click the strip, to the right of the property name, that previews the color. This will open the *Color Picker*, shown in Figure 4-21. The Color Picker is available in several places in the Unreal Editor where there is a need to select a color.

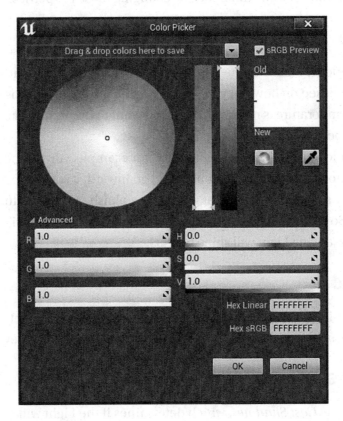

Figure 4-21. *The Color Picker*

The Color Picker actually gives you several ways in which you can select a color. You can select one from the color wheel. You can adjust the saturation and the brightness using a pair of sliders. You can set the Hue, Saturation, and Brightness values directly. It is another place where you can set the Red, Green, and Blue values. And finally, you can use the hexadecimal representation of a color if you wish.

Source Angle

The next two properties are *Source Angle* and *Source Soft Angle*. These affect how soft the shadows produced by the Directional Light are. The higher the value, the softer the edges of the shadows will be. The default value of 0.5357 for Source Angle is meant to represent how shadows should look in sunlight.

Be aware that these properties take advantage of a new computer graphics technology called *raytracing*, which is only supported by the latest graphics cards. If you haven't bought an expensive graphics card or a new gaming computer recently, there's a good chance you won't see any difference by changing these properties.

Temperature

The next two properties relate to the *Temperature* of the Light. Temperature changes the color of the Light based on how hot you tell the Engine the light source is supposed to be. By default, Temperature is not used, but if you want to use it, you can check the *Use Temperature* property.

If you've ever looked at the fire in a fireplace, for example, you will notice it's made up of different colors. Most of it is red, but as you go inward, it starts to get more orange, and then you may see wisps of purple and blue. The bluish parts are actually the hottest parts of the fire. So as the Temperature setting is decreased, the Light will shine redder, and as it is increased, the Light will shine bluer.

Affects World

The next property is *Affects World*. This simply toggles whether the Light is enabled or disabled. If this is unchecked, it will be as if the Light isn't even in the Level.

Cast Shadows

The next property is *Cast Shadows*, which determines if the Light will cause shadows to be cast when objects block the Light's path. You would want this checked for a more realistic environment. However, shadows are processor intensive, so if you were in need of performance savings, you might choose to uncheck this for some of the Lights in your Level.

When this property is checked, there are a couple more properties you can configure relating to casting shadows. These are *Cast Static Shadows* and *Cast Dynamic Shadows*, which can be found by expanding the Light category. Cast Static Shadows determines whether or not this light should cast a shadow when shone on static objects, such as a Static Mesh Actor whose Mobility is set to Static. Cast Dynamic Shadows determines whether or not this light should cast a shadow when shone on dynamic objects, such as a Static Mesh Actor whose Mobility is set to Stationary or Moveable.

Indirect Lighting Intensity

The next property is *Indirect Lighting Intensity*. If some light gets reflected off of another surface, that reflected light is called "indirect lighting" and can also light up objects in the Level. This property will determine how much this reflected light affects the other objects it shines upon.

Volumetric Scattering Intensity

The last property in the Light category is *Volumetric Scattering Intensity*. This property applies to fog, which will be covered in the next section. When light passes through fog, it will scatter in various directions. The higher the Volumetric Scattering Intensity, the more the light will scatter.

Point Light

The *Point Light* emanates light in all directions. It has many of the same properties that the Directional Light has, with a few additional ones as well, as seen in Figure 4-22.

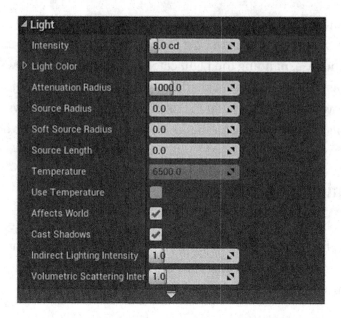

Figure 4-22. *The Light category properties of a Point Light*

The first of these is the *Attenuation Radius*. This determines how far from the source the Light will still affect objects in your Level. In the Level Editor, this is represented by a blue sphere (Figure 4-23). The higher the Attenuation Radius, the larger the sphere will be, and the farther the light will extend from its source.

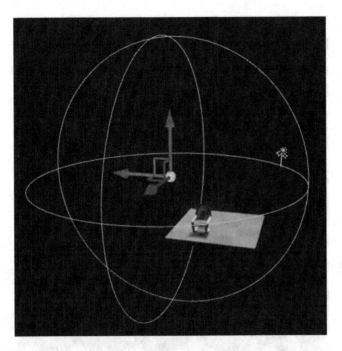

Figure 4-23. *The attenuation sphere surrounding a Point Light*

The next three properties are *Source Radius, Soft Source Radius,* and *Source Length.* The light from a Point Light will actually emanate from a single point in the Level. However, let's say you have a Light that is supposed to be coming from a long, thin fluorescent bulb, and it is above a very shiny floor. If there were a reflection of the bulb in the floor, you would want it to be in the same shape as the bulb. You can use these three properties to adjust the size and shape that the light source will appear in reflections.

Spot Light

The *Spot Light* is very similar to the Point Light, except that instead of shining light in all directions, it shines it in a specific direction, in a cone shape, as seen in Figure 4-24. The Spot Light has all the same properties as the Point Light, with the addition of two more properties – the *Inner Cone Angle* and the *Outer Cone Angle.*

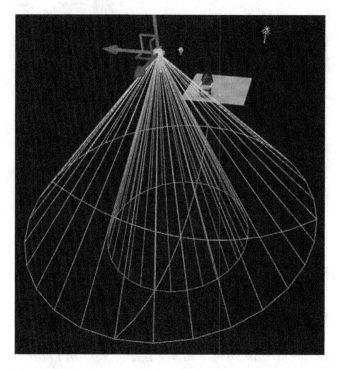

Figure 4-24. *A Spot Light Actor*

Within the Inner Cone of the Spot Light, the light will be at its brightest and will be just as bright at any spot within the Inner Cone. From the outer edge of the Inner Cone to the outer edge of the Outer Cone, the Intensity of the light will gradually fall off to nothing.

So you can use the Inner Cone Angle and the Outer Cone Angle to set the size of these cones and determine how much of the light is at full brightness and how much of the light is part of the gradual falloff portion.

Rect Light

The next light is the *Rect Light*. This Actor emits light in a rectangular shape. The first of its unique properties are *Source Width* and *Source Height*. These are used to represent the size of the light source. For example, a 90-inch television would require a larger Source Width and Source Height than a 24-inch television would.

The next two properties are *Barn Door Angle* and *Barn Door Length*. A barn door, in the context of lighting, is a set of flaps attached to the front of the light. They are usually used on studio lights, and they help the photographer, cinematographer, and so on make subtle adjustments to the lighting by adjusting the angle of the flaps. You can use the Barn Door Angle and Barn Door Length properties to emulate those kinds of effects.

The next property is *Source Texture*. You can apply a texture to the light, just like you would with a Material, and then the light will look as if it is being filtered through that texture.

Sky Light

The *Sky Light* (Figure 4-25) is used to represent the reflection of light from the atmosphere or faraway objects in the sky such as clouds or mountaintops. To determine at what distance this Light should appear to emanate from, we need to define at what distance the sky should be considered to start.

Figure 4-25. A Sky Light Actor

By default, the Sky Light's *Source Type* property will be set to "SLS Captured Scene," which just means that the sky will be defined as any point that is the *Sky Distance Threshold* away from the Sky Light Actor. So if the Sky Light is placed at the center of the Level, with a Sky Distance Threshold of 150,000, you are saying that the sky should begin 150,000 units from the center of the Level.

There is also the option to change the Source Type to "SLS Specified Cubemap" and then provide a file called a Cubemap to define the area that should be considered the sky. Cubemaps, however, are beyond the scope of this beginner-level book.

Fog

Atmospheric Fog

The *Atmospheric Fog Actor* is used to add a realistic looking atmosphere to a Level, as seen in Figure 4-26. The Atmospheric Fog Actor can be found in the Visual Effects tab in Place Mode of the Modes Panel.

The Directional Light Actor can be used to represent sunlight, but this alone won't make the Level look like it's outside. Atmospheric Fog will add a blue sky and a sun disc and will cause objects to get a little foggy when they are far away in the distance.

Figure 4-26. *The Atmospheric Fog Actor adds an atmosphere to the Level*

Sun Disc

By default, the sun disc of the Atmospheric Fog will appear on the horizon, giving a look of sunrise or sunset. But it is possible to combine the Atmospheric Fog Actor with the Directional Light Actor, which will cause the sun to appear in the sky, like it does in

Figure 4-27. To do so, check the property *Atmosphere/Fog Sun Light* of the Directional Light Actor. This property can be found in the Light category, after clicking the arrow to expand the menu.

Figure 4-27. *Here, the Engine is using the rotation of the Directional Light to determine where to place the sun disc in the sky*

If the Atmosphere/Fog Sun Light property is checked, the Atmospheric Fog will use the rotation of the Directional Light to determine where the sun disc should be placed in the sky. The Engine will look at the direction that the light rays from the Directional Light are set to hit the Level and then calculate where in the sky the Sun should be for that to make sense. If you use the Rotation Tool on the Directional Light to change the angle of the light rays, it will change the location of the sun disc in the sky.

Atmospheric Fog Properties

The first property under the Atmosphere category (Figure 4-28) is *Sun Multiplier*. The higher its value, the brighter the sky and the fog will appear. In other words, you can use it to make the Level look more or less sunny.

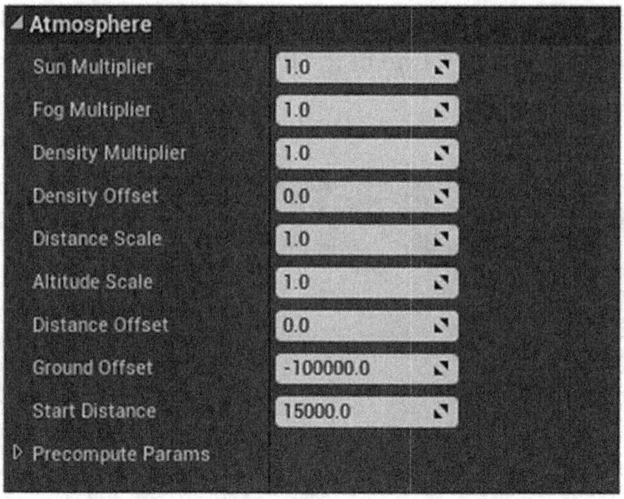

Figure 4-28. *The properties of an Atmospheric Fog Actor*

The next three properties affect the fog only. They are also somewhat subtle in their effects, especially when the fog is far away. The *Fog Multiplier* property affects how much the light affects the fog. Higher values will make the fog seem brighter. The *Density Multiplier* affects how dense the fog is. Higher values will make the fog denser, and lower values will make it less dense. The *Density Offset* affects the opacity of the fog. Higher values will make the fog more opaque, while lower values will make the fog more transparent. Basically, these three properties will make the fog seem more or less thick in subtly different ways.

The next property is *Distance Scale*. This will affect the scale of the units of any other properties of the Actor that have to do with distance. For example, changing the Distance Scale from 1 to 2 will cause any distance units to be double in length. Setting the Distance Scale higher is useful when you have a large Level, and it would be easier to work with larger units of distance.

The *Altitude Scale* is just like the Distance Scale except it only affects the Z-axis, whereas the Distance Scale affects all three dimensions.

Next is the *Ground Offset* property. This tells the Engine where sea level should be considered to be at in our Level. This is important to the Atmospheric Fog Actor, as the fog will only appear at places above sea level. The default value is -100,000. This is saying that sea level starts at -100,000 on the Z-axis. So if the ground of our Level is placed at 0 on the Z-axis, this means that our Level is 100,000 centimeters, or 1000 meters, above sea level.

The *Start Distance* property controls how far away from the camera the Level will start to appear foggy. Higher values will make the fog appear distant, and lower values will make the fog appear close.

Under the *Sun* category, the first property is *Sun Disc Scale*. The Sun Disc Scale property is very straightforward. It simply defines the size of the sun disc. Increasing its value will make the sun appear bigger in the sky (Figure 4-29), and decreasing its value will make the sun appear smaller.

Figure 4-29. *Setting the Sun Disc Scale to a high value will make the sun appear large in the sky*

Exponential Height Fog

The *Exponential Height Fog Actor* is used to add regular fog to your Level. The reason it has "Height" in its name is that the altitude will affect the thickness of the fog. Lower altitudes will have thicker fog, while higher altitudes will have thinner fog. The altitude is calculated relative to the Fog Actor's position.

Now let's take a look at some of its properties. The first property in the *Exponential Height Fog Component* category is *Fog Density*. This one is pretty self-explanatory. The higher the value, the denser, or thicker, the fog will be.

The next property is *Fog Height Falloff*. This property controls how quickly the fog changes thickness as the altitude changes. Higher values cause the fog to change quickly with only small changes in altitude, while lower values make it so that large changes in altitude are required to see any change in fog thickness.

Next, the three properties under *Second Fog Data* allow you to create a second layer of fog. *Fog Density* and *Fog Height Falloff* work the same way as they do for the first fog layer. *Fog Height Offset* sets the Z value of the second fog relative to the location of the first fog. For example, if Fog Height Offset is set to 100, then the second fog will be 100 centimeters above the first fog.

The next property, *Fog Inscattering Color*, simply sets the color of the fog. The color can be set either by the Color Picker or by setting its RGBA properties.

The next property, *Fog Max Opacity*, sets how opaque the fog can get at its thickest point. With a value of 1.0, the fog will be able to be fully opaque at low altitudes, meaning you won't be able to see through it at all. With a value of 0, the fog will be completely invisible at any altitude.

The next property, *Start Distance*, is used the same with the Exponential Height Fog Actor as it is with the Atmospheric Fog Actor. With a value of 0, the player will be directly inside the fog, while higher values will cause the fog to appear at a distance.

Finally, the *Fog Cutoff Distance* property determines how far away an object has to be to not have any fog effect applied to it. Objects beyond the distance specified will not be affected by the fog.

Player Start Actor

If a Level does not contain a *Player Start Actor*, the player will begin the Level at position (0,0,0). If you want to have control over where the player will start the Level, you need to place a Player Start Actor.

The Player Start Actor can be accessed from the Modes Panel under the Basic tab. Wherever you place it is where the player will start when the Level begins. It can also be used to specify the direction the player should be facing when the Level starts. The light blue arrow coming out of the Actor indicates the direction (Figure 4-30). You can rotate the Actor to change the direction the arrow is pointing.

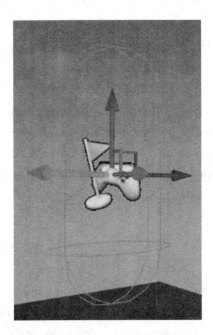

Figure 4-30. *The Player Start Actor*

If you ever place your Player Start Actor somewhere in the Level where it intersects with another object, the icon of the game controller will change to a label that says "Bad Size" (Figure 4-31). To make sure the player doesn't start the Level stuck in something, move the Player Start Actor to a position where the icon shows the controller instead.

Figure 4-31. *If the Player Start Actor intersects with another object, it will display a "Bad Size" label*

While you are developing your Levels, you will often want to test something or look at something in-game right in the spot you are at in the Viewport at that moment instead of wherever the Player Start Actor might be. To do so, right-click the Viewport and then choose *Play From Here* toward the bottom of the menu.

If you want to move around the Viewport and continually start the Level at wherever you are at that moment, you can go to the dropdown menu to the right of the Play button and choose *Spawn player at...* ➤ *Current Camera Location*. When you want to go back to using the Player Start Actor, go back to the dropdown menu and choose *Spawn player at...* ➤ *Default Player Start*.

Components

Components are various objects or functionality that can be attached to Actors. There are many different kinds of Components. Some of the types of Components are objects that are also used as Actors on their own. For example, you could attach a Static Mesh as a Component to another Actor. Or, you could attach a Light as a Component to another Actor.

Other Components, such as *Movement Components*, do not have their own Actor type and are only used as Components on other Actors. For example, a *Rotating Movement Component* attached to an Actor will cause that Actor to rotate, but doesn't have any use on its own.

Adding Components

When you want to attach a Component to an Actor, select that Actor, then go over to the Details Panel and click the green button that says *Add Component*. You'll get a long list of different Components you can add, grouped by category (Figure 4-32). There will also be a search bar that you can use to quickly find a type of Component by name.

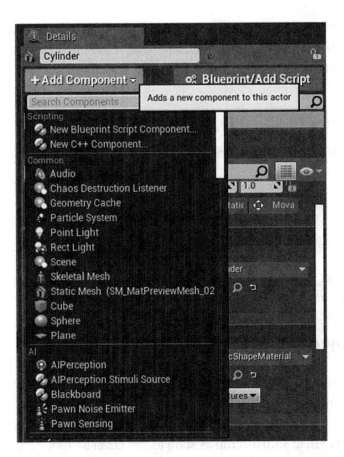

Figure 4-32. *Use the Add Component button in the Details Panel to add a component to an Actor*

To add a Static Mesh from the Content Browser as a Component, after clicking Add Component, instead of choosing one of the pre-made meshes available in the Modes Panel, click the generic "Static Mesh." This will add an empty Static Mesh Component to the Actor. You can then choose which Static Mesh to use by using the Static Mesh section of the Details Panel.

Component Structure

Below the Add Component button is a section where you can see the Component structure of an Actor (Figure 4-33). There is a parent-child relationship where Components can have sub-Components which, in turn, can have their own sub-Components. Sub-Components will appear underneath their parent Components and will be indented further to the right than their parent. If you move or rotate a Component, it will move or rotate all of its sub-Components as well.

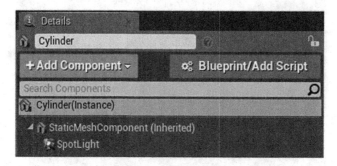

Figure 4-33. *The Component structure of an Actor. Here, a Spot Light is a child of a Static Mesh, which is a child of an Actor named "Cylinder"*

Rotating Movement Component

A *Rotating Movement Component* will cause the Actor it is attached to to rotate. It can be added by clicking "Add Component," going down to the "Movement" category, and selecting "Rotating Movement." If the Mobility setting of the Actor has been set to Moveable, it will begin to spin around as soon as the Level begins.

The Rotating Movement Component has some properties you can edit (Figure 4-34). The first property is *Rotation Rate*, which specifies how much to rotate the Actor and in which direction. Whatever angle you enter, it will rotate the Actor that many degrees per second. For example, setting the rotation around the Z-axis to 180 degrees will cause the Actor to spin one full 360-degree rotation, in that direction, every two seconds.

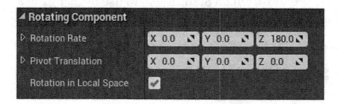

Figure 4-34. *The properties of a Rotating Movement Component*

Another property you can edit is the *Pivot Translation*. By default, with this at (0,0,0), the Actor will rotate around its center. However, you can enter X, Y, and Z values to change the pivot point to a different location. For example, a value of 100 for the X value will cause the Actor to rotate around a point 100 units, along the X-axis, from the center of the Actor.

Volumes

In the Unreal Engine, a *Volume* is a 3D area of space that is invisible to the player and serves a specific purpose depending on its type. A Volume is actually another type of Brush. However, for the remainder of this book, Volume Brushes will be referred to as simply Volumes in order to avoid confusion with Geometry Brushes. You can access a variety of Volumes from the Volumes tab in the Modes Panel (Figure 4-35).

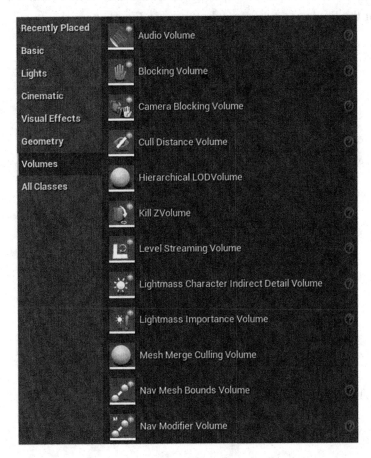

Figure 4-35. *There are several Volumes available in the Volumes tab of Place Mode*

Blocking Volumes

A *Blocking Volume* will prevent Actors from being able to enter that Volume. So you can use them as a type of force field or just to block off areas of your Level where you don't intend for players to go.

A *Camera Blocking Volume* is just like a Blocking Volume except it only blocks Cameras. This is useful in third-person games when you want to keep the Camera confined to certain parts of the Level.

Trigger Volumes

Perhaps the most important type of Volume is the *Trigger Volume*, shown in Figure 4-36. Trigger Volumes are used to trigger something called an *Event* when an Actor enters or exits them. In the next chapter, *Blueprints*, you will learn how to define a set of instructions for the Engine to perform when certain Events occur.

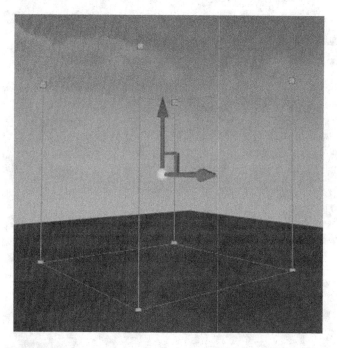

Figure 4-36. *A Trigger Volume*

For example, if you had a haunted house in your Level, you could place a Trigger Volume in the doorway of the entrance and name it "PlayerEntersHouseVolume." Then, using a Blueprint, you would be able to define an Event, and name it something like "PlayerEntersHouseEvent," that should fire off a set of instructions any time the player enters the PlayerEntersHouseVolume.

Those instructions could be anything you want, such as playing a scary sound file, or having the Mesh of a bat fly around the room, or playing a video, and so on. The end result would be that any time the player enters that doorway, something specific happens.

To give you another example, let's say you have a racing game. You could place a Trigger Volume at the finish line so that when the player reaches that point it will trigger the Event that handles the end of the race.

Pain Causing Volumes

A *Pain Causing Volume* will cause Damage to an Actor who enters that volume. For example, you could surround a fire with a Pain Causing Volume so that a player takes Damage if they "enter the fire." Damage is a built-in concept in the Unreal Engine, and you can use Blueprints to define what happens when an Actor takes Damage, such as subtracting from their health based on the amount of Damage done.

The first property of Pain Causing Volume is simply called *Pain Causing* (Figure 4-37). This will determine if the Volume will actually apply Damage to Actors that enter it. By unchecking this, it will disable the Pain Causing feature of the Volume.

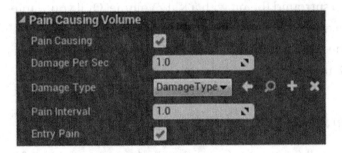

Figure 4-37. *Properties of a Pain Causing Volume*

The next property is *Damage Per Second*. This determines the rate at which the Actor inside the Volume is damaged. But note that it does not determine the *interval* at which the Damage is applied. That is set by the *Pain Interval* property.

For example, with them both set to 1, every second a point of Damage will be applied. If the Pain Interval was changed to 0.5, then Damage would be applied every half-second. However, now only half a point of Damage would be applied each time, so that, overall, the Actor is still only receiving 1 point of Damage per second. If the Pain Interval was changed to 2, then Damage would only be applied every 2 seconds, but it would apply 2 points of Damage each time.

An easy way to calculate how much Damage will be applied at each interval is to multiply the two values together. So if the Damage Per Second is 2, and the Pain Interval is 4, then 8 points of Damage will be applied at each interval.

The *Damage Type* allows you to change the overall way that Damage by the Volume is handled by the Engine. However, in almost all cases, you will just want to leave this on the default.

The *Entry Pain* property specifies whether or not Damage should be applied to the Actor immediately upon entering the Volume. With Entry Pain checked, the Actor will receive Damage immediately and then again after every interval. With Entry Pain unchecked, the Actor will not receive any Damage until the first interval has elapsed.

Kill ZVolume

The *Kill ZVolume* will destroy any Actor that enters it. It is useful for defining any places in your Level that mean instant death. For example, if you had a pit of lava in your Level, you might want to surround the pit with a Kill ZVolume. Or if you wanted to kill a player that had fallen off a ledge into a bottomless pit, you could use a Kill ZVolume.

You can define in Blueprints what should happen when the player is destroyed, such as displaying a Game Over menu.

Physics Volume

The *Physics Volume* allows you to change the physics of the space within the Volume.

Its first property is *Terminal Velocity* (Figure 4-38). Terminal velocity is the maximum speed that something can reach when it's falling, or, put another way, the maximum speed something can reach due to the forces of gravity.

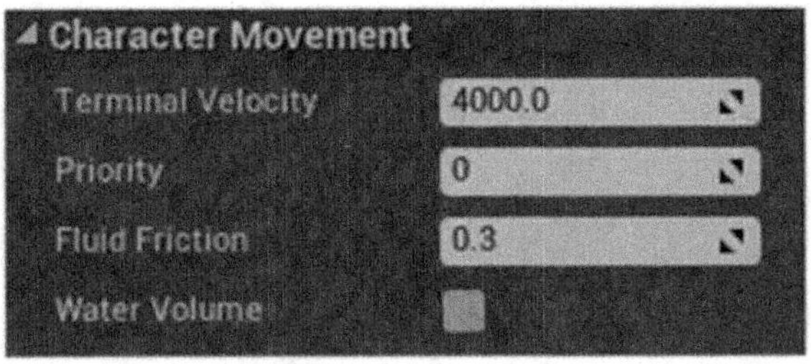

Figure 4-38. *Properties of a Physics Volume*

When something falls, if nothing interrupts the fall, the object will continue to accelerate until it reaches the Terminal Velocity, and then it will no longer accelerate; it will fall at a constant speed. In the real world, all objects falling toward the Earth have the same terminal velocity. But this value will be different on other planets that have different amounts of gravity.

So you could use the Terminal Velocity property to better mimic an alien world, or you could use it to produce other effects. For example, reducing the Terminal Velocity of the Volume to something really low, so that objects fall very slowly through it.

The next property is *Priority*. This is used when two Physics Volumes are overlapping, in order to determine which Volumes' settings should be used for that overlapping space. The higher the value, the higher the priority. So if a Physics Volume with a Priority of 0 overlapped a Physics Volume with a Priority of 1, only the settings for the Volume with a Priority of 1 would be honored within the overlapping space.

The next property is *Fluid Friction*. This is used to mimic the friction that occurs when something passes through something semi-solid. For example, trying to walk through water is a lot more difficult than walking through air, because there is a lot more friction. Walking through mud is more difficult than walking through water. The higher the Fluid Friction, the slower that objects will pass through it.

Last is the *Water Volume* property. This specifies whether or not the space that the Volume is defining is supposed to be occupied by water or a water-based liquid. For example, this could be used in Blueprints to specify that anytime the character is within a "water" volume, the character should begin to swim.

Summary

In this chapter, you got an in-depth look at several types of Actors available in UE4. In the next chapter, you will learn how to script logic for your game using Unreal Engine's visual scripting system, Blueprints.

CHAPTER 5

Blueprints

In this chapter, you will learn about *Blueprints*, a visual scripting system used to script logic in Unreal. You will learn about Level Blueprints, Blueprint Classes, variables, arrays, functions, flow control, Timelines, how to debug Blueprints, and more.

Introduction to Blueprints

In the Unreal Engine, a *Blueprint* is an asset that contains data and instructions.

So far, this book has mainly shown you how to construct environments that can be used for games. But the environment is only one half of a game. The other half is the logic that determines how the environment can be interacted with and how the game is actually played. This is where Blueprints come into play.

Using Blueprints, you can keep track of health, energy, score, and so on. You can also specify game logic, like the requirements for completing a puzzle, what happens when that puzzle is complete, what happens when you shoot an enemy, and so on.

Level Blueprint vs. Blueprint Classes

There are two main types of Blueprints – the Level Blueprint and Blueprint Classes.

A *Level Blueprint* is used to hold data and instructions for a particular Level. It might hold data such as the time remaining to complete the Level, or the number of keys you've collected in that Level, and so on. It's also used to store instructions that pertain only to that Level. For example, let's say there was a spot in a Level where there was a bridge, and when the player crosses that bridge, a meteor flies across the sky. If that's a one-time unique occurrence just for that spot in that Level, it would make sense to store those instructions in the Level Blueprint for that Level.

© David Nixon 2020
D. Nixon, *Beginning Unreal Game Development*, https://doi.org/10.1007/978-1-4842-5639-8_5

Blueprint Classes are a way to turn any Actor or asset into a Blueprint. The Engine comes with several pre-made Blueprint Classes, such as Pawn, Character, Player Controller, Game Mode Base (all of which will be covered in the next chapter), and many more. However, you can also create your own Blueprint Classes. This allows you to create objects with custom traits and behaviors.

Let's say, again, that you are building a haunted house. And let's say you want to have a chair that floats up and down. Let's also say that you want your character to be able to shoot the chair and, eventually, destroy it. You can achieve all of this by creating a Blueprint Class out of the chair Mesh.

Within the Blueprint, you could specify that the chair should move straight up and down, over and over again, starting from wherever it is placed in the Level. You could also specify that it should contain a variable called Health with a default value of 100. You could also say that any time the chair was hit by a projectile, that 10 should be subtracted from its Health. Finally, you could specify that if the Health of the chair ever gets to 0 or below, the chair should be destroyed.

One of the great things about Blueprint Classes is that you can use them to create as many copies, or instances, of your creation as you want. Using the haunted chair as an example, once you completed the Blueprint, it would be available to you in the Content Browser, and then each time you dragged it into the Viewport, it would create a new instance of the chair. Each chair would float up and down, starting from the position they were placed, and each chair would have their own copy of the Health variable. So if you damaged one of the chairs, its Health would be 90, while the other chairs would still have a Health of 100.

Level Blueprint Editor

To open a Level Blueprint, go up to the Toolbar and expand the menu of the Blueprints button. Then click "Open Level Blueprint." This will open the *Level Blueprint Editor*.

Event Graph

Inside the Level Blueprint Editor is the *Event Graph*. The Event Graph is the area of a Blueprint where you script the logic. If you're a programmer, the logic can be scripted in pure code using C++. However, Epic Games has developed a visual scripting system that allows non-programmers to script logic and can be convenient even for experienced programmers.

Nodes

The scripting system works by using various *Nodes* that each serve a specific purpose and connecting those Nodes together. By default, the Level Blueprint starts off with two commonly used Nodes in the Graph, as seen in Figure 5-1. They are disabled to start with, but can be used right away by connecting them to another Node.

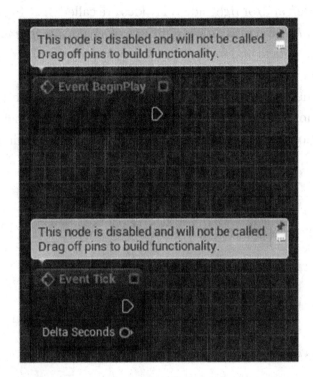

Figure 5-1. *The Event BeginPlay Node and Event Tick Node start in the Level Blueprint by default*

The first Node is the *Event BeginPlay Node*. An *Event Node* is a Node that is activated when a certain event occurs. So an Event BeginPlay Node, inside of a Level Blueprint, will be activated by the event of the Level first starting. You can recognize an Event Node by its top strip which will be the color red and will have an icon of an arrow inside of a diamond symbol.

The second default Node is also an Event Node. The *Event Tick Node* is a Node that is activated on every tick of gameplay. Before every frame of the game is drawn on the screen, any logic connected to the Event Tick Node will be executed. This is useful in situations where you need to constantly check certain conditions that, when met, will have an immediate effect on the game, such as the main character colliding with something harmful.

Pins and Wires

The icons along the left and/or right sides of Nodes are called *pins*. Pins on the left side of a Node are *input pins,* and pins on the right side of a Node are *output pins*. Pins are used to input/output data to and from Nodes and to specify the order in which Nodes should be executed.

Pins can be connected to one another with *wires*. To create a wire, left-click a pin and then drag the mouse while still holding the LMB. This will drag a wire out of that pin (Figure 5-2). If you hover over another pin and release the LMB, it will connect the end of the wire to that pin.

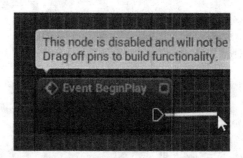

Figure 5-2. *Wires can be dragged out of pins*

Pins with a white icon that looks like a Play button are *execution pins*. Execution pins on the left side of a Node are *input execution pins*. When a wire connected to an input execution pin is activated, it will trigger execution of that Node. Execution pins on the right side of a Node are *output execution pins*. Wires connected to an output execution pin will activate once that Node has finished executing. Output execution pins can only be connected to input execution pins and vice-versa. By chaining Nodes together through their execution pins, you can define a series of Nodes that should be executed, one after the other, every time the first Node in the series is activated. The first Node in a chain will always be an Event Node.

Pins with a circular icon are *data pins*. Data pins are used to pass data between Nodes. Output data pins can only be connected to input data pins and vice-versa. Whatever data is contained in the output data pin gets sent to the input data pin it is connected to.

Adding Nodes

To add a new Node to the Event Graph, you will need to select that Node from the Node Menu (Figure 5-3). The Node Menu can be brought up by right-clicking any empty space in the Graph or by releasing the LMB over any empty space when dragging out a wire from an output execution pin. When doing the latter, the Node you add will automatically be connected to the wire.

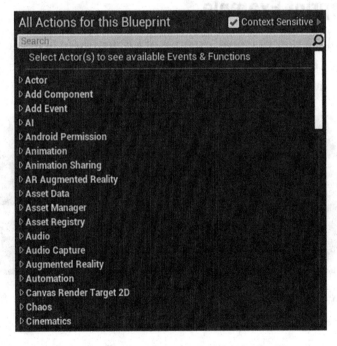

Figure 5-3. You can add Nodes from the Node Menu

There are many Nodes available to choose from in the Node Menu. They are organized into categories, but if you know at least part of the name of the Node you're looking for, you can use the search box at the top of the Node Menu to search for it.

Compiling

Before you can test any new logic you have created, you must compile the Blueprint. *Compiling* just means that the Engine will convert the logic into machine code that the computer can understand. In order to compile the Blueprint, simply go up to the toolbar of the Blueprint Editor and click the Compile button (Figure 5-4). If there is any new logic that hasn't been compiled yet, the Compile button will contain a question mark icon.

Figure 5-4. *The Compile button*

Simple Blueprint Example

Here is a simple, albeit non-practical, example of a Blueprint to help you gain familiarity. Figure 5-5 shows a Level Blueprint whose logic specifies that the game should exit two seconds after the Level begins.

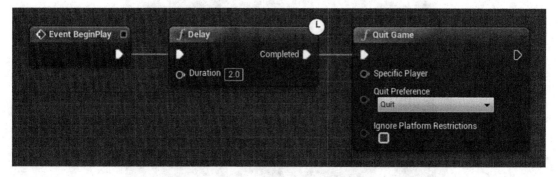

Figure 5-5. *This logic will cause the game to exit two seconds after the Level begins*

As mentioned earlier, the Event BeginPlay Node will be executed when the Level first begins. As a consequence, any Nodes connected to the Event BeginPlay Node through execution pins will get executed as well.

The Event BeginPlay Node is connected to a *Delay Node*. The Delay Node is a *Function Node*. Function Nodes are light blue and have an icon of a lowercase "f." A Function Node is a Node that performs a specific task when executed. The task of a Delay Node is to wait for a specified amount of seconds before passing execution on to the next Node.

In this example, a value of 2 seconds has been specified. A Delay Node doesn't delay the execution of all logic in the game, just within the flow of wires it's connected to.

After a two-second delay, execution will pass to the *Quit Game Node* which will cause the game to exit.

Variables

Variables are what Blueprints use to store data. Just like in algebra, where you might use a variable named X to store a number, you can use variables in Unreal to store data. But in Unreal, variables can hold other kinds of data in addition to numbers, such as text.

To create a variable in Unreal, first look on the left side of the Blueprint Editor for the *My Blueprint* tab (Figure 5-6). Within the My Blueprint tab is a Variables sub-tab. Clicking the plus sign on that tab will create a new variable which can then be named.

Figure 5-6. *You can add new variables in the My Blueprint tab*

Data Types

A variable's *data type* determines what kind of data it can hold. One way of setting the data type is to click the rectangle to the left of the variable's name, and then choose the data type from the menu that appears. The menu will contain a list of all the basic data types in Unreal, as shown in Figure 5-7. Each data type can be identified by a unique color.

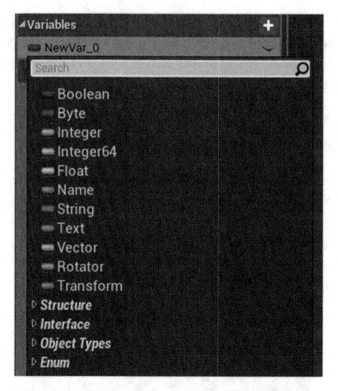

Figure 5-7. *Each data type in Unreal can be identified by a unique color*

The first one on the list is the *Boolean* data type, which is identified by the color red in Unreal. A Boolean data type is simply used to hold a value of *True* or *False,* and those are the only two values it can hold. Because of this, a Boolean data type takes up very little space in memory.

The next four data types in the list – Byte, Integer, Integer64, and Float – are all used to hold numbers. But they each hold different kinds of numbers and each take up different amounts of space in memory as a result.

Byte is the smallest of the four, meaning it takes up the least amount of space in memory. This is because a Byte can only store a whole number between 0 and 255, inclusive. So if you needed a variable to store, for example, some choice that the player makes in the game, and there are only a limited amount of choices the player can make, a Byte might be a good data type to use to store this choice, with each number corresponding to one of the choices the player could make.

Like Byte, the *Integer* data type is used to store whole numbers. But unlike Byte, it can hold numbers between about negative 2 billion and positive 2 billion. Because of this, however, it will also use more memory than a Byte.

Integer64 has a range between about negative 9 quintillion (18 zeroes) and positive 9 quintillion. Again, the trade-off for that extra range is an increase in the memory required.

Float is short for "floating point number." A "floating point" is just another name for a decimal point. So a Float is used to hold numbers that have a decimal place. Unlike the Integer data type, it can be used to store numbers that aren't whole, such as 3.5, or 24.743, and so on. Because of this, it requires more memory than an Integer.

The next three data types are used to store text. The largest of the three is the *Text* data type. Because this requires the most amount of memory of the three, it should only be used for its specific purpose, which is to store data that will be displayed on the screen to the player. The Text data type is useful for displaying text because it has, among other things, localization features, which allows it to display text in a way that is custom for that player's region or language.

The *String* data type is used to store text that you can perform manipulation functions on. These functions include extracting a substring of text from the larger portion; changing the case of the text, meaning uppercase or lowercase; reversing the text; and so on. The String type is smaller than the Text type, so if you might have a need to perform these functions on the text, and the text isn't going to be displayed on the screen, you would store the text in a String variable.

The smallest of these three data types is the *Name* data type. The Name type doesn't have the localization or other features that the Text data type has to display text on the screen, and it also doesn't have the manipulation functions of the String data type. However, it does take up the least amount of memory of the three. So you would use the Name data type for any text that doesn't require the features of the String or Text data types.

The *Vector* data type is used to store three Float values. This is useful for defining a point in space, an RGB value, or anything that is defined with three values.

The *Rotator* data type is used to store numbers that describe an object's rotation in 3D space.

The *Transform* data type is used to hold data that describes an object's position, rotation, and scale in 3D space.

Get Node

A *Get Node* is a Node whose only purpose is to output the value of a variable (Figure 5-8). It will contain just a single pin, an output data pin. It has no execution pins. A Get Node can be thought of as always active, because it will output the current value of the variable, every tick of gameplay, to whatever pin it is connected to.

Figure 5-8. *A Get Node for a Float variable named "Delay Duration"*

To create a Get Node for a specific variable, left-click the variable in the My Blueprint tab and drag it into the Event Graph. When you release the LMB, click "Get" from the menu that appears. This will create a Get Node. Another way to do this is to hold down the *Ctrl* key when dragging the variable into the Graph, and then when you let go of the mouse, it will automatically create a Get Node for the variable.

Set Node

A *Set Node* is used to change the value of a variable (Figure 5-9). It contains an input data pin which is used to specify what value the variable should be changed to. The value will be changed once the Node is activated through its input execution pin. The Node also contains an output data pin so the new value can be passed on to another Node if you wish.

To create a Set Node for a specific variable, left-click the variable in the My Blueprint tab and drag it into the Event Graph. When you release the LMB, click "Set" from the menu that appears. This will create a Set Node. Another way to do this is to hold down the *Alt* key when dragging the variable into the Graph, and then when you let go of the mouse, it will automatically create a Set Node for the variable.

Figure 5-9. *A Set Node for a Float variable named "Delay Duration"*

Default Value

A *default value* is a value that will be assigned to a variable as soon as the variable is created. The default value can be set in the Details Panel, on the right side of the Blueprint Editor, under the "Default Value" category (Figure 5-10). If you see the text "Please compile the blueprint," it means that you haven't compiled the Blueprint since that variable was created. Once you compile the Blueprint, that text will go away and a box will appear where you can enter the default value.

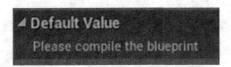

Figure 5-10. *When you create a new variable, you will need to compile the Blueprint before you can give that variable a default value*

Updated Blueprint Example

Expanding on the Blueprint example from the previous section, Figure 5-11 shows an example of using a variable to specify the duration that the Delay Node should delay.

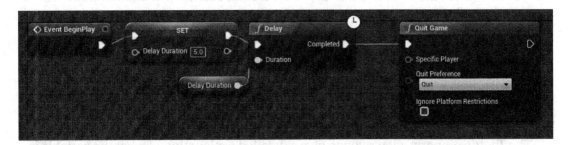

Figure 5-11. *The Duration property of the Delay Node is now set by a variable*

The Set Node sets a Float variable named "Delay Duration" to a value of 5.0. A Get Node for the "Delay Duration" variable passes the value of that variable to the Delay Node. So now, the Delay Node will delay for 5 seconds instead of the 2 seconds that were "hardcoded" into the Node in the previous example.

Variable Properties

In addition to the default value, there are other properties of variables that you can set in the Details Panel (Figure 5-12). Some data types will have different properties than others.

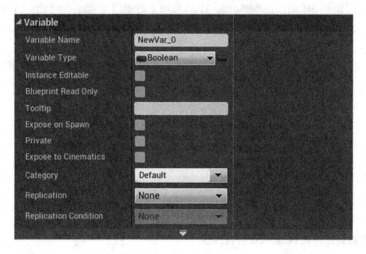

Figure 5-12. *Properties of a Boolean variable*

The first two properties, *Variable Name* and *Variable Type*, are the same properties that you can edit in the My Blueprint tab, so the Details Panel is just another place where you can set them.

The *Instance Editable* property will be covered in the section on Blueprint Classes.

The *Blueprint Read Only* property can be used to make the variable read-only, meaning its value can't be changed; it will always contain its default value. With this checked, if you added a Set Node to the Blueprint for the variable, you would get an error when trying to compile the Blueprint.

The *Tooltip* property allows you to give a detailed explanation of what the variable is and what it is used for. This is useful not only when you are working on teams – so that the people you are working with can more quickly understand what you've created – but also for yourself, so that when you come back to the variable at a later time, you can quickly remember its use.

To create a tooltip, just type the message into the Tooltip box, and when the variable is hovered over in the My Blueprint tab, or when a Set Node for that variable is hovered over, it will display the tooltip message that you've created.

The *Expose on Spawn* and *Expose to Cinematics* properties involve more advanced topics and won't be covered in this book.

The *Private* property determines if other Blueprints can access the variable. With this unchecked, other Blueprints will be able to access the variable. With it checked and set to Private, other Blueprints would not be able to access the variable.

The *Category* property allows you to group your variables into categories if you wish. This is for organizational purposes within the Editor. To place a variable into a category, select an existing one from the dropdown or create a new one by typing its name into the box. Once a variable has been placed into a category, it will appear under a heading for that category in the My Blueprint tab.

The next two properties are *Slider Range* and *Value Range*. These properties are only for numerical data types.

Starting with the Value Range property, this allows you to set a minimum and maximum value that the variable is allowed to contain. If you set the Value Range to 0 to 10, you won't be able to set the variable to anything other than those numbers and the numbers in between. If you go down to the Default Value, for example, and try to set that to 11, it won't let you.

The Slider Range property determines what value you can set the variable to when using a slider. If you set the range to 3 to 5, for example, and try to use the slider on the Default Value to set the number, it will only go between 3 and 5. But if you enter a number manually, you can still enter any number not restricted by the Value Range or the limits of the data type itself.

The *Replication* property is used in multiplayer games that are running over a network. This specifies whether or not the variable should be replicated over the network. So if it's a variable that would affect all the players in the game, it would need to be replicated over the network. But if it's a variable that only affects an individual player, it would probably not need to be replicated over the network.

If a variable is set to be replicated, the *Replication Condition* property can be used to set the conditions under which the variable should be replicated.

Arrays

An *array* is a list of variables of the same data type. You can have an array of Integers, an array of Strings, and so on.

This is useful whenever you need to store a group of something. For example, you could use an array of Integers to store the combination to a safe. Or you could use an array of Strings to store the dialogue of a character for a certain scene.

To create an array, first create a regular variable with the data type you want the array to use, and then click the icon to the right of the Variable Type property in the Details Panel and select the "Array" icon (Figure 5-13).

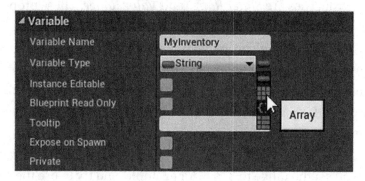

Figure 5-13. *Changing a regular variable into an array*

Arrays are made up of slots that each store one of the values of the list. The proper term for one of these slots is an *index*. Arrays in Unreal are "zero based" which means the first index is 0. So the second index is 1, the third index is 2, and so on. Each value stored in the array is known as an *element* of the array.

ForEachLoop Node

The *ForEachLoop Node* is used to iterate through the elements of an array. It has an input pin called *Array* where you can input the array you wish to use. It has an output execution pin called *Loop Body* that will be activated once for each element in the array. Each time the Loop Body pin fires, the Node's *Array Element* pin will contain the value of the current element, and the Array Index pin will contain the index number of the current element. The output execution pin *Completed* will fire once all the elements have been iterated through.

The example shown in Figure 5-14 will loop through an array of Strings named "My Inventory" and output each value to the screen.

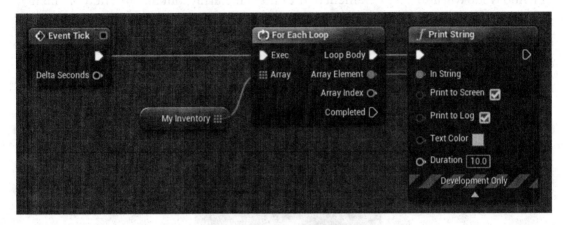

Figure 5-14. *The ForEachLoop Node will loop through every element of an array*

Add Node

The *Add Node* can be used to add another element to the end of an array. It has an input pin for the array itself and an input pin for the variable containing the value to add.

In Figure 5-15, whatever value the variable "New Item" contains will be added to the end of an array named "My Inventory" whenever the *P* key is pressed on the keyboard.

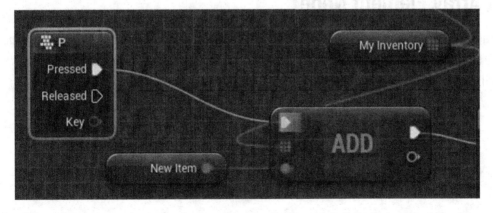

Figure 5-15. *Pressing P will cause New Item to be added to the end of the My Inventory array*

Insert Node

The Add Node will add a new element to the end of the array, but to add a new element somewhere in the middle, you need to use the *Insert Node* (Figure 5-16). It has a pin to specify the array, a pin to specify the value you want to add, and a pin to specify at which index the value should be inserted.

Figure 5-16. *The Insert Node*

When a value is inserted, the length of the array increases by one, all the values at the specified index and above get moved one index higher, and then the new value is assigned to the specified index. So the Insert Node inserts values in between other values without erasing any data.

Set Array Element Node

If you want to replace the value of a certain index, you need to use the *Set Array Element Node* (Figure 5-17). Unlike the Insert Node, this Node will overwrite the value at the specified index and won't change the location of any of the other values.

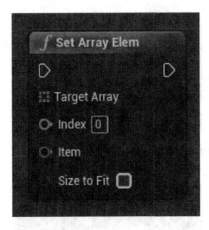

Figure 5-17. *The Set Array Element Node*

The Set Array Element Node has a *Size to Fit* pin. As an example, let's say that at the time the Node fires, the array being used has four elements (indices 0 to 3). Also, let's say you specify that you want the new value to go into index 6. If Size to Fit is False, this won't work, because index 6 doesn't exist. The game won't crash, the array simply won't change in any way. But if Size to Fit were True in this scenario, the length of the array would increase to 7, so that there is an index 6. Index 6 would get set to the new value specified, and indices 4 and 5 would simply remain empty.

Removing Elements from an Array

When you want to remove elements from an array, there are a few ways to do this. The *Clear Node* (Figure 5-18) simply deletes all the elements of an array. The *Remove Index Node* (Figure 5-19) will delete the element at the specified index, and then shift any values at higher indexes down one. The *Remove Item Node* (Figure 5-20) deletes elements based on their values, deleting any element whose value matches the one specified. The Remove Item Node also has a Boolean pin that outputs True or False based on if any matches were found.

Figure 5-18. *The Clear Node*

131

Figure 5-19. *The Remove Index Node*

Figure 5-20. *The Remove Item Node*

Retrieving Elements from an Array

When you want to retrieve the value of a certain element, you need to use a Get Node (Figure 5-21) and specify the index of the element, and it will output its value. This is a different kind of Get Node than the one created by dragging the variable into the graph. This Get Node can be found in the Utilities ➤ Array category of the Node Menu.

Figure 5-21. *The Get Node in the Utilities ➤ Array category*

Contains Item Node

When you just want to know whether or not an array contains a certain value, you can use the *Contains Item Node* (Figure 5-22). You specify the value you want to search for, and it will output True if that value was found and False if it was not.

Figure 5-22. *The Contains Item Node*

Find Item Node

If you need to know the index that a certain value is located at, you can use the *Find Item Node* (Figure 5-23). This will return the index of the first element of the array that matches the value specified. If no match is found, this will return a value of -1.

Figure 5-23. *The Find Item Node*

Length Node and Last Index Node

You can use the *Length Node* (Figure 5-24) when you want to know how many elements an array has and the *Last Index Node* (Figure 5-25) when you want to know its highest index number. Because arrays in Unreal Engine are zero based, the last index of an array will always be one less than its length.

Figure 5-24. *The Length Node*

Figure 5-25. *The Last Index Node*

Functions

A *function* is a procedure or routine meant to carry out a specific task or series of tasks. Functions are not unique to Unreal Engine. A function is a concept that comes from mathematics and computer science. In computer science and programming, a function is a specific block of code. By extension, in Unreal Engine, a function is a specific Event Graph of Nodes. The entire Event Graph for a function gets *encapsulated* (contained) within a single Node that can then be used without having to worry about the details inside it.

To create a new function, go to the My Blueprint tab, look for the Functions category, and then click the Add button (Figure 5-26). Whenever you create a new function, it will automatically open that function's Event Graph and add its *Entry Node* (Figure 5-27). The Entry Node is the Node that will fire whenever the function is called.

Figure 5-26. *New functions can be added in the My Blueprint tab*

Figure 5-27. *The Entry Node for a function named "Welcome Message"*

Function I/O

Functions can have inputs and outputs so that data can be passed into and out of the function. To add an input or output, go to the Details Panel and click the Add button under the Inputs or Outputs category, depending on which you want to create (Figure 5-28). You can then define the name and data type of the input/output.

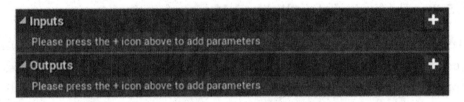

Figure 5-28. *Clicking these Add buttons will create either an input or output for your function*

When an input is created, looking "outside" of the function, at its single-node encapsulated form, you will see the input created as an input pin. "Inside" of the function, the data that gets passed to that input pin can be retrieved through a corresponding output pin that gets added to the Entry Node.

Creating an output variable will create a *Return Node* within the function. The Return Node will always be the last Node of a function, and it will contain input pins for each of your output variables so that you can pass that data back out of the function (these will appear as output pins on the Function Node itself).

Function Example

As an example, Figure 5-29 shows a function that takes a name as input and then outputs a message using that name.

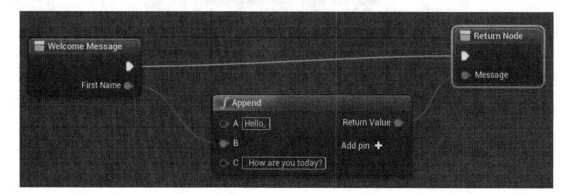

Figure 5-29. *The "inside" of the Welcome Message function*

It has one input – a String variable named "First Name" – and one output, a String variable named "Message." It retrieves First Name from the Entry Node and passes that to an Append Node where it combines the name with other Strings to form a greeting. That greeting is then passed to the Return Node. Figure 5-30 shows an example of the function in use.

Figure 5-30. *The Welcome Message function in use*

As soon as the Level begins, it will call the Welcome Message function. The name "David" is passed in as the value of First Name. This is the value that will be retrieved from the Entry Node within the function. The message that is created inside the function, and gets passed to the Return Node, is the message that is being retrieved here and then passed to the Print String Node.

Advantages of Using Functions

Using functions has many advantages. The main advantage is *reusability*. For example, if you wanted to use the preceding Welcome Message function dozens of times throughout your game, with several different characters with different names, you don't want to have to write the logic every single time, for each character, every time it is used. It would be easier to just write it once and be able to use it over and over again. This also makes it much easier to make changes, since the change only needs to be made in one place.

Another advantage is *reliability*. If you use a function that's already been used, and thus tested, over and over again, there's a much better chance that that function is free of mistakes than logic you just wrote. For example, many of the built-in functions in Unreal Engine have now been used repeatedly by numerous companies and developers, and thus any bugs they may have once contained have already been reported and fixed.

A third advantage of functions is *readability*. While the Welcome Message function example is very small, functions could contain hundreds or even thousands of Nodes. But no matter how many nodes a function contains, it will always get condensed down into just one Node. So by hiding away the "guts" of your logic in this way, it makes it much easier to understand the logic of your game at a high level.

Function Properties

In the *Graph* category (Figure 5-31), the first property, *Description*, is used to briefly explain what the function does. Whatever this is set to will appear in the tool tip message that pops up whenever you hover over a function. So if you come back to this function later, or someone you're working with comes across it, this makes it much easier to quickly understand what a function does without having to open it up and analyze its logic.

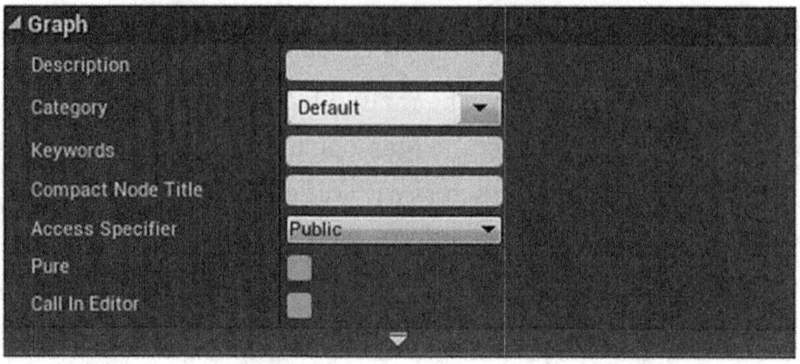

Figure 5-31. *Function properties*

The *Category* property is used to organize your custom-made functions. For example, you could assign a function to a category called "String," and then in the My Blueprint tab, it will group the function under that category, along with any other functions you assign to that category.

The *Keywords* property can be used to add a list of keywords to the function which can be useful if you search for the function later.

If you give the *Compact Node Title* property a value, it will display the Function Node in a compact form, with the value you entered being displayed in the background.

The *Access Specifier* property is used to specify what Blueprints are allowed to call this function. With this set to *Public*, any Blueprint is allowed to call this function. With this set to *Private*, only the Blueprint that the function belongs to is allowed to call it. For example, if a function was created in the Level Blueprint, and Access Specifier is set to Private, you will only be able to call the function from the Level Blueprint and no other.

The *Protected* setting is like the Private setting, except that the function can also be called from Blueprints derived from the owning Blueprint. Derived Blueprints will be discussed in Chapter 6.

The next property deals with the concept of *Pure* vs. *Impure* functions. A Pure function cannot modify any of the variables of its Blueprint, while an Impure function can.

The final property is *Call In Editor*. So far, we've just been looking at Level Blueprints. But as we'll see later on, every Actor can have their own Blueprint as well. So if this was a Blueprint for an Actor, and the Call In Editor property was checked, then you could click an instance of that Actor in the Viewport, and in the Details Panel, there would be a button that could be clicked to run this function.

Local Variables

In addition to having a Variables tab within its My Blueprint window, functions also have a Local Variables tab (Figure 5-32). *Local variables* are variables that can only be used within that particular function and aren't accessible to the rest of the Blueprint. Because of this, local variables are more memory efficient than regular variables. They also help keep your Blueprint more organized.

Figure 5-32. *The Local Variables tab within a function*

Flow Control

In the Node Menu, under "Utilities," there is a category called *Flow Control*. This category contains several different Nodes that you can use to control the flow of execution in your Blueprints. This is essential to creating logic.

Branch Node

The first node in the list is the *Branch Node* (Figure 5-33). The Branch Node takes in a Boolean value as its input and then continues execution either through the True output execution pin if the Boolean value is True or through the False output execution pin if the Boolean value is False.

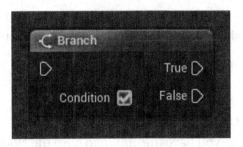

Figure 5-33. *The Branch Node*

For example, when the player tries to open a door, you could have a Branch Node with a Boolean variable that stores whether or not the player has the key. You could connect the False pin to a Node that will play the sound of a locked door trying to be opened and connect the True pin to the sound of a door being unlocked.

Do N Node

The *Do N Node* (Figure 5-34) means "Do N times" where "N" is the number of times this Node should allow execution to pass through it before it begins to block execution. For example, if N is 5, then the first 5 times execution flows into the Enter pin, it will flow out of the Exit pin. However, the sixth time and beyond that, the flow will not continue out of the Exit pin.

Figure 5-34. *The Do N Node*

So execution will be blocked in a Do N Node after the Nth time the Node has been activated, unless execution flows into the Reset pin of the Node. When execution flows into the Reset pin, the counter will be reset to 0, and the Node will be able to execute N more times.

The Counter pin will output an Integer representing the number of times the Do N Node has been activated since the game began or since the last time the Node was reset.

DoOnce Node

The *DoOnce Node* (Figure 5-35) is just like a Do N Node where N = 1, with the exception that with the DoOnce Node, you have the option to have the Node start closed. By having the Node start closed, this means that execution must flow through the Reset pin before execution will flow through the Completed pin, even the first time.

Figure 5-35. *The DoOnce Node*

DoOnce MultiInput Node

The *DoOnce MultiInput Node* (Figure 5-36) is like the DoOnce Node except that it allows for multiple In/Out pairs. Additional pairs can be added using the "Add pin" button at the bottom. So if execution flows into the A In pin, it will flow out of the A Out pin. If execution flows into the A In pin a second time, without a reset, nothing will happen, but execution will still be able to flow through the B pins and the C pins.

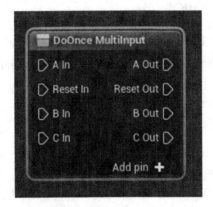

Figure 5-36. *The DoOnce MultiInput Node*

If execution flows into the Reset In pin, all of the pairs will get Reset. The DoOnce MultiInput Node also differs from the DoOnce Node in that it has a Reset Out pin that will be executed when the Reset In pin is executed.

141

FlipFlop Node

The *FlipFlop Node* (Figure 5-37) simply alternates between having execution flow out of the A pin and the B pin every time the Node is activated. The first time execution flows into the FlipFlop Node, it will flow out of the A pin, and the second time execution flows into the FlipFlop Node, it will flow out of the B pin, and then the third time, it will flow out of the A pin again, and so on.

Figure 5-37. *The FlipFlop Node*

The FlipFlop Node has a Boolean output called *Is A* that will output a value of True if execution is currently being routed through the A pin and False if execution is being routed through the B pin.

ForLoop Node

With a *ForLoop Node* (Figure 5-38), the Loop Body execution output pin is fired a certain number of times, starting from an Integer defined by the First Index and then increasing by 1 until it gets to the Integer defined by the Last Index. The Index pin will output an Integer specifying the index of the current loop. The Completed pin will be executed after the final loop is completed.

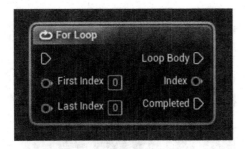

Figure 5-38. *The ForLoop Node*

ForLoopWithBreak Node

The *ForLoopWithBreak Node* (Figure 5-39) is just like the ForLoop Node, except that it is possible to break the loop before it is finished. If execution flows into the Break pin, the loop will stop immediately and the remaining loops will not be executed.

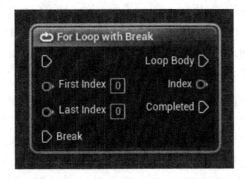

Figure 5-39. *The ForLoopWithBreak Node*

Gate Node

A *Gate Node* (Figure 5-40) is a Node that can be set to opened or closed. When the Gate is open, execution flow entering the Enter pin will flow out of the Exit pin. When the Gate is closed, any execution flow entering the Node will stop there, and the Exit pin will not fire.

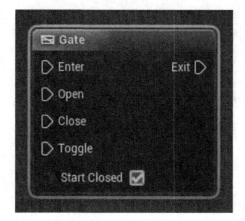

Figure 5-40. *The Gate Node*

The next three input pins are used to set the status of the Gate. Any time execution flows into the Open pin, it will open the Gate, and any time execution flows into the Close pin, it will close the Gate. If execution flows into the Toggle pin, it will set the status to whatever it is currently not. So if the Gate was open, the Toggle pin would close it, and if the Gate was closed, the Toggle pin would open it. The Start Closed property will determine whether the Gate starts out Open or Closed.

MultiGate Node

With a *MultiGate Node* (Figure 5-41), execution enters a single execution input pin, but it will flow out of only one of the execution output pins. You can use the Add pin button to add as many execution output pins as you like.

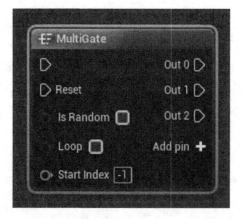

Figure 5-41. *The MultiGate Node*

If Is Random is unchecked or set to False, then execution will flow out of the output pins in sequential order, starting at the Start Index. With a Start Index of -1, it's the same as saying that you're not specifying a Start Index, so it will just go with the default which is 0. Loop will determine whether or not the sequence should start over or if the Node should just block further execution flow.

If Is Random is set to True, then instead of going in sequential order, output will flow out of the pins in random order until each pin has been used. At that point, the Node will either need to be reset or start a new loop, depending on what Loop was set to.

Retriggerable Delay Node

The *Retriggerable Delay Node* (Figure 5-42) is just like the Delay Node, except that the delay can be reset or "retriggered" if another pulse enters the execution input pin before the delay has finished counting down. So if the duration of the delay is set to 10 seconds, and the Node is activated, and then after 7 seconds the Node is activated again, the delay will start counting down from 10 again.

Figure 5-42. *The Retriggerable Delay Node*

Sequence Node

With the *Sequence Node* (Figure 5-43), every time execution flows into the Node, it will flow out of every single one of the output pins. Again, you can use the Add pin button to add as many output pins as you want. When execution flows into the Node, it will fire each of the pins sequentially; however it will do so without any delay, so from the player's perspective, it will appear as if each of the pins fired at the same time.

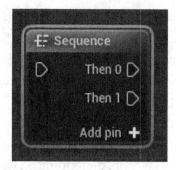

Figure 5-43. *The Sequence Node*

WhileLoop Node

Once the *WhileLoop Node* (Figure 5-44) has been activated, the Loop Body pin will fire over and over again, as long as the Boolean value connected to the Condition pin is True. Before each loop iteration, it will check the value of Condition, and once the Condition is False, it will break the loop and execution will flow out of the Completed pin. It's important to make sure that there is definitely some way for the Condition to eventually evaluate to False, or you will end up with an infinite loop.

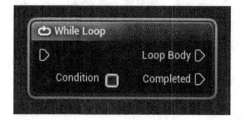

Figure 5-44. *The WhileLoop Node*

Switches

Switches are a way to route the flow of execution based on the value of whatever variable you pass into the Switch. For example, if you create a *Switch on Int Node* (Figure 5-45), you can connect an Integer variable to the Selection pin, and then when the Node is activated, it will read in the value of the Integer and, based on that value, route execution to one of the output pins.

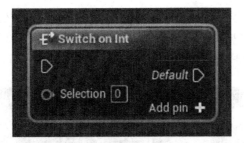

Figure 5-45. *The Switch on Int Node*

By default, the only output pin is the Default pin. The Add pin button can be used to create more output pins and will create them starting with the value of the Node's Start Index property and then incrementing by 1 each time the button is clicked. If you want to delete one of the pins you added, you just need to right-click that pin and click "Remove execution pin."

You can also do a Switch on other data types. For example, you could use the *Switch on Name Node* (Figure 5-46). This will work the same way as the Switch on Int Node, with the exception that you will need to specify the text to compare against for each of the output pins. You can do that by going over to the Details Panel, expanding the Pin Names property, and entering the text you want each pin to check for.

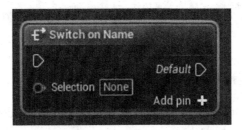

Figure 5-46. *The Switch on Name Node*

Accessing Actors Within Blueprints

To really get use out of your Blueprints, you're going to want to be able to access the Actors in your Level in order to be able to read their data, make decisions based on that data, and to manipulate the Actors in different ways.

In order to get access to an Actor within a Blueprint, that Actor needs to be selected in the Level Editor when you right-click the Event Graph of the Blueprint. When you do so, the Node Menu will have some options at the top relating to that Actor. You can create an Event based on the Actor, you can call a Function on the Actor, and you can also get a reference to the Actor (Figure 5-47). Note that for this to work, the Context Sensitive checkbox needs to be checked.

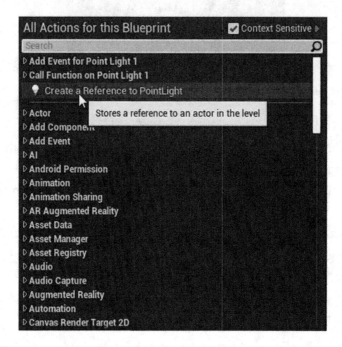

Figure 5-47. *You can get a reference to the currently selected Actor through the Node Menu*

Getting a Reference to an Actor

The example shown in Figure 5-48 uses a reference to a Light Actor to turn that light off two seconds after the Level begins.

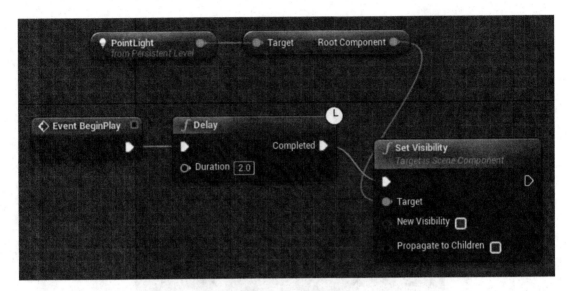

Figure 5-48. *This logic will turn a Light Actor off two seconds after the Level begins*

The *Set Visibility Node* takes in a Root Component as the "Target" to perform the action on, and its New Visibility Boolean will determine whether the Node will set the visibility of the target component to True or False. Note that when connecting the reference to the Light Actor to the Target pin, the Engine automatically created a Node in between. This is because the Set Visibility function technically sets the visibility of Components, not the Actors themselves, so the Node is just getting the Root Component of the Light Actor so that the Root Component can be passed in as the target component.

Creating an Event from an Actor

To create an Event from an Actor, select the Actor in the Level Editor, open the Node Menu in the Blueprint, make sure Context Sensitive is checked, then select "Add Event for [Actor Name]." From there, if you expand the Collision menu, there will be an option to create an *On Actor Begin Overlap Event* (Figure 5-49). This Event will fire whenever another Actor overlaps with this Actor. This Event is often used with Trigger Volumes.

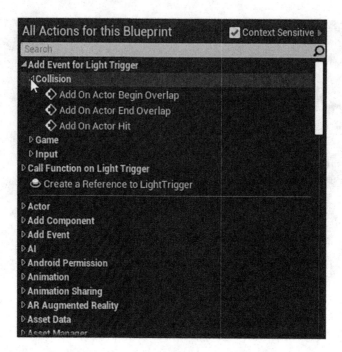

Figure 5-49. *Adding an Add On Actor Begin Overlap Node*

The example in Figure 5-50 uses Events to turn a Light on and off when an Actor enters and exits a Trigger Volume named "LightTrigger."

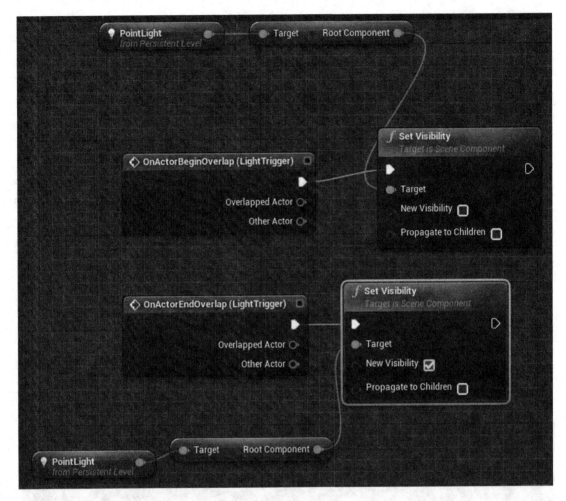

Figure 5-50. *This logic will turn a light off when an Actor enters a Trigger Volume and will turn it back on once that Actor leaves the Trigger Volume*

Blueprint Classes

With *Blueprint Classes*, you can create Blueprints out of existing Actors. By creating a Blueprint from an Actor, you can add data and functionality to that Actor, essentially creating your own custom version of that Actor type.

Unreal comes with several built-in Blueprint Classes, such as Pawn, Character, Player Controller, Game Mode Base, and many more. We'll start to see some of these in the next chapter, but this section will focus on creating your own Blueprint Classes.

To create a Blueprint from an Actor, select it, and then in the Details Panel, click the blue "Blueprint/Add Script" button (Figure 5-51). Then select the folder path where you want to save the Blueprint, give it a name, and click "Create Blueprint."

⚙ Blueprint/Add Script

Figure 5-51. *The Blueprint/Add Script button*

So far in this book, the only Blueprints have been Level Blueprints, which only have an Event Graph. But for Blueprints of Actors, there is also a *Viewport* tab and a *Construction Script* tab. The Viewport tab allows you to see what your Actor looks like and also allows you to add Components to it. The Construction Script is something that will be run just before the Actor gets created, so it's useful for performing any initialization you might need to do on the Actor to get it ready for gameplay.

Blueprint Class Example

The example in Figure 5-52 is a Blueprint that has been created from a Point Light Actor. The logic will cause the Light to turn on and off every second.

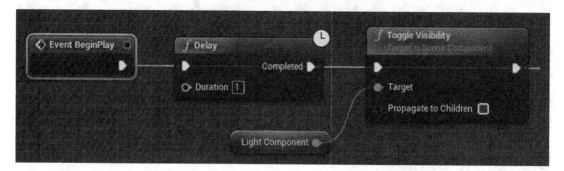

Figure 5-52. *This logic will cause a Light Actor to turn on and off every second*

The *Toggle Visibility* function is like the Set Visibility function, except instead of using it to specifically set a visibility property to True or False, it will simply toggle the property to the opposite of whatever it's currently set to. So if the visibility was True, the function would set it to False, and vice-versa.

Because this is the Blueprint for the Point Light, the Editor assumed that the Light is the desired target and automatically connected the Light Component of the Light to the Target pin when the Toggle Visibility Node was created.

When the game loads and the Actor is first created in memory, its Event BeginPlay Node will fire. Then the Delay Node will delay flow for one second before the Toggle Visibility Node is activated. The output execution pin of the Toggle Visibility Node has been connected to the input execution pin of the Delay Node. This creates a loop that will cause the Light to turn on and off every second for the duration of the Actor's existence.

Instances

One of the major advantages of Blueprint Classes is that they are reusable. The preceding Blueprint of a custom Light Actor can be used just like any other Actor. If you browse to it in the Content Browser, you can drag and drop as many instances of it as you want. An *instance* is an individual copy of an object made from a Blueprint.

So if you dragged five copies of the Light into the Viewport, let's say, you would have five instances of it in your Level, each with their own copy of the Nodes in the Blueprint they were created from. Think of, for example, identical human quintuplets. Each was created from the same Blueprint (their DNA), but each of them can exist independently in the world.

Instances made from the same Blueprint have the same variables, but they maintain their own copies of that variable, so the value stored in that variable can be different for each instance, a concept explained in the following section.

Instance Editable Variables

When you add a variable to a Blueprint Class, it is, in essence, adding a custom property to that Actor. The example in Figure 5-53 builds upon the earlier example and adds a Float variable named Light Toggle Duration to the Blueprint and uses that variable as the Duration of the Delay Node.

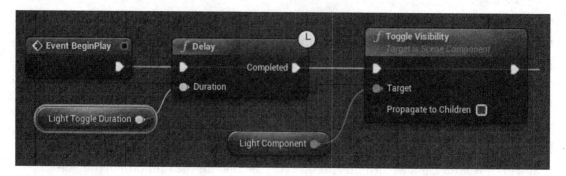

Figure 5-53. *A Float variable named Light Toggle Duration has been added to this example*

Right now, this isn't doing anything different than it was doing before, but that can be changed by making this variable *Instance Editable.*

There are two ways to make a variable Instance Editable. One way is to use the icon in the My Blueprint tab, which will toggle between the image of an eye open and an image of an eye closed. When the eye is open, that means that the variable is Instance Editable. You can also use the Instance Editable checkbox in the Details Panel.

If a variable is set to Instance Editable, its value can be changed in the Level Editor. With the Light Toggle Duration variable set to Instance Editable, if you select an instance of the Light Blueprint in the Level Editor, that variable will now appear in the Details Panel, as shown in Figure 5-54.

Figure 5-54. *The variable named Light Toggle Duration now appears in the Details Panel when an instance of the Light Blueprint is selected in the Level*

Now you have the ability to easily set a different duration for each instance of the Actor. You could drag in several instances of the Actor, give them each a different Light Toggle Duration, and they will all turn on and off at different rates. This is the power of Blueprint Classes. You can create your own custom Actors, reuse them as many times as you like, and modify their individual properties.

Timelines

Timelines are used to create simple animations, such as changing the location, rotation, or color of an object. To add a new Timeline Node, right-click the graph, select "Add Timeline…" from the bottom of the menu (Figure 5-55), and give the Timeline a name. To edit a Timeline, double-click it to open it in the *Timeline Editor*.

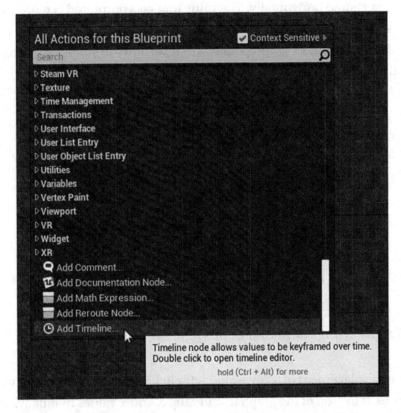

Figure 5-55. *A new Timeline Node can be added from the Node Menu*

Tracks and Keys

To add a new *track* to a Timeline, use one of the buttons in the upper-left corner of the Timeline Editor (Figure 5-56). A track is used to specify what value or values the Timeline should be outputting at any given point in time. For example, the first button with the "f" on it is used to add a *Float track* which is used to output single Float values.

Figure 5-56. *These buttons are used to add new tracks to a Timeline. The first button creates a Float track*

A track is represented by a graph. The time, in seconds, from the start of the Timeline, is represented horizontally. The value that gets outputted is represented vertically. To specify what value should be outputted at what time, you need to add a *key* to that point on the track's graph (Figure 5-57). To add a key, hold down *Shift* on the keyboard and left-click the graph.

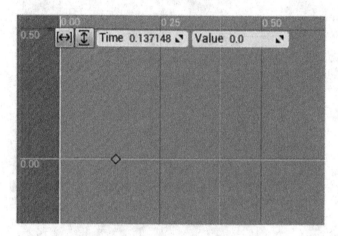

Figure 5-57. *The orange diamond in this figure is called a key*

To change the placement of a key, either left-click it and drag it to where you want or use the boxes at the top of the graph to enter the X and Y values manually. To move around the graph, right-click and drag the mouse. To zoom in and out, use the scroll wheel of the mouse, just like in a Blueprint graph.

Timeline Example

Figure 5-58 is an example of a Timeline that is used to animate a Light Actor, so that its light starts out completely dark, gradually gets brighter, and then gradually gets dimmer again. The Timeline consists of a single Float track that will be used to feed values into the Light's Intensity property.

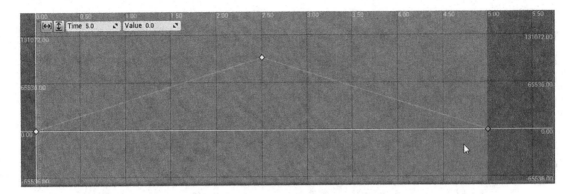

Figure 5-58. *The line that connects the keys in a Timeline is called a curve*

The line that connects the keys is called a *curve* and represents what value the Timeline Node will output at any given time during the animation. In this case, at the start of the animation, the Timeline Node will output zero, then it will gradually output a higher and higher value, until at 2.5 seconds, it is outputting a value of 100,000. Then, for the next 2.5 seconds, the value gradually decreases, until it reaches zero again.

This value will get outputted from an output pin on the Timeline Node. For each track you create, it will create a new output pin on the Timeline Node that will have the same name as the track and will output the value for that track. In Figure 5-59, the output of the track is connected to a pin that will set the Intensity property of the Light Component of a Light Actor.

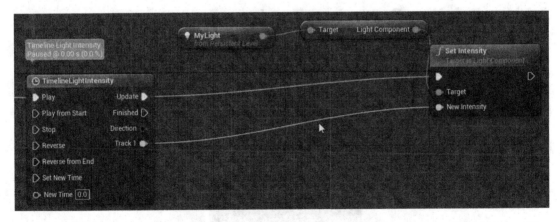

Figure 5-59. *Due to the curve of the track created for this Timeline, this logic will cause a light to gradually get brighter, then gradually get dimmer again*

157

When the Play execution pin is activated, it will cause the Timeline to start playing. For the next 5 seconds (the length of the Timeline), for each tick of gameplay, the Update pin will fire, causing the Set Intensity Node to fire. Each time the Set Intensity Node fires, it will receive a different value from the track based on that track's curve and the current playback point of the Timeline.

That's the basics of how Timelines work. You create a curve on a track to output different values across time and then use those values to update some property during each tick of gameplay.

Other Types of Tracks

The preceding example used a Float track, but there are other types of tracks as well. If you wanted to create a track to change a Vector value, such as an object's location, you would use the button to the right of the Float track button to create a *Vector track*. By gradually changing an object's location over time, you can create a simple movement animation.

To the right of that is a button that is used to create an *Event track*, which can be used to specify at what points in time certain Events should fire. To the right of that is a button used to create a *Color track* which can be used to gradually turn one color into another color.

Add an Existing Curve to a Track

The button to the right of the Color track button can be used to add an already existing curve to a new track. If you select a curve asset in the Content Browser and then click the button, it will create a new track and add that curve to it.

To add an existing curve to the *current* track, select the curve in the Content Browser, then click the arrow beneath the text "External Curve" to the left of the track you want the curve added to (Figure 5-60).

Figure 5-60. *Existing curves can be added to a track*

To save a curve you create so it can be used again later in the preceding manner, right-click the graph and select "Create External Curve" to save the curve as an asset in the Content Browser.

Timeline Options

To the right of the create track buttons, there are a few options you can set for your Timeline (Figure 5-61). The first box allows you to set the length of the Timeline. To the right of that is the *Use Last Keyframe?* option. If this is unchecked, the very last tick of the animation will be ignored. This is useful when looping, to prevent skipping in the animation when the loop starts over.

Figure 5-61. *Timeline options*

If the *AutoPlay* option is checked, the Timeline will begin playing as soon as the Level (or Actor) is created, even if it's not connected to an Event BeginPlay Node. With the *Loop* option checked, the animation will start over from the beginning once it reaches the end. The *Replicated* option will cause the animation to be replicated across all clients during a multiplayer game.

The final option is *Ignore Time Dilation*. "Time dilation" is a feature in UE4 where you can slow down or speed up time in your game. With this option checked, the Timeline will ignore any time dilation settings and just play at normal speed.

Timeline Node Pins

When the *Play* pin (Figure 5-62) fires, the Timeline will start playing from its current position. So let's say the Timeline starts at zero, and the Play pin fires, and then two seconds into the animation the *Stop* pin gets executed. At that point, the animation will pause at the two-second mark. If the *Play From Start* pin was executed, the animation would go back to the zero-second mark and play from there. But if the Play pin was executed at that point, the animation would continue playing from the two-second mark.

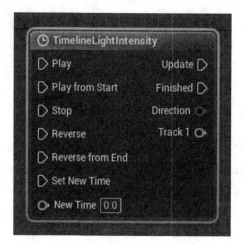

Figure 5-62. *The pins of the Timeline Node*

The *Reverse* pin will cause the animation to start playing in Reverse from its current position, and the *Reverse from End* pin will move the animation to the end and then start playing in Reverse from there. The *Set New Time* pin will move the animation to whatever time is specified in the *New Time* pin.

The *Finished* pin fires when the animation is complete. The *Direction* pin will contain a value of either Forward or Reverse, based on which direction the Timeline is playing at that particular moment.

Debugging Blueprints

If your Blueprints aren't behaving the way you expect, there is a feature called "debugging" you can take advantage of to help diagnose the problem. With debugging, you can watch the flow of execution move through your Blueprint in real time, as the game runs, or you can pause the game and view the state of the Blueprint at that time. You will be able to see what Node is currently being processed, which Nodes were already processed and in what order, and what values the Blueprint's variables currently contain. You can also step through the Blueprint one frame at a time or, using Breakpoints, one Node at a time.

When viewing a Blueprint while the game is running, every time a Node is activated, the wire leading into its execution pin will pulsate for a few seconds and change color, as seen in Figure 5-63. Some types of Nodes will display extra information. For example, the

Delay Node will display how much time is remaining until the delay finishes, also seen in Figure 5-63.

Figure 5-63. *A Level Blueprint shown while the game is running. Execution has just flowed into the Delay Node, as indicated by the pulsating wire and the information above the node*

While the game is running, you can pause or stop it from the Toolbar of the Level Editor or Blueprint Editor. While paused, you have the option to resume, frame skip, or stop (Figure 5-64). Clicking the *Frame Skip* button will advance the game by one frame of gameplay, then pause the game again.

Figure 5-64. *While the game is paused, these controls will be available in the Toolbar*

While the game is running or paused, you can hover over the name of a variable in a Get or Set Node to see the value of the variable at that time, as seen in Figure 5-65. You also have the option to *watch* a variable by right-clicking its name in a Get or Set Node and then clicking "Watch this value." This will cause the value of the variable to be displayed above the Node at all times, without having to hover over it (Figure 5-66).

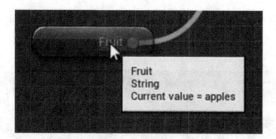

Figure 5-65. *Hovering over a variable while the game is running or paused allows you to see the variable's current value*

Figure 5-66. *Watching a variable causes that variable's value to be displayed at all times*

In order to debug an instance of a Blueprint Class, you must specify the instance in the *Debug Filter* dropdown menu on the right side of the Blueprint's Toolbar (Figure 5-67). You can use the magnifying glass icon to the right of the dropdown to take you directly to that instance within the Level.

Figure 5-67. *Use this dropdown to select which instance of the Blueprint to debug*

Breakpoints

A *Breakpoint* will cause execution of the game to pause automatically when it reaches the Node on which that Breakpoint has been placed.

To add a Breakpoint, right-click a Node and select "Add breakpoint" from the menu. Alternatively, you can select a Node and press F9 on the keyboard to toggle a Breakpoint on or off for that Node.

If a Node has a Breakpoint attached, there will be a red circle in the upper-left corner of the Node. Once that Node is reached, execution will pause, and there will be a red arrow pointing at the Node, as shown in Figure 5-68.

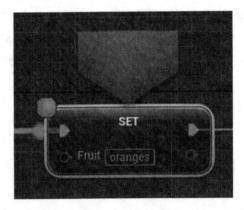

Figure 5-68. *The Breakpoint attached to this Node has caused execution to automatically pause here, as indicated by the red arrow*

When execution is paused due to a Breakpoint, additional controls appear in the Toolbar that aren't available when you pause execution manually (Figure 5-69).

Figure 5-69. *These controls are available when execution flow reaches a Breakpoint*

The *Find Node* button will take you directly to the Node that execution is currently paused at. This is useful for large Blueprints with hundreds or even thousands of Nodes. If the current Node is a custom function, you can use the *Step Into* button to open that function and see execution flow at that level of detail. If you currently have a function open and want to go back to the Node that calls the function, you can click the *Step Out* button. For all Nodes, you can click the *Step Over* button to execute that Node and move to the next Node where execution will pause once more.

Summary

In this chapter, you got a solid foundation in the complex topic of Blueprints. In the next chapter, you will build upon this foundation and continue your study of Blueprints by learning how you can use them to create players and an input system.

CHAPTER 6

Players and Input

Even the most breathtaking Levels aren't of much use if your game doesn't have rules, things you can control, and a way to input that control. This chapter will teach you about Game Modes, which define the rules for the game; about Pawns and Characters, which are objects you can take possession of in the game; and how to set up a robust input system to control those objects.

Game Modes

A *Game Mode* is an Actor that can be used to define and enforce the game's set of rules. These rules may include how many lives the player starts with, whether or not the game can be paused, if there are any time limits, the conditions needed to win the game, and so on. The Game Mode can be set on a per-level basis, and you can use the same Game Mode for multiple Levels. In fact, the primary purpose of a Game Mode is to store data and logic that applies to more than one Level and thus isn't appropriate for a Level Blueprint.

To use the Game Mode Actor, you will want to create a Blueprint Class from it. Just like with any other Blueprint, you can create variables to store data and Nodes to add functionality. For example, you could create an Integer variable called "Start Time" that specifies the amount of seconds that the game timer should start with, and you could use the Event Graph to define how a player wins the game and what should happen when they do.

Game State

Before continuing the discussion on Game Mode, you should be aware of a closely related concept, Game State, so you don't get confused. Game State is used to share and sync certain Game Mode data with all clients on the server during an online multiplayer game. The data it shares should be game-wide data that all connected clients need to

© David Nixon 2020
D. Nixon, *Beginning Unreal Game Development*, https://doi.org/10.1007/978-1-4842-5639-8_6

know but that isn't specific to any one player. This includes things like if the game has started, how long it has been running, how long each player has been connected, and the base class of the Game Mode. For this reason, in multiplayer games, Game Mode is stored on the server while Game State is stored on the server *and* replicated to each client.

Create a New Game Mode Blueprint

To create a new Blueprint Class from the Game Mode Actor, go to the Content Browser and browse to the folder you want to put the Blueprint in. Then click the green Add New button and select Blueprint Class (Figure 6-1).

Figure 6-1. *Creating a new Blueprint Class*

This will open a window where you can choose the parent class you want to derive the new Blueprint from (Figure 6-2). At the top, there is a list of commonly selected parent classes, and below that is a searchable list of all the classes that can be used. In the list of common classes, click the Game Mode Base button. To edit the Blueprint, simply double-click it to open it in the Blueprint Editor.

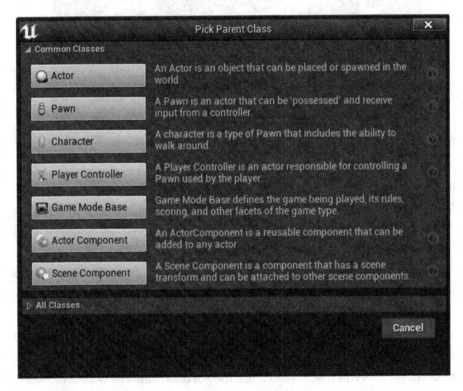

Figure 6-2. *Selecting a parent class for the Blueprint Class*

Game Mode Properties

The Game Mode class comes with some default properties that can be edited in the Details Panel of the Blueprint Editor.

First is the *Classes* category, as shown in Figure 6-3. The properties under the Classes category define various gameplay classes that your game will use. For example, the *Default Pawn Class* specifies the Actor that the Player will start off controlling in the game. The *HUD Class* defines what kinds of text overlays you will have during gameplay such as health, lives, score, timer, and so on.

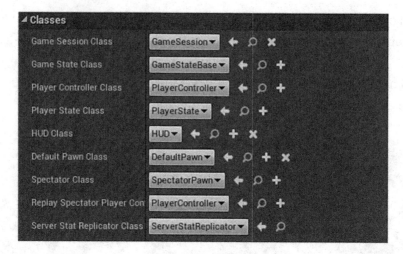

Figure 6-3. *You can set the game's default classes in the Game Mode*

There are already defaults for each of the classes. But if you wanted to change, for example, the HUD that a Game Mode used, you could create a new HUD Blueprint Class, and once you saved it, you would be able to select it from the dropdown, telling the Game Mode to use that HUD and not the default.

The next category is *Game,* and it has only one property, *Default Player Name* (Figure 6-4). This will simply assign a default name to any players who connect to the server with no name specified.

The next category is *Game Mode.* The first property is *Use Seamless Travel.* This has to do with how players transition between Levels in multiplayer games. With this unchecked, players will disconnect from the server while a new Level loads and then reconnect to the server once the Level has loaded. With Seamless Travel enabled, the new Level will load in the background, and there is no disruption in the server connection. For multiplayer games in Unreal Engine, using Seamless Travel is recommended.

The next property is *Start Players as Spectators.* A *Spectator* simply refers to someone in an online multiplayer game who is connected to the server and can view the game in some form but cannot currently play the game. With this unchecked, players will spawn into the game as soon as they connect to the server. With this checked, players who connect to the server will start as Spectators and must spawn into the game manually.

The next property, *Pauseable,* simply determines whether or not the game is allowed to be paused.

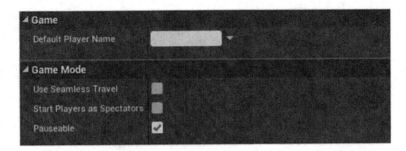

Figure 6-4. *The Game and Game Mode categories*

Assigning Game Modes

After you create a Game Mode Blueprint, you still need to tell the Engine you want to use it. One option you have is to assign it as the default Game Mode for the game that all the Levels will use by default, unless otherwise specified.

To set the default Game Mode, go up to the Menu Bar, click Edit, and then Project Settings. Then select Maps & Modes from the list on the left. On the screen that comes up, there will be a Default GameMode property that you can set (Figure 6-5).

Figure 6-5. *You set the Game Mode to use in the Maps & Modes tab of Project Settings*

You can also choose to override the default Game Mode on a per-level basis. First, with the Level open that you want to use a different Game Mode for, go up to the Toolbar and click Settings and then World Settings (Figure 6-6). This will open the World Settings tab within the Details Panel. On this tab, there is a property called *GameMode Override* (Figure 6-7). By default, this is None, which means the Level will use the Default GameMode. But you can choose to override the default by assigning another GameMode using the dropdown.

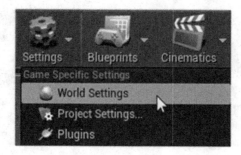

Figure 6-6. *Opening the World Settings tab*

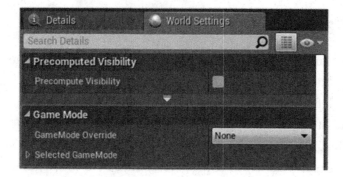

Figure 6-7. *A GameMode Override can be set in the World Settings tab of the Details Panel*

Pawns

A *Pawn* is an Actor that can be controlled, either by a human player or the computer. Pawns are used for the Actor that you play as in the game and also for AI-controlled allies and enemies.

As you saw in the previous section on Game Modes, the default Game Mode starts with a default Pawn Actor. You've probably already used this Pawn to fly around your practice Levels, even though you can't see it because (1) it doesn't have a Static Mesh defined and (2) the camera is attached to it in a first-person perspective.

You can, however, create your own Pawn Actors, by creating a new Blueprint Class out of the existing Pawn class. Then you would assign the new Pawn as the Default Pawn Class in the Game Mode. To create a new Pawn class, first go to the Content Browser and navigate to the folder you want the Blueprint to be created in. Then click Add New, hover over Blueprints, and select Blueprint Class. Then select the Pawn class as the Parent Class for the Blueprint. To edit the Blueprint, double-click it to open it in the Blueprint Editor.

In the Viewport tab of the Blueprint Editor, you will see that the Actor starts out consisting of just a single component, the *DefaultSceneRoot* component. This is an advanced topic, so don't worry about what the DefaultSceneRoot is, just know that every Pawn will have one.

Adding a Static Mesh Component to a Pawn

The first thing you may want to consider adding to your Pawn is a Static Mesh Component, so that the Pawn actually looks like something and isn't invisible. To do so, simply click Add Component and select Static Mesh, as shown in Figure 6-8.

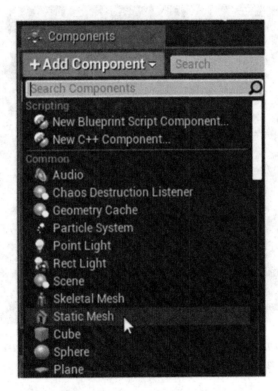

Figure 6-8. *Adding a Static Mesh Component to an Actor*

This will add a Static Mesh Component, but you will still need to define which Static Mesh the component should use. To do that, go to the Static Mesh category of the Details Panel and select one using the dropdown.

Adding a Camera Component to a Pawn

If you are using a Pawn for a human player, you will want to add a *Camera Component* to it, in order to define the perspective that the player will see from. To do so, click Add Component, go down to the Camera category, and select Camera.

Wherever you place the lens of the Camera icon is where the player will see out of. So if you wanted a first-person perspective, you would place the Camera so that the lens was located at the same place as where the Mesh's eyes are supposed to be (Figure 6-9). Or you could position the Camera elsewhere and have it pointing at the Mesh in order to give it a third-person perspective.

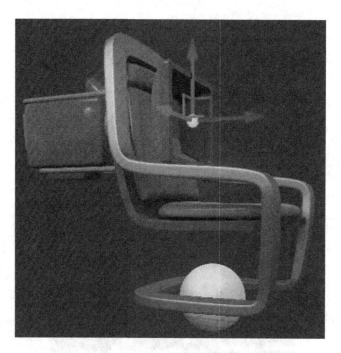

Figure 6-9. *This Pawn has a chair for its Mesh. If the chair had eyes in its front, this Camera placement would give a first-person perspective*

Adding a Spring Arm Component to a Pawn

When you are setting up a third-person perspective, you will also want to use a *Spring Arm Component*. The Spring Arm Component will allow the Camera to automatically make adjustments in cases where the line of sight between the Camera and the mesh gets obscured. The Spring Arm Component can also be found under the Camera category.

You will need to attach the Camera to the Spring Arm in order for it to be of use. To do that, select the Camera Component in the Components window, and drag it onto the Spring Arm Component (Figure 6-10). Once the Camera is attached, you can't use the Move Tool to move it around. At that point, if you want to adjust how far away the Camera is positioned, you will need to set the Target Arm Length property of the Spring Arm, which sets the default length of the Spring Arm (Figure 6-11).

Figure 6-10. *The Camera Component attached to the Spring Arm Component*

Camera		
Target Arm Length	300.0	
▷ Socket Offset	X 0.0	Y 0.0	Z 0.0
▷ Target Offset	X 0.0	Y 0.0	Z 0.0

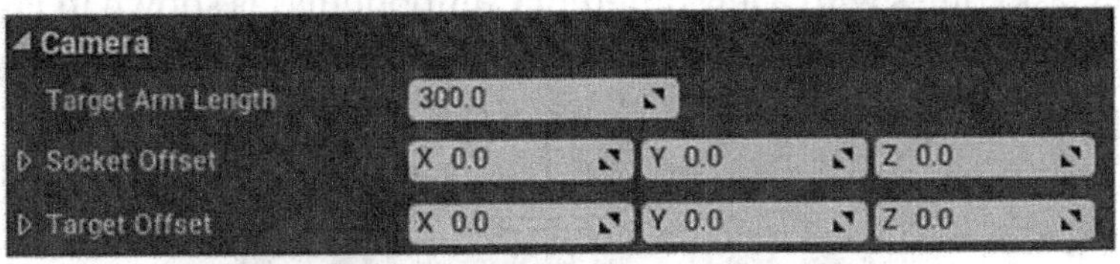

Figure 6-11. *Properties of the Spring Arm Component*

The Camera will normally be the default length away from the Mesh, but that could change if the Spring Arm needs to adjust because the view of the Camera gets blocked. For example, if a wall gets between the Camera and the Mesh, the Spring Arm will automatically shorten in order to bring the Camera in close enough to be able to see the Mesh again. Then, when the wall was no longer an issue, the Spring Arm would lengthen back to the Target Arm Length.

Characters

A *Character* is a type of Pawn that has all the features and functionality of a Pawn, plus additional ones. Specifically, a Character is a type of Pawn that is meant to have bipedal movement. Bipedal refers to walking on two legs, so you would use the Character class to represent humans and other creatures with human-like movement, like walking and jumping.

You can create your own Character class the same way as the Game Mode and Pawn class. Go to the Content Browser, go to Add New, select Blueprint Class, and select Character as the Parent Class. As always, double-click it to open it in the Blueprint Editor.

Don't forget to assign your new Character as the Default Pawn Class in the Game Mode. Remember that a Character is a type of Pawn. The Character class is a child of the Pawn class. So the Default Pawn Class can be set to a Pawn class or any child of a Pawn class.

Character Components

The Character class comes with a few different Components, as shown in Figure 6-12. The *Capsule Component* is used as the boundaries of the Character for the purposes of detecting collisions.

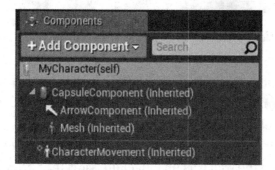

Figure 6-12. *The default Components of a Character*

The *Arrow Component* is used to indicate which direction should be considered facing forward for the Character. So if you had a Mesh of a human, you would want the arrow to be coming straight out of the front of its body.

The *Skeletal Mesh Component* can be used to assign a Skeletal Mesh to the Character.

Character Movement Component

Perhaps the most important component of the Character is the *Character Movement Component*. This is what gives the Character its movement capabilities. If you click it, you can edit several properties relating to its movement (Figure 6-13).

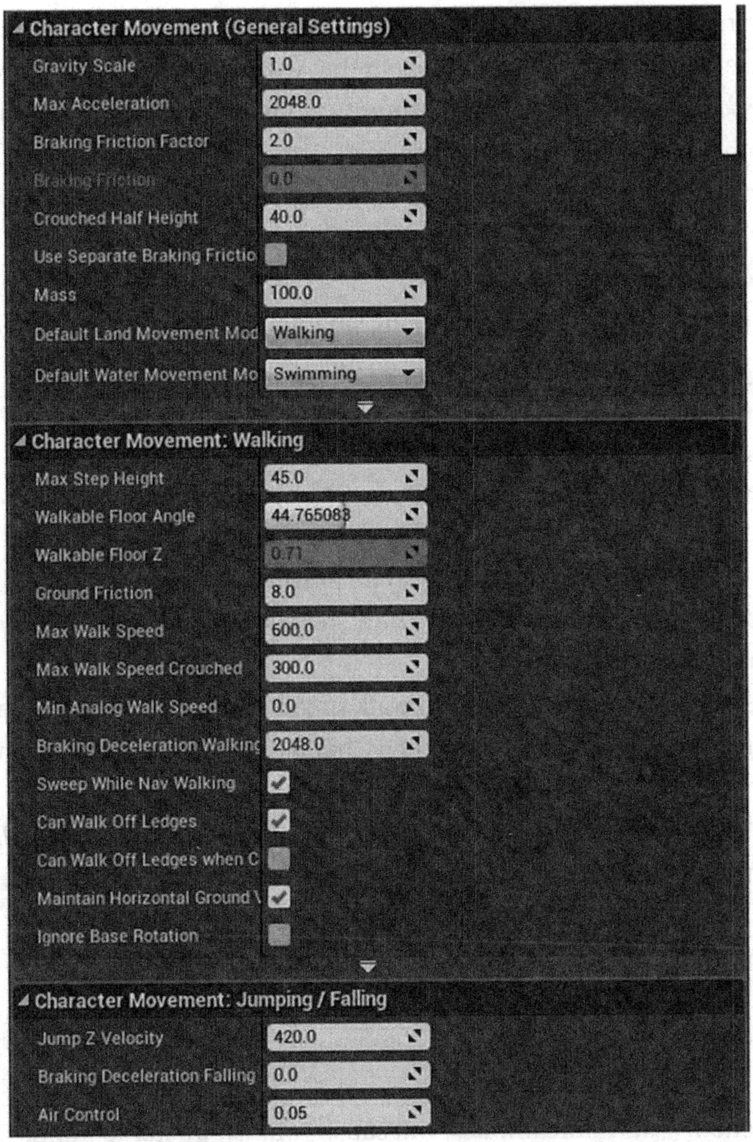

Figure 6-13. *Character Movement properties*

The *Gravity Scale* property determines how much of an effect gravity will have on this Character. *Max Acceleration* determines the maximum acceleration that this Character can achieve for any type of movement, whether it be walking, swimming, and so on.

Braking Friction Factor determines how much the Character will glide when attempting to slow down its speed. If *Use Separate Braking Friction* is unchecked, the Braking Friction Factor will be multiplied against all other friction forces (ground, wind, etc.) to get the actual friction coefficient that will be used. If Use Separate Braking Friction is *checked*, the Braking Friction property alone will be used as the friction coefficient, with all other friction forces ignored.

The *Crouched Half Height* property is used to tell the engine where the middle of the Character should be calculated at when the Character is crouching. This is used for collision detection purposes.

The *Mass* property will set the mass of the Character which determines things like how much force is required to move it, and so on.

The *Default Land Movement Mode* and *Default Water Movement Mode* properties are simply used to specify what kind of default movement the character should have when they are on land or in the water. So these default to Walking and Swimming.

Next is the *Character Movement: Walking* category. *Max Step Height* determines how tall a step has to be before the Character can no longer automatically ascend it when walking. *Walkable Floor Angle* determines how steep a sloped floor can be before a Character can no longer walk up it.

You can set the Character's maximum walk speed and the max walk speed when the Character is crouched. You can set whether a Character will walk off a ledge when they reach the end of it or if that will block the Character's movement.

There are several properties relating to jumping and falling, such as the *Jump Z Velocity* which will determine how high your Character can jump and the *Air Control* property which determines how much control you have over your Character when it is in the air. There are also some properties for swimming, flying, and so on.

Creating a Jump Input

The Jump function, as its name implies, will cause your Character to jump. The Jump function is one of many movement functions available to the Character class that is not available to the regular Pawn class.

Adding the nodes shown in Figure 6-14 to the Event Graph of the Character Blueprint will cause the Character to jump when the *Space Bar* is pressed.

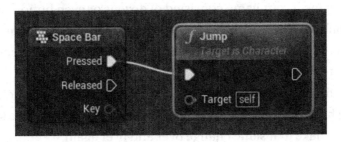

Figure 6-14. *Pressing the Space Bar will cause the Character to jump*

Controllers

A *Controller* is an Actor that is used to possess a Pawn and control its movement and actions. There are two types of Controllers – the *Player Controller*, which is used to take input from a human and use that to control a Pawn, and the *AI Controller*, which is used to implement AI control over a Pawn.

You can create a Player Controller Blueprint by creating a new Blueprint Class and using Player Controller as the Parent Class. To use it, you will need to set it as the Player Controller Class in the Game Mode Blueprint (Figure 6-15).

Figure 6-15. *Setting the Player Controller Class in the Game Mode*

Advantages of Using a Controller

As you learned in the last section, you can define the input for a Pawn directly in its own Blueprint. But imagine if your game consisted of dozens or even hundreds of characters that the player could control and they all shared many of the same movements. For example, think of the Lego games, like *Lego Star Wars*, which have dozens of characters you can switch between.

If you were defining the input inside the Pawn, you would have to define it over and over again for each and every Pawn. Then, if you wanted to make even a small change, you would have to make that same change over and over again.

By defining your input inside of a Player Controller instead, you only need to define it in one place, and if you ever need to make a change, you only need to make the change in one place. Then you would be able to use that input on any Pawn that the Player Controller possesses.

Adding Input to a Player Controller

If you tried to add jump functionality, like was done in the previous section, to a Player Controller Blueprint immediately, you won't be able to because the Jump function belongs to the Character class. The Jump Node won't even be available as a selection in the Node Menu.

You would first need to get access to the Character so that you can access its Jump function. This can be done with a *Get Player Character* function. This function will return the Character that the specified player is using. Player index 0 is for player 1 and player index 1 is for player 2 and so on. If the Pawn that the player is using is a Character, the Return Value will contain that Character; otherwise it will return a Null value.

If the Return Value pin contains a valid Character, when you drag off the pin and access the Node Menu, the Jump Node will be available because you are in the context of a Character. Figure 6-16 shows an example of adding jump functionality to a Player Controller.

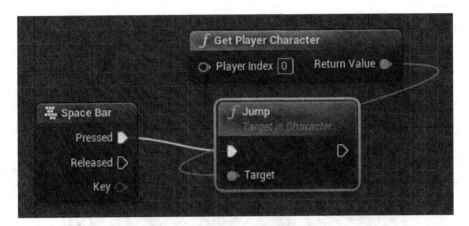

Figure 6-16. *The Jump function is only available to the Character class*

This provides the same functionality as in the previous example, but now that functionality has been abstracted out to a higher level which will allow you to easily use it with any Character you wish.

Input Mapping

Imagine you were creating a multiplayer game that could support eight players. You would need eight different Player Controllers – one for each human player that is playing the game. If each Player Controller contained the Jump functionality from the previous section, and you wanted to change what key caused the player to jump from the Space Bar to some other key, you would need to make that change eight times.

But with Input Mapping, you can define what key or keys correspond to what behavior by mapping the keys to a name that you create. Then, you can refer to that name in Player Controller Blueprints instead of hardcoding the specific key to use. If you ever want to change which key corresponds to which action, you will only need to make that change in one place.

Action Mappings vs. Axis Mappings

In the Level Editor, go to Edit ➤ Project Settings. Under the Engine category, click Input. This will bring up the screen where you can create Input Mappings. These are divided into two categories – Action Mappings and Axis Mappings (Figure 6-17).

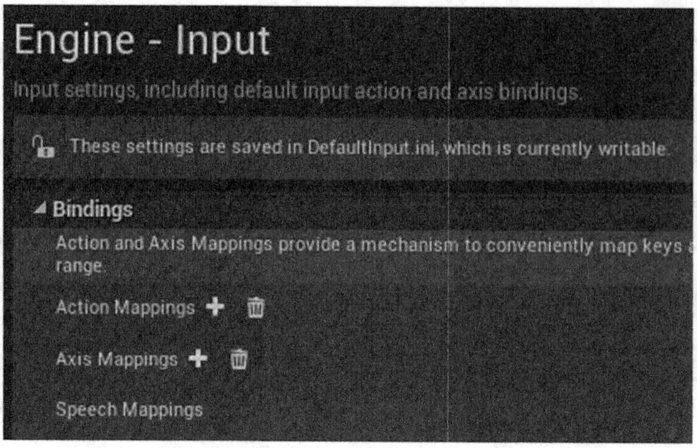

Figure 6-17. *You can map inputs in the Engine category of the Project Settings*

Action Mappings are for key or button presses and releases where holding down the key/button for any length of time doesn't make a difference and there is no direction associated with the input. For example, if you wanted your character to throw a punch and you wanted the player to have to press a button for each punch, you would use an Action Mapping. On a keyboard, you might use the P key or a mouse click for this. On a gamepad, such as an Xbox controller, you would use one of the face buttons on the right, such as the A button.

Axis Mappings are used in situations where holding down the key provides a continuous stream of input and/or the direction of the input matters. For example, you would often use this for walking, where if you hold the key continuously, the character will continue to walk until you let go, and it matters which direction you are trying to go. On a keyboard, the W, A, S, and D keys are usually used for this purpose where W and S represent opposite Y-axis directions and A and D represent opposite X-axis directions. On a gamepad, such as an Xbox controller, this is usually accomplished using the left analog stick or the directional pad.

Creating New Input Mappings

To create a new mapping, under the Bindings category, click the plus sign next to the type of mapping you want to create (Figure 6-18). If you don't see the new mapping right away, click the triangle to the left of the label to expand the section.

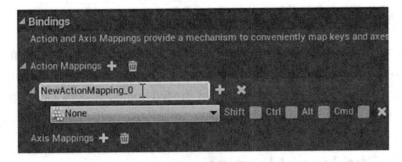

Figure 6-18. *Creating a new input mapping*

The first box is used to give the mapping a name. Underneath that box is a row where you define a key or button to use that will trigger the action. There are also a series of checkboxes you can check to require that additional keys be held at the same time as the one defined, such as *Shift, Ctrl,* or *Alt.*

If you want another key or button to also trigger the same action, just click the plus sign next to the name of the mapping to define another input.

You don't need to save your changes here because any changes made in the Project Settings are automatically saved as they are made. When you are done, you can simply close the Project Settings window.

Once you create a mapping, it will be available in the Node Menu, and you can use it in place of the keyboard Nodes used in the previous examples. See Figure 6-19.

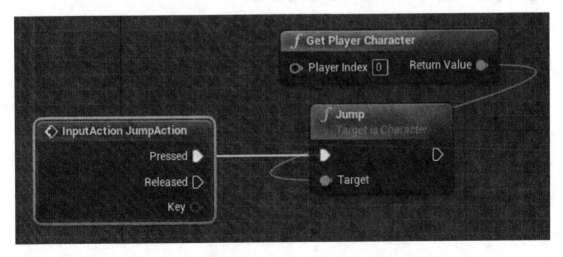

Figure 6-19. *Using a mapped action instead of hardcoding the key to use*

Setting Up Basic Character Movement

This section will go through the entire process of setting up basic Character movement. In addition to the jump functionality already covered, you will learn how to move your Character around using the *W*, *A*, *S*, *D* keys, or the left analog stick of a gamepad, and how to make your Character look around using the mouse or the right analog stick.

Setting Up the Input Mapping

Go to Edit ➤ Project Settings ➤ Input. Set up an Action Mapping named "JumpAction" like was done in the previous section. Refer to Figure 6-20 for reference.

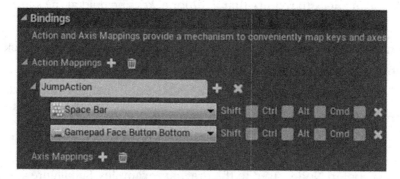

Figure 6-20. *Mapping inputs for a jump action*

Movement requires detecting a continuous input, so the movement behaviors will use Axis Mappings. Add an Axis Mapping and name it "LookUpDown." To look up and down, we want our player to be able to use either the mouse, by dragging it up or down, or the right thumbstick of a gamepad, by tilting it up or down. So click the plus sign to the right of the mapping twice, and select "Mouse Y" for the first input and "Gamepad Right Thumbstick Y-Axis" for the second input (Figure 6-21).

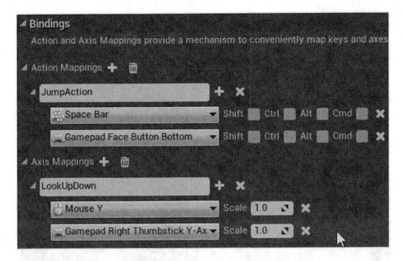

Figure 6-21. *Adding mappings for having the Character look around*

To the right of the mappings, you will see a *Scale* property. This will determine both the magnitude and direction of the axis input. So if you set the scale of the mouse to 2.0 but left the gamepad at 1.0, then the mouse would cause the player to look up and down twice as fast as using the gamepad.

If you make the Scale negative, it will reverse the direction of the movement applied. With the gamepad scale set at 1.0, tilting the stick up will cause the player to look up, and tilting the stick down will cause the player to look down. If it was set to -1.0, it would invert those controls. The mouse Y-axis is inverted by default, so you will need to set that to negative if you want to make it standard.

Continue to add Axis Mappings for the remaining movements until your mappings look like they do in Figure 6-22.

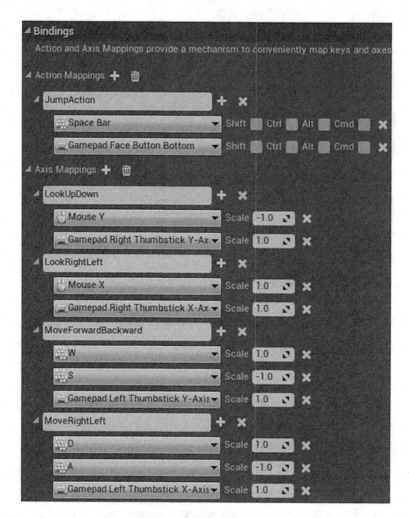

Figure 6-22. Complete input mapping for a Character

Using Input Mappings in Blueprints

Now that you have the input mappings set up, you will need to edit your Player Controller Blueprint so you can specify the behaviors that these mapping names actually correspond to. Before you do that, it will help to place your Character into a variable that you can access it from, so that you don't need to keep calling the Get Player Character function over and over.

So in the Event Graph of the Player Controller Blueprint, add a Get Player Character Node. Drag off the Return Value pin and select *Promote to variable* from the top of the menu (Figure 6-23). This will create a variable and store the Character in it. In the My Blueprint tab, rename the variable from "NewVar_0" to "MyCharacter."

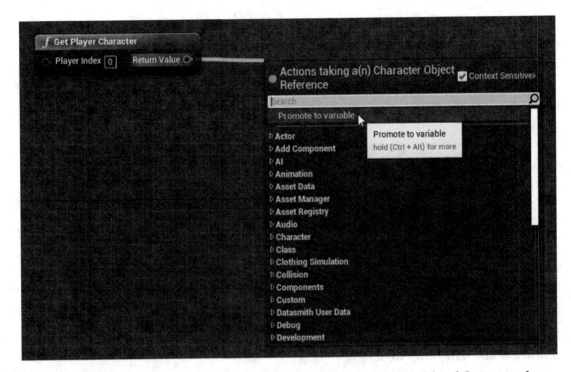

Figure 6-23. *Selecting Promote to variable will create a variable of the same data type as the pin*

Connect the output execution pin of the Event BeginPlay Node to the input execution pin of the Set Node. Now, as soon as the Player Controller is created, it will get a reference to the Character and store it in a variable which you can easily access (Figure 6-24).

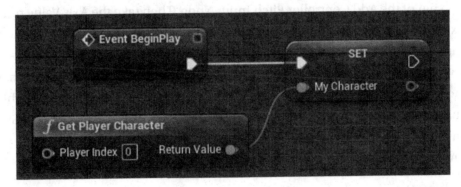

Figure 6-24. *This will get a reference to the Character and store it in a variable as soon as the Level begins*

185

Go back to the My Blueprint tab, drag the MyCharacter variable into the Event Graph, and create a Get Node. Drag off the pin of the Get Node and add a Jump Node. Open the Node Menu and search for the "JumpAction" mapping that you created earlier. Add that Node and connect its Pressed pin to the input execution pin of the Jump Node, as shown in Figure 6-25.

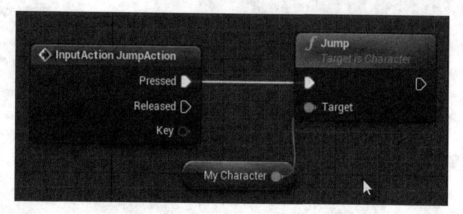

Figure 6-25. *The jump logic*

Setting Up the Look Movements

In the Node Menu, search for the "LookUpDown" mapping and add that Node. Drag another wire off the MyCharacter node, so you can access the Character's functions, and search for a function called *Add Controller Pitch Input*. The word "pitch" in this context refers to the kind of up and down rotational movement that we're looking to produce.

Connect the output execution pin of the InputAxis LookUpDown Node to the input execution pin of the Add Controller Pitch Input Node. Then take the Axis Value pin of the InputAxis LookUpDown Node, which contains the Scale value you specified in the Input Mappings, and connect it to the Val pin of the Add Controller Pitch Input Node.

Now add the Node for the LookRightLeft mapping you created and connect that to a function called *Add Controller Yaw Input* which is used to control left and right rotational movement. Remember that you need to drag out of the My Character Get Node in order to access Character functions.

Your Event Graph should now look similar to Figure 6-26.

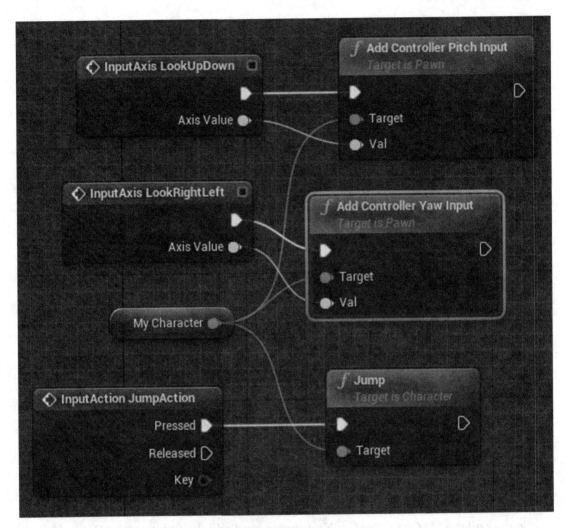

Figure 6-26. *The logic for the look movement*

There's one more thing you will need to do to get this look functionality working with these functions. Compile and save the Blueprint, and then open your Character Blueprint. In the Details Panel, under the Pawn category, make sure that the two properties *Use Controller Rotation Pitch* and *Use Controller Rotation Yaw* are both checked, like they are in Figure 6-27.

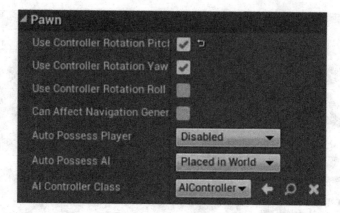

Figure 6-27. *Make sure the first two properties here are checked*

Setting Up the Walking Movements

Reopen the Player Controller Blueprint. Create another copy of the My Character Get Node to prevent the Event Graph from getting too messy. Add the Node for the MoveForwardBackward mapping and connect that to a function called *Add Movement Input.* Connect the Axis Value pin to the Scale Value pin.

For this to work, you need to provide the Add Movement Input Node with additional information. You need to tell it which direction to move the Character relative to the world. You already know what direction you want to move relative to the character – forward or backward – but which direction is that as far as the Level is concerned? That depends on the direction that the character is facing. So you will need to get the Vector that represents that direction and hook it into the *World Direction* pin.

So drag off the My Character Get Node again, and add the function *Get Control Rotation.* This will tell you how the Character is rotated relative to all three axes. But all you care about at this point is which direction the character is facing. So to get that information, drag off the Return Value pin and add the *Get Forward Vector* function.

This will extract the forward Vector from out of the Rotation value. Now connect the Return Value pin of the Get Forward Vector Node to the World Direction pin of the Add Movement Input Node.

The setup for left and right movement is the same, except you need to use the *Get Right Vector* function instead of the Get Forward Vector function. When you are finished, the logic for the walking movements should look something like Figure 6-28.

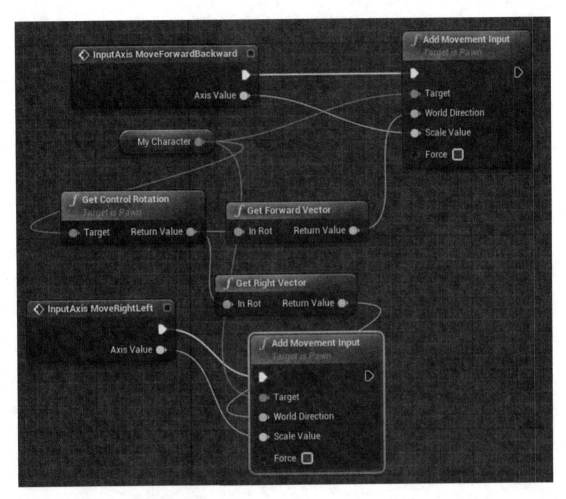

Figure 6-28. *The logic for the walking movement*

Summary

In this chapter, you learned how to define the rules for your game and how to set up characters that you can control. In the next chapter, you will learn about collisions and about Unreal Engine's built-in damage system.

CHAPTER 7

Collisions

Collisions are an integral part of game development. In this chapter, you will learn how Unreal Engine handles collisions and how to apply that knowledge. First, you will get a high-level technical overview of collisions and the various collision settings available in UE4. Then, you will be shown an example to demonstrate how these settings work. Finally, you will be shown how collisions can be applied in a real-world example, where colliding with an enemy causes damage to the player.

Collisions Overview

In the Details Panel, under the Collision category, you can edit the Collision properties of an Actor.

Hit Events and Overlap Events

If two Actors are set to block one another when they come into contact, then, when they collide, they will impede each other's movement, and a *Hit Event* will be generated *if* Hit Events are enabled for that Actor.

To enable Hit Events for an Actor, check the *Simulation Generates Hit Events* checkbox under the Collision category, as shown in Figure 7-1. For an Actor's Hit Event to fire, only the Simulation Generates Hit Events checkbox for that Actor needs to be checked. The other Actor's checkbox only needs to be checked if you want that Actor's Hit Event to fire as well.

191

© David Nixon 2020
D. Nixon, *Beginning Unreal Game Development*, https://doi.org/10.1007/978-1-4842-5639-8_7

Figure 7-1. *To enable Hit Events for an Actor, check the Simulation Generates Hit Events checkbox*

On the other hand, if two Actors are set to *overlap* with one another, then, when they collide, they will *not* impede each other's movement and will overlap with one another instead. This will generate an *Overlap Event* if Overlap Events are enabled for *both* of the Actors.

To enable Overlap Events for an Actor, check the *Generate Overlap Events* checkbox under the Collision category. Again, for an Actor's Overlap Event to fire, both the Actors involved in the collision must have Generate Overlap Events checked.

Hit Events and Overlap Events can be used like any other Event Node and thus can be used to define what should happen when a collision occurs.

Collision Presets

When you expand the menu under the Collision Presets property, you will find a long list of collision properties that can be automatically set by choosing from a list of presets. Or they can be individually set by choosing "Custom" and setting them one by one.

Collision Enabled Property

The *Collision Enabled* property is another way to set the block and/or overlap behaviors of the Actor (Figure 7-2). This has four possible settings. When this is set to *Collision Enabled*, it means that the Actor is enabled for both *Query Collisions* and *Physics Collisions*. Query Collisions just refer to overlap collisions and Physics Collisions refer to blocking collisions.

Figure 7-2. *The Collision Enabled property*

With Collision Enabled set to *Physics Only*, the Actor will be able to block other Actors, and fire Hit Events, but it won't be able to fire Overlap Events. If it is set to *Query Only*, the Actor will be able to fire Overlap Events but won't be able to block other Actors and won't be able to fire Hit Events. If it is set to *No Collision*, the Actor won't be able to block other Actors and won't be able to fire Overlap Events or Hit Events.

Object Type Property

If the Actor is a Pawn or a Pawn sub-type, such as a Character, you would set the *Object Type* (Figure 7-3) to Pawn. If the Actor is a Vehicle, you would set the Object Type to Vehicle. If the Actor is a Destructible Mesh, a topic that hasn't been covered, you would set it to Destructible.

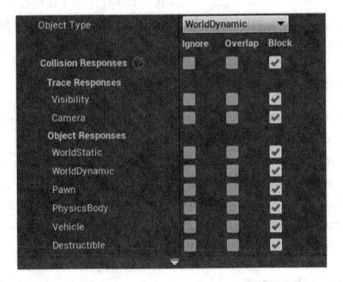

Figure 7-3. *The Object Type property and Collision Responses*

For all other Actors, if the Actor doesn't move, you would set the Object Type to *WorldStatic*. If the Actor does move, you would set it to either *WorldDynamic* or *PhysicsBody*. You would use WorldDynamic for Actors that move due to an animation or a Blueprint script and PhysicsBody for Actors that will move due to physics, such as gravity or the force of another object.

193

The Object Type doesn't do anything itself inherently. Its purpose is simply to be able to place each Actor into a specific group, so that you can use the section below it to specify how the different types should interact with each other when they collide.

This section has a row for each of the six Object Types. Each row is used to specify the behavior that should occur when the Actor collides with the Object Type of that row. You can set each row to either *Ignore*, *Overlap*, or *Block*. The first row of checkboxes, labeled *Collision Responses*, can be used as a "select all" for each column. For example, if you click the Overlap checkbox, it will check the Overlap box in every row.

So if you wanted blocking and Hit Events to occur when the Actor collides with an Actor of the type WorldDynamic, you would check the Block column of the WorldDynamic row. If you wanted the two Actors to overlap and to generate Overlap Events, you would check the box in the Overlap column instead. If you wanted the two Actors to overlap, but not generate any Overlap Events, you would check the Ignore checkbox.

Note that the behavior that will actually occur depends on the preceding settings for *both* the Actors involved in the collision. For example, both Actors must be set to block the other's type in order for blocking to actually occur and for Hit Events to fire. Similarly, if one of the Actors is set to Ignore the other, then Overlap Events won't fire even if the other Actor is set to Overlap.

Trace Responses

The Trace Responses section is used to determine the Actor's visibility to other Actors. If the Actor doing the looking is a camera, you would use the Camera row, and for all other Actor types, you would use the Visibility row.

If the Actor is set to Ignore, it will be invisible to other Actors. If it is set to Overlap, it can be seen by other Actors, but it can also be seen through. So you would use this for a glass wall, for example. If it is set to Block, then it can be seen, but it cannot be seen through. So you might use this for a brick wall, for example.

Collision Preset Property

Again, if you want to be able to set the preceding properties manually, you need to set the Collision Preset to Custom. But you can also use the dropdown to select from a long list of presets. Each preset will automatically select some combination of the properties.

For example, with *BlockAll* as the preset, it will automatically set the Collision Enabled property to Collision Enabled, it will set the Object Type to WorldStatic, and it will set all of the responses to Block. If *OverlapAll* is selected, it will set Collision Enabled to Query Only, it will set the Object Type to WorldStatic, and it will set all of the responses to Overlap. If *OverlapAllDynamic* is selected, it will choose the same settings as OverlapAll, except it will set the Object Type to WorldDynamic.

Can Character Step Up On Property

The *Can Character Step Up On* property (Figure 7-4) is used to specify whether or not a Character will step onto the top of the Actor when it walks into it or if it will block the Character's movement. This is assuming that the two Actors' Object Types are set to Block one another. Otherwise, this property doesn't apply. Also, at very small heights, a Character will step onto an Actor when it walks into it regardless of what this property is set to.

Figure 7-4. *The Can Character Step Up On property*

So if the Actor is tall enough, with Can Character Step Up On set to *No*, if a Character walks into the Actor, it will block the Character's movement. But if it is set to *Yes*, when a Character walks into the Actor, it will step *onto* the Actor instead.

If Can Character Step Up On is set to *(Owner)*, then the Actor will use the same setting as its parent. If it doesn't have a parent, then setting this to (Owner) is the same as setting it to Yes.

Block vs. Overlap Example

The interaction between Object Types, Collision Responses, Hit Events, and Overlap Events that was covered in the previous section can be confusing, so let's take a look at an example. Imagine there is a cube mesh resting on the ground and that a sphere mesh, that has Simulate Physics and Enable Gravity checked, is placed above the cube, as shown in Figure 7-5. When the Level starts, the sphere will fall, and whether the cube blocks its movement or not will depend on the collision settings of the two Actors.

Figure 7-5. *Whether the cube will block the sphere or not depends on the two Actors' collision settings*

So now, imagine the sphere's Object Type is set to PhysicsBody and its WorldStatic Collision Response is set to Block (Figure 7-6). Also imagine that the cube's Object Type is set to WorldStatic and its PhysicsBody Collision Response is set to Block (Figure 7-7). With these Actors set to block each other's type, when the Level begins, and the sphere falls, its movement will be blocked by the cube, and it will come to rest on top of it, as shown in Figure 7-8.

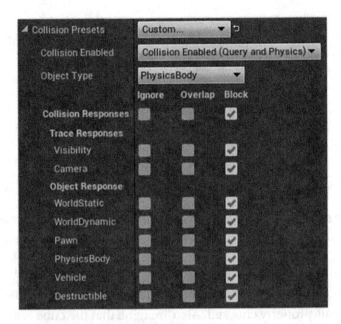

Figure 7-6. *The collision settings of the sphere*

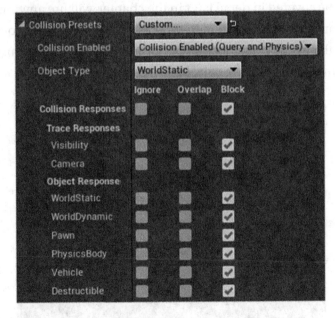

Figure 7-7. *The collision settings of the cube*

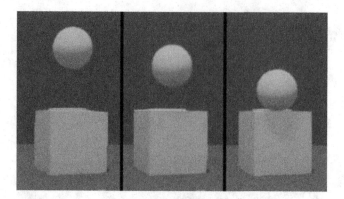

Figure 7-8. *The cube will block the sphere's movement because both Actors are set to block one another*

Also, because these Actors block one another, this will cause any Hit Events to fire at the moment that the two objects collide. Imagine that the cube has its Simulation Generates Hit Events property checked. Also, imagine that the cube is an instance of a Blueprint and that it has the nodes shown in Figure 7-9 in its Event Graph. The Event Hit Node, which will be covered in detail later in the chapter, will fire anytime the Actor has a blocking collision with another Actor. In this case, when the sphere collides with the cube, it will print the word "Hello" to the screen, and it will actually print it several times as the sphere bounces on top of the cube before coming to rest (Figure 7-10).

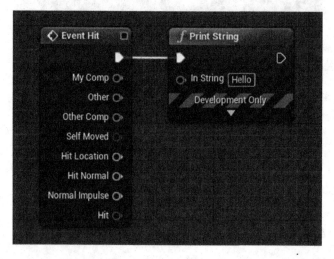

Figure 7-9. *When the Event Hit Node fires, the word "Hello" will be printed to the screen*

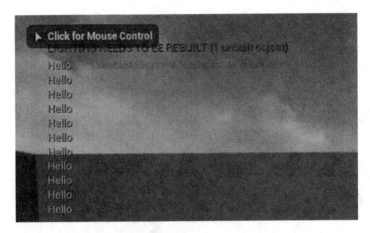

Figure 7-10. *The word "Hello" is printed to the screen multiple times as the sphere bounces on the cube and causes multiple collisions to occur*

Now imagine that the cube's PhysicsBody Collision Response is set to Overlap (Figure 7-11). When the Level begins, the sphere will now fall right through the cube, as shown in Figure 7-12, even though the sphere is still set to block WorldStatic objects. Again, this is because both Actors must be set to block one another for blocking to occur. Also, because an overlapping collision occurred, and not a blocking collision, the Event Hit Node won't fire, and the word "Hello" won't be printed to the screen.

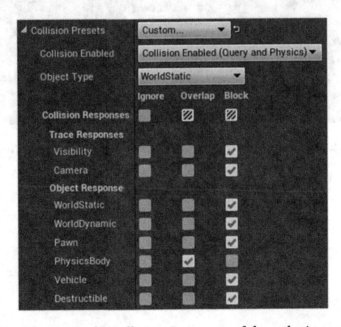

Figure 7-11. *The PhysicsBody Collision Response of the cube is now set to Overlap instead of Block*

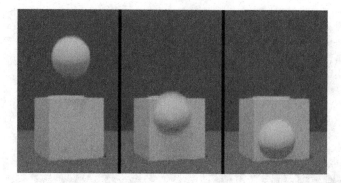

Figure 7-12. *The two Actors now overlap with each other instead of blocking each other*

Now let's say that, instead of an Event Hit Node in its Blueprint, the cube had an Event ActorBeginOverlap node in its place (Figure 7-13). Also, assume that Generate Overlap Events is checked for both the cube and the sphere. Now when the sphere falls through the cube, the word "Hello" will be printed to the screen as soon as the two Actors first overlap with one another (Figure 7-14).

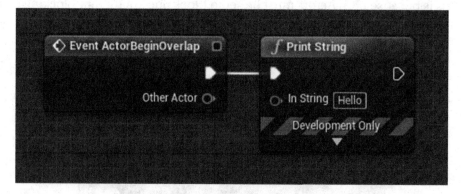

Figure 7-13. *The same logic as before but with an Event ActorBeginOverlap node instead of an Event Hit Node*

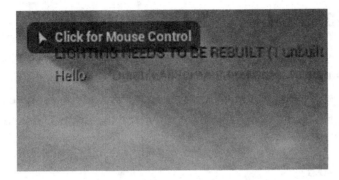

Figure 7-14. *The word "Hello" is printed to the screen as soon as the overlap collision occurs*

Finally, imagine that the sphere's WorldStatic Collision Response was now set to Ignore (Figure 7-15). In this case, the sphere will fall through the cube just like before, but this time, the word "Hello" *won't* be printed to the screen. This is because if either Actor is set to ignore the other, no collision events will occur.

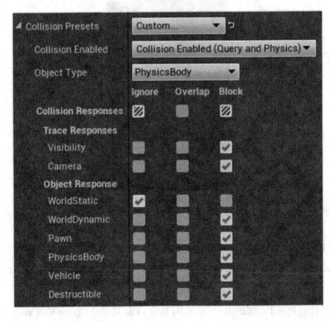

Figure 7-15. *The sphere's WorldStatic Collision Response is now set to Ignore instead of Block*

Causing Damage Due to Collisions

This section will demonstrate a practical use for collisions by showing you how you could deduct health from a Character when it collides with an enemy or some harmful object. Before we get to the example, however, let's learn about a couple of nodes in detail – the Event Hit Node, which we saw earlier, and the Apply Damage Node.

Event Hit Node

An *Event Hit Node,* inside an Actor's Blueprint, will fire any time that Actor registers a Hit Event. The Node contains several output pins, as you can see in Figure 7-16.

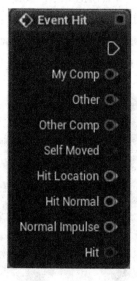

Figure 7-16. *The Event Hit Node*

The *My Comp* pin will return which Component of this Actor was hit. The *Other* pin will return the other Actor that collided with this Actor. The *Other Comp* pin will return the Component of the other Actor that was hit.

The *Self Moved* pin is a Boolean that will tell you if the collision was directly caused by the player. If the player collides with the Actor, or if a projectile fired from the player collides with the Actor, this will return False. For any other collisions, this will return True.

The *Hit Location* pin is a Vector value that will return the X, Y, and Z coordinates of the location where the hit occurred. The *Hit Normal* pin is a Vector value that will return the direction of the impact. So it will return the angles relative to the X, Y, and Z axes. The *Normal Impulse* pin will return how much force the impact had in the X, Y, and Z directions.

The *Hit* pin contains even more data about the collision. If you drag off the pin and select "Break Hit Result," it will create a *Break Hit Result Node* containing many more details about the collision should you need to access that information (Figure 7-17).

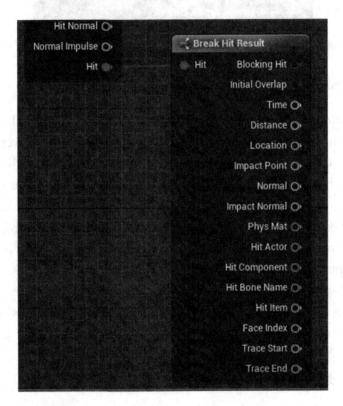

Figure 7-17. *The Break Hit Result Node*

Apply Damage Node

The *Apply Damage Node* (Figure 7-18) will activate a *Damage Event* for whatever Actor is passed into its *Damaged Actor* pin. The Apply Damage Node will also pass the data from its other pins to the Damage Event. It is then up to the Actor receiving the Damage to define in its Blueprint how it should handle that incoming information.

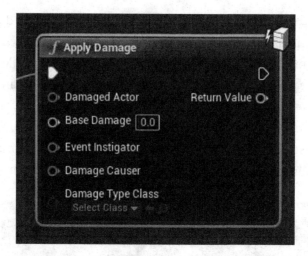

Figure 7-18. *The Apply Damage Node*

The *Base Damage* pin is used to specify how much Damage should be applied. So you would specify higher Base Damages for Actors that should be more powerful or harmful. Note that this value is arbitrary until you give it some meaning with further logic.

Imagine that the Damage is supposed to be the result of a Character firing a projectile and hitting an Actor with that projectile. In that situation, the Character who fired the projectile would be considered the *Event Instigator,* and the projectile itself would be considered the *Damage Causer*. So if you needed to pass that information into the Damage Event, you would use those pins.

Using a *Damage Type Class* is optional, but if you want, you could create Blueprints that specify different types of Damage and then use this pin to specify which type of Damage this is supposed to be.

Damage Example

In this example, we will use a Cube Mesh to represent an enemy or some sort of object that would cause harm upon contact. The cube's Simulation Generates Hit Events property has been checked, and it is set to block all other Actor types.

The cube has been converted into a Blueprint Class by clicking the blue "Blueprint/Add Script" button in the Details Panel. In the cube's Blueprint, an Event Hit Node has been added that will cause an Apply Damage Node to fire, as seen in Figure 7-19. The Other pin of the Event Hit Node has been connected to the Damaged Actor pin of the Apply Damage Node, meaning that whatever Actor collides with the cube will register a Damage Event.

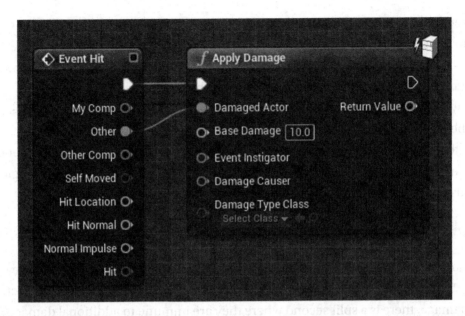

Figure 7-19. *The logic in this Cube's Blueprint will cause Damage to be applied to any Actor that collides with it*

In the Character Blueprint, a Float variable named "Health" has been added and given a default value of 100. An *Event AnyDamage Node* has been added that will fire any time the Character registers a Damage Event. The Event AnyDamage Node will trigger a Set Node that will set the Health variable to whatever its current value is minus the amount of Damage received in the Damage Event. This calculation is performed by a *Float Minus Float Node*. See Figure 7-20.

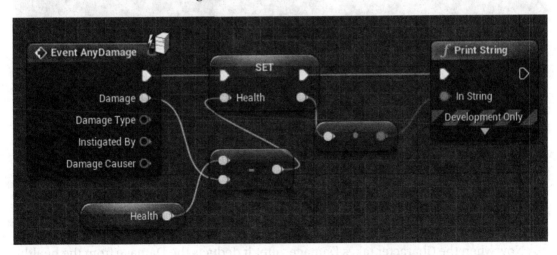

Figure 7-20. *When this Character takes Damage, the value of that Damage will be subtracted from the Character's Health variable*

After the new value of the Health variable is set, a Print String Node will print this value to the screen so the player can see how much health the Character has remaining. When connecting the pin containing the value of the variable to the In String pin, a Node was automatically created in between to convert the data from a Float to a String.

However, there is still a slight problem with this example. If the Character runs into the cube even for a half-second and the game is running at 30 frames per second, that means that the Event Hit Node is going to fire 15 times, because that is the number of frames of gameplay that is occurring during that half-second. With the current logic, this will cause the Character to get health deducted 15 times.

Making a Character Temporarily Invincible

The solution is to make your Character temporarily invincible after every time they receive Damage. You've probably noticed in several games that when your Character takes damage, there is a split second where they are immune to additional damage. This is to get around this problem of the game registering multiple collisions for what you and I would think of as just a single collision.

This can be accomplished by using a DoOnce Node and a Delay Node, as shown in Figure 7-21.

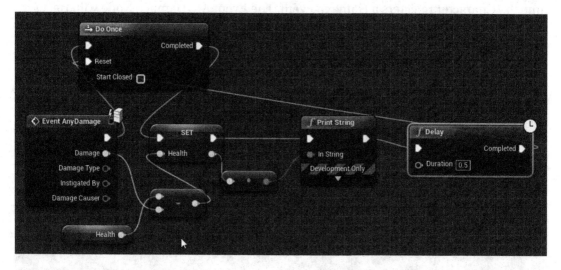

Figure 7-21. *This will make the Character invincible for a half-second after it takes Damage*

Now when the Character takes Damage, after it deducts the Damage from the health and prints the health to the screen, there will be a half-second delay during which the

DoOnce Node will be closed. Any Damage Events that fire during that half-second will be blocked by the closed DoOnce Node. Then, after the half-second has expired, the DoOnce Node will get reset, and Damage Events will once again affect the Character.

Destroying a Character

The logic shown in Figure 7-22 can be added to the preceding example to destroy the Character once the Character's Health reaches zero.

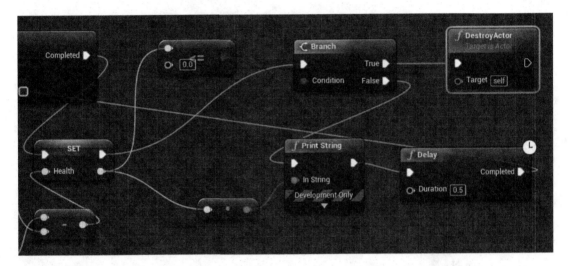

Figure 7-22. *This logic will destroy the Character when its Health reaches zero*

Instead of going straight to the Print String Node after setting the new Health value, the Blueprint will first check to see if the Health has reached zero yet. It does this by using a *Float Less-Than-Or-Equal-To Float Node* that will look at the Float value in its first input pin and tell you if that value is less than or equal to the Float value in its second input pin.

If the Health variable is less than or equal to zero, the Branch Node will route execution to a *DestroyActor Node* which will destroy the Actor in its Target pin. Otherwise, the Branch Node will route execution to the Print String Node as before.

Summary

In this chapter, you learned about collisions in Unreal Engine, how to work with them, and how to configure various collision settings. In the next chapter, you will learn how to use the UMG Editor to create menus, HUDs, and other user interfaces for your game.

CHAPTER 8

User Interfaces

In this chapter, you will learn how to create user interfaces for your game, such as menus and HUDs (head-up displays). *Menus* are used when the player needs to make a choice from a list, such as choosing between "Start New," "Continue," and "Options" at the beginning of a game. *HUDs* are used to show information to the player while the game is in progress. For example, health, ammo, score, time remaining, and so on.

Unreal Motion Graphics (UMG) Overview

History of Unreal Interfaces

There are a few different ways to create menus and HUDs in Unreal Engine. The original way was to create a HUD Blueprint. Then, you would script the User Interface elements in this Blueprint, and then go into the Game Mode and set that HUD Blueprint as the default for the Game Mode.

This method is outdated, but it is covered here so that if you run across a HUD Blueprint, you know what it is, and also so you don't wonder why we aren't setting the HUD Class in the Game Mode like we are the other classes.

In Unreal Engine 3, Epic Games released the *Slate* framework, which was an improved method for creating UI elements, but one that was still pure scripting.

Finally, in Unreal Engine 4, they built a framework on top of Slate called Unreal Motion Graphics, or *UMG* for short. What's great about UMG is that it's a visual system for creating UI elements. This makes it much quicker to create your layouts and much easier to see what the result will be.

209

© David Nixon 2020
D. Nixon, *Beginning Unreal Game Development*, https://doi.org/10.1007/978-1-4842-5639-8_8

Widget Blueprints

To use UMG, you will first need to create a *Widget Blueprint*. A Widget Blueprint is where you will design the layout you want to use for your HUD, menu, and so on. If you're not familiar with the term widget, in the context of computing, the definition of a widget is "a component that enables a user to perform a function." That's basically what a widget is in UMG. For example, you might create a menu widget that enables a user to choose from a list of options.

Another thing you should know about widgets in UMG is that widgets can, and often do, contain other widgets. For example, a menu widget would probably be made up of multiple button widgets. And then the menu widget itself could be placed inside another menu widget as a sub-menu, and so on.

To create a Widget Blueprint, go to the Content Browser, click the "Add New" button, scroll down to "User Interface," and select "Widget Blueprint" (Figure 8-1).

Figure 8-1. *Adding a new Widget Blueprint*

In order for a widget to appear in-game, it will need to be called from another Blueprint, such as the Level Blueprint or the Blueprint of a Pawn. Figure 8-2 shows an example of calling a widget named "My Widget" from a Character Blueprint.

Figure 8-2. *This logic renders a Widget Blueprint named "My Widget" in memory and adds it to the screen*

The *Create Widget Node* will create a copy of the widget specified in its *Class* pin. The *Owning Player* pin specifies the Player Controller that the widget should be applied to. If nothing is connected, it will be applied to the default Player Controller.

The *Add to Viewport Node* will display the widget passed into its Target pin on the screen. When you want to remove a widget from the Viewport, you need to use the *Remove From Parent Node* and connect the widget you want removed to that Node's Target pin.

Widget Blueprint Editor

To edit a widget, double-click it to open it in the *Widget Blueprint Editor*. This editor is divided into two tabs – the Designer tab, where you construct the interface, and the Graph tab where you can script logic for the interface. You can switch between the two by clicking their buttons in the upper-right (Figure 8-3).

Figure 8-3. *These buttons are used to switch between the Designer tab and Graph tab*

The main window of the Designer tab is the *Visual Designer* in the center (Figure 8-4). This is where you will create the layouts for your interfaces.

Figure 8-4. *The Visual Designer*

In the upper-left is the *Palette* window (Figure 8-5). This window contains pre-made widgets that you can drag and drop into the Visual Designer to construct your layouts.

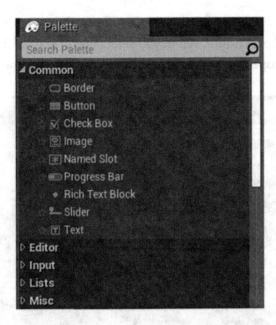

Figure 8-5. *The Palette window*

Below that is the *Hierarchy* window (Figure 8-6). This window is very similar to the World Outliner in the Level Editor. It organizes the elements in the Visual Designer and shows their parent-child relationships.

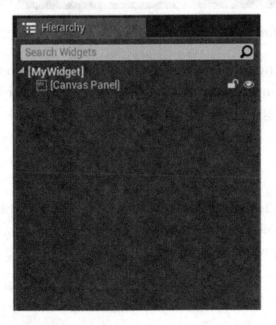

Figure 8-6. *The Hierarchy window*

213

To the right of the Visual Designer is the *Details* window (Figure 8-7). This is just like its counterpart in the Level Editor. When you select one of your widgets, you will be able to view and edit the properties of that widget in the Details window.

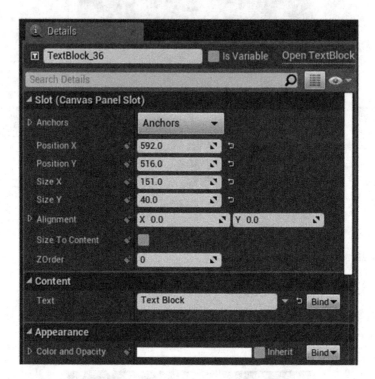

Figure 8-7. *The Details window*

At the bottom are two windows that can be used to animate your layouts. For example, if you had a menu, you could make it fly in from the edge of the screen or something, if you wanted, instead of it just appearing.

Root Widget

A Widget Blueprint will always consist of at least a *Root Widget,* which will have the same name as the Widget Blueprint itself. The Root Widget will always be the first element listed in the Hierarchy window, as shown in Figure 8-8.

Whenever you create a new Widget Blueprint, it will, by default, start out with a *Canvas Panel* added as a child of the Root Widget. The Canvas Panel will be covered in detail in the next section, so, for now, just know that it is a container that is used to hold other widgets.

Figure 8-8. *The Root Widget of a Widget Blueprint named "MyWidget" with a Canvas Panel child*

Color and Opacity

If you select the Root Widget, you can view and edit its properties in the Details window. Most of these categories are common to several types of widgets and will be covered later in the chapter.

In the *Appearance* category, shown in Figure 8-9, the first two properties are *Color and Opacity* and *Foreground Color*. Both of these colors can be set either by clicking the colored strip and using the Color Picker or by expanding their respective menus and setting the red, green, blue, and alpha settings directly.

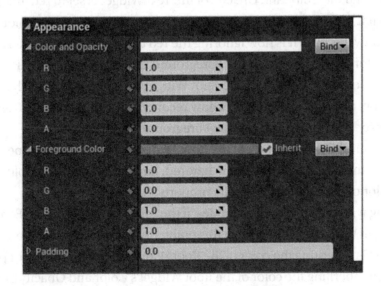

Figure 8-9. *The Appearance category for a Root Widget*

Whatever color you set the *Color and Opacity* to in the Root Widget will be applied to all child widgets. That color will be combined with the color of the child itself, with the color white being ignored. Here are a few examples to clarify this.

Imagine that a Text Widget has been added as a child of the Canvas Panel. Because the Canvas Panel is a child of the Root Widget, by extension, the Text Widget is now also a child of the Root Widget. If the color of the Root Widget is white, and the color of the Text Widget is blue, then the white will be ignored, and the text will appear blue. Conversely, if the Root Widget is set to blue, and the Text Widget is set to white, the white of the Text Widget will be ignored, and the text will again appear blue.

But now let's say that the Root Widget is set to blue, and the Text Widget is set to yellow. These two colors will combine, and the text will appear green. So again, the Color and Opacity of the Root Widget gets combined with the color of the child, with the color white being ignored.

Foreground Color

The *Foreground Color* property of the Root Widget is similar to the Color and Opacity property, except that it will only be applied to children whose color property is set to *Inherit*. Note that not all color properties have an Inherit property, so you won't be able to apply this to all types of widgets.

If the Color and Opacity of the Root Widget is set to white and the Foreground Color is set to yellow, and the Color and Opacity of the Text Widget is set to red, the text will appear red. But if the Inherit property of the Text Widget is checked, the color of the text changes to yellow, because it is now ignoring the red color and instead inheriting from the next highest color property which is the Foreground Color property of the Root Widget.

Now, if the Color and Opacity of the Root Widget is changed to blue, the text will appear green because the Text Widget is now receiving the blue from the Color and Opacity property and the yellow from the Foreground Color property.

The Foreground Color property of the Root Widget has an Inherit property itself. If this is checked, the color set there will be ignored, and the Foreground Color will instead inherit the color of the Color and Opacity property.

Continuing with the preceding examples, if the Inherit property of the Foreground Color of the Root Widget was checked at this point, the text will appear blue again, because the Text Widget is inheriting the color of the Root Widget's Foreground Color property, which is in turn inheriting the color of the Root Widget's Color and Opacity property.

Padding

The *Padding* property simply sets the padding around the content of the widget. If you expand the property, you can set the padding of each side individually.

Is Focusable

The *Interaction* category contains just one property, *Is Focusable* (Figure 8-10). If this is checked, the widget will be able to attain *focus*. A widget can attain focus by being clicked or navigated to by the keyboard. A widget that has focus will be able to accept input from the keyboard.

Figure 8-10. *The Interaction category*

For example, if a button has focus, then pressing Enter on the keyboard will cause that button to be pressed. If Is Focusable is unchecked, the widget will not be able to be navigated to, and if it is clicked, it will still register click events, but it will not take focus away from whatever other widget currently has it.

Canvas Panel

Whenever you create a new Widget Blueprint, it will automatically add a *Canvas Panel* to the Root Widget by default. However, you can delete it if you want, and you can manually add Canvas Panels to the layout via the Panel category of the Palette.

In the context of UMG, a *Panel* is a container that is useful for aligning widgets and moving widgets as a group. Each Panel has its own unique type of slot, which gives its children different positioning and sizing capabilities.

For example, when a widget is added to a Canvas Panel, it is placed inside of a *Canvas Panel Slot* (Figure 8-11). A Canvas Panel Slot allows for absolute positioning, meaning you can specify the exact location you want the widget to be located within the Canvas Panel. If you added a widget to a *Grid Panel*, however, it would go into a *Grid Slot*, and you would specify the widget's location by row and column instead of by exact pixels.

Canvas Panel Slot Properties

You can position a widget inside of a Canvas Panel using the *Position X* and *Position Y* properties. You can size the widget to an exact size using the *Size X* and *Size Y* properties.

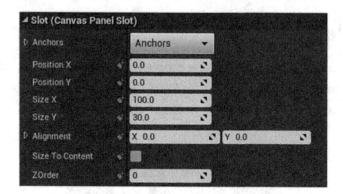

Figure 8-11. *The properties of a Canvas Panel Slot*

Anchors

Up at the top of the Slot category are *Anchors*. Anchors are a way to specify where on the edge of the Panel the location of a Widget should be measured from, in the scenario that the window size or screen size changes.

An *Anchor Medallion* will appear in the spot where the Slot is anchored. For example, if a button is placed into a slot and anchored to the top-left of the screen, an Anchor Medallion will appear in the top-left corner of the Visual Designer (Figure 8-12). If you ran the game, no matter how you resized the window, the button would stay in the same position relative to the top-left corner.

Figure 8-12. *An Anchor Medallion*

By clicking the Anchors button, you can choose a different location to anchor the widget. You could anchor it to the top-center edge, to the upper-right corner, and so on. There are also six Anchors available that will anchor the widget to two sides of the canvas. The Anchor in the bottom-right of the Anchor Menu will anchor the widget to all four corners of the canvas and stretch and shrink it in all directions as you resize the window.

The coordinate system that the Position X and Position Y properties use is based on where the widget is anchored to. So when a slot is anchored to the top-left, the position (0,0) is located in the top-left. But if the slot were anchored to the top-right, then position (0,0) would be located in the top-right, and so on.

The question of which point on the widget should be used as the Anchor's location is determined by the *Alignment* property. The Alignment property uses a coordinate system where (0,0) represents the top-left corner of the widget, and (1,1) represents the bottom-right.

So if a slot is anchored to the top-left, and its position is set to (0,0), when its Alignment is set to (0,0), its top-left corner will align with the top-left corner of the Canvas, as shown in Figure 8-13.

Figure 8-13. *A Button Widget anchored to the top-left, at position (0,0) and alignment (0,0)*

If the Alignment was changed to (1,1), its bottom-right corner will be aligned with the corner of the Canvas (Figure 8-14).

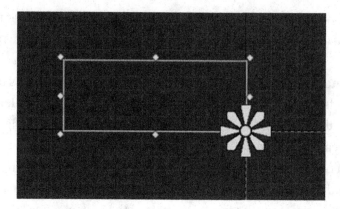

Figure 8-14. *A Button Widget anchored to the top-left, at position (0,0) and alignment (1,1)*

If it were changed to (0.5,0.5), the center of the slot will be aligned with the corner (Figure 8-15).

Figure 8-15. *A Button Widget anchored to the top-left, at position (0,0) and alignment (0.5,0.5)*

Size to Content

Normally, a Text Widget will not resize its box even if the text inside it is too large to hold. In this scenario, you could manually resize the box using the Size X and Size Y properties. But if you want the box to be exactly big enough to show the text inside of it, you can check the *Size to Content* property, and it will automatically adjust the size. Note that when the Size to Content property is checked, the Size X and Size Y settings will be ignored.

ZOrder

The *ZOrder* property determines the order in which widgets get drawn to the screen and, thus, for widgets in the same location, determines which widget overlaps which. Lower numbers get drawn first.

If you have a button whose ZOrder is 0, and some text whose ZOrder is 1, then the button will be drawn first, followed by the text. So if these are in the same location, the text will overlap the button since it gets drawn last, as shown in Figure 8-16.

Figure 8-16. *A Button Widget with a ZOrder of 0 and a Text Widget with a ZOrder of 1*

But if the ZOrder of the button was changed to 2, then the button would now get drawn last and thus appear on top, as shown in Figure 8-17.

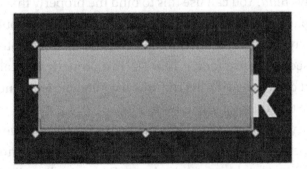

Figure 8-17. *A Button Widget with a ZOrder of 2 and a Text Widget with a ZOrder of 1*

Common Widget Properties

This section will cover properties that are common to all widgets in UMG.

Behavior Category

Starting with the *Behavior* category, shown in Figure 8-18, the first property is *Tool Tip Text*. By adding text to this property, it will cause that text to appear whenever the user hovers the mouse over the widget. This is useful for providing further clarity to the user about how to use the widget or what its purpose is.

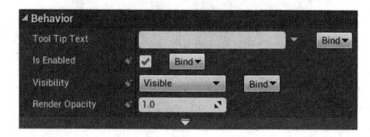

Figure 8-18. *The Behavior category*

To the right of the Tool Tip Text property, and several other properties as well, is a dropdown that says *Bind*. You can use this to bind the property that it's next to to a variable. For example, you could create a Text variable, and if you bound that to the Tool Tip Text property for a button, then whatever text was stored in the variable would automatically be used as the text for the Tool Tip Text property. This allows widgets to have properties that can change during runtime if your game logic ends up changing the value of the variable that the property is bound to.

The next property is *Is Enabled*. If this is unchecked, it will disable the widget, meaning it cannot be interacted with by the user. So widgets like buttons, checkboxes, sliders, and so on will not be able to receive input. For example, a disabled button will be a darker shade of gray than an enabled button, and if you click it, it won't change color like an enabled button because it is not registering the click.

The next property is *Visibility*. By default, it is set to *Visible* which means it can be seen by the user, interacted with by the user, and it takes up space in the layout. If a widget is set to *Collapsed*, it will be invisible to the user, it cannot be interacted with by the user, and it won't take up any space in the layout. If a widget is set to *Hidden*, it will be invisible to the user, and cannot be interacted with by the user, but it will take up space in the layout.

222

A setting of *Not Hit-Testable (Self & All Children)* is essentially the same as making the widget not focusable and not enabled, with the exception being that its appearance won't change, so it won't be grayed out like a widget normally would be when disabled. The final value, *Not Hit-Testable (Self Only)*, is the same as the previous value except that it won't apply to child widgets.

Render Transform Category

The next category is *Render Transform* (Figure 8-19). If you expand the *Transform* menu, you will see four properties, Translation, Scale, Shear, and Angle.

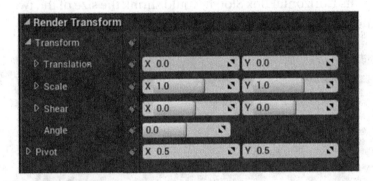

Figure 8-19. *The Render Transform category*

With the *Translation* property, you can change the location of the widget. With the *Scale* property, you can change the size of the widget. These work very similar to the Position and Size properties inside of a Canvas Panel Slot. But the transform that occurs within a slot is known as a *Layout Transform*, as opposed to a *Render Transform*. The difference is that a Layout Transform can affect and be affected by the other widgets in the layout, while a Render Transform will ignore the layout.

For example, imagine there were three buttons in a row, side by side, inside a Horizontal Box Panel, as shown in Figure 8-20 (Horizontal Box Panels will be covered later in the chapter).

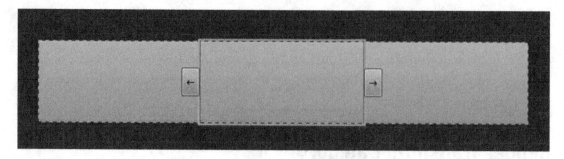

Figure 8-20. *Three Button Widgets in a Horizontal Box Panel*

If you increased the size of the middle button with a Layout Transform, by adjusting the properties of its Horizontal Box Slot, it would shrink the size of the two buttons beside it (Figure 8-21).

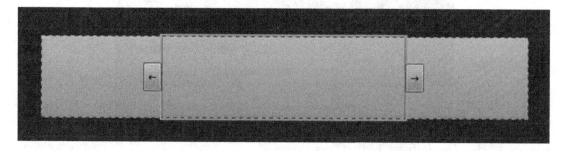

Figure 8-21. *The size of the middle button has been increased via a Layout Transform*

Also, the size you could increase the middle button would be limited by the size of the Horizontal Box that it's in. However, if you change its size using a Render Transform, by adjusting the Scale property of the Render Transform category, the other two buttons will be ignored, as will the bounds of the Horizontal Box (Figure 8-22).

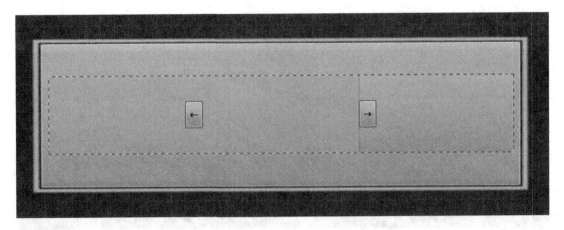

Figure 8-22. *The size of the middle button has been increased via a Render Transform*

Most of the time, you will want to use Layout Transforms to set the position and size of your widgets, but Render Transforms can be useful in some situations, such as animating your widgets.

The next property is *Shear*. You can use the Shear property to distort the widget diagonally, as shown in Figure 8-23.

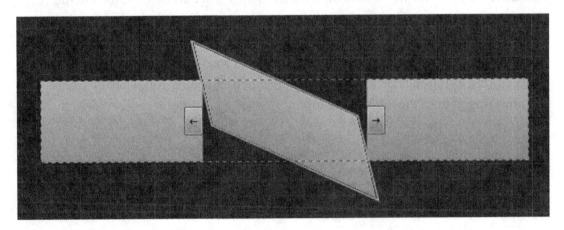

Figure 8-23. *The Shear property can be used to skew the shape of widgets*

The *Angle* property can be used to rotate the widget (Figure 8-24).

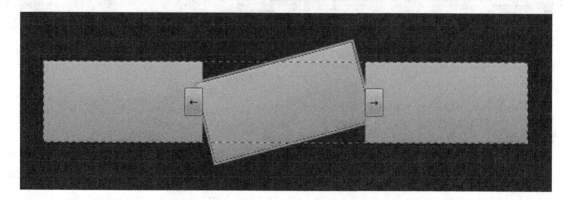

Figure 8-24. *Changing the Angle property will rotate a widget*

Finally, there is the *Pivot* property. Just like the Alignment property of the Canvas Panel Slot, this uses a coordinate system of (0,0) to indicate the top-left of the widget and (1,1) to indicate the bottom-right of the widget. By default, it is set to (0.5,0.5) which places the pivot point in the center of the widget. So with the pivot point in the center, if you were to, for example, rotate the widget, it would rotate around its center. If you scaled the widget, it would expand outward from the center and inward toward the center.

But if you were to change this to (0,0), then the pivot point would now be the top-left corner of the widget. Now if you rotate it, instead of it rotating around its center, it will rotate around its top-left corner, as shown in Figure 8-25. When you scale the widget, it will now expand from the left and the top.

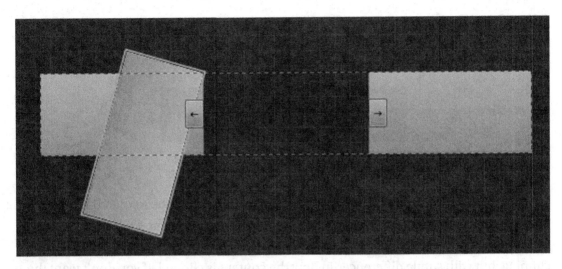

Figure 8-25. *This button had its Angle property changed while its Pivot point was set to (0,0)*

Performance Category

The next category, *Performance*, has just one property, *Is Volatile* (Figure 8-26).

Figure 8-26. *The Performance category*

The Is Volatile property is used with the *Invalidation Box* widget in the Optimization category of the Palette. The purpose of the Invalidation Box is to cache its children widgets, meaning save them in memory. This will increase performance if those widgets don't change often. But if one of those child widgets does change often, such as one that animates and needs to be drawn differently each frame, you would not want to try to cache that widget. In that scenario, you would set the widget's Is Volatile property to True, to prevent it from being cached.

Clipping Category

The next category, *Clipping*, has just one property of the same name (Figure 8-27).

Figure 8-27. *The Clipping category*

Content that overflows the bounds of a widget will normally be rendered anyway, but you can use the Clipping property to hide this overflow content. This can be done by setting the value of the property to *Clip to Bounds*. The next three values also turn on clipping, but with subtle differences in how the content is clipped. If you don't want the widget to clip its content, set the Clipping property to *Inherit*, which causes the widget to inherit the clipping bounds of its closest parent.

Navigation Category

The next category is *Navigation* (Figure 8-28). This category affects how the user can navigate to the different widgets using their keyboard.

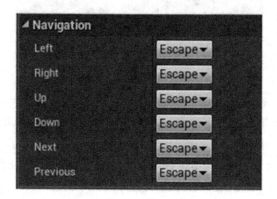

Figure 8-28. *The Navigation category*

By default, all the properties here are set to *Escape*. Escape basically means that you are able to escape that widget in that direction. For example, if a button's *Left* property is set to Escape, this means that if that button has focus and you press left on the keyboard, focus will move left to the next widget. But if you were to change the Left property to *Stop* instead, then navigation can no longer move to the left through the widget.

The *Wrap* setting can be used with certain Panels, such as a Uniform Grid Panel. This needs to be set on the Panel itself. For example, if you had a Uniform Grid Panel that contained a grid of buttons, and you set its Left and Right navigation properties to Wrap, then when the player pressed left on the keyboard when focused on one of the left-most buttons, focus will wrap around to the first button on the other side, and vice-versa.

By setting the value to *Explicit*, you can specify the widget you want the focus to move to when navigation moves in that direction. Simply choose the name of the widget you want focus to move to in the dropdown that appears (Figure 8-29).

Figure 8-29. *When navigating to the right from this widget, focus will move to a widget named "Button2"*

Localization Category

The final category is *Localization* (Figure 8-30). This just has one property, *Flow Direction Preference*.

Figure 8-30. *The Localization category*

In most Western languages, words and menus are read from left to right, but in some languages, words and menus are read from right to left. This property can be used to change the direction that the widgets in your menu flow in, based on the preferences of the local culture.

Visual Designer

The *Visual Designer* is the main window of the Designer tab. If you hold down the RMB and drag, you can pan about the window. If you use the scroll wheel on the mouse, you can zoom in and out. In the upper-left corner, it will tell you just how much you are zoomed in or out.

In the upper-right corner, there is a row of buttons that pertain specifically to the Visual Designer. The first pair of buttons, shown in Figure 8-31, concerns localization. If you are planning to release your game in different languages, you can load the translations for the game into your Project. Once you do so, there are features that allow you to preview those different languages inside the Editor without having to run the game.

Figure 8-31. *Use these buttons to preview different languages*

If you click the button that currently says "None," it will expand a dropdown menu where you can quickly switch between the languages you have available. If you select "Region & Language," it will open the Editor Preferences to the page where you can set the *Preview Game Language* for the Editor as a whole. If you have a preview language set, you can click the button of the Earth in the Visual Designer to toggle between the default language and the preview language.

The next button to the right is used to toggle dashed outlines on and off (Figure 8-32). By default, you will see a dashed line represent the border of a panel. Clicking this button will turn those dashed lines off, which helps you better visualize how your layout will actually look in-game.

Figure 8-32. *Use these buttons to toggle dashed outlines and toggle the widget locking system*

The next button has to do with the widget locking system. If you look in the Hierarchy window, you will see an icon of a padlock next to each widget. If you click the icon, it will switch to the locked position indicating that the widget is now locked. Normally, locked widgets, and their children, can't be selected in the designer. However, you can use the button of the padlock, in the upper-right, to toggle the entire locking system on or off. With it off, all locks on widgets will be ignored, and you will still be able to select them.

The next pair of buttons (Figure 8-33) is used to toggle between Layout Transform and Render Transform, and you can use the shortcut keys W and E as well.

Figure 8-33. *Use these buttons to toggle between Layout Transform and Render Transform*

As discussed in the previous section, a Layout Transform is when you adjust the positioning and so on of a widget within its slot, which causes the widget to be bound by the layout. A Render Transform is when you make those adjustments within the Render Transform category, which causes the widget to ignore the layout.

Note that if you use Render Transform here, it will NOT change the way the sizing control behaves when you click and drag the edges of a widget, it will still behave like a Layout Transform. So these buttons only affect positioning.

To the right of those buttons is a pair of buttons used to set Grid Snapping (Figure 8-34). This works just like Grid Snapping does in the 3D Viewport. This first button turns snapping on and off, and the second button sets the Snap Size.

Figure 8-34. *Use these buttons to set Grid Snapping*

To the right of that is the *Zoom to Fit* button (Figure 8-35). This will center the layout on the screen and zoom in to it. It will zoom in until the layout fills the screen or reaches a 1:1 aspect ratio, whichever comes first.

Figure 8-35. *The Zoom to Fit button*

Two buttons to the right is a button with two triangles on it (Figure 8-36). This button concerns device safe zones, which is an advanced topic and won't be covered in this book.

Figure 8-36. *The Landscape/Portrait and Flip Safe Zones buttons*

The button to the left of that one, with the icon of a painting, can be used to toggle between Landscape and Portrait mode. It will be disabled if you aren't simulating a device that supports those modes.

You can change the device and screen size you are simulating by using the dropdown to the right that says "Screen Size" (Figure 8-37). There are options for various phones, tablets, laptops, monitors, and TVs. The resolution and aspect ratio of the screen size you choose can be seen in the bottom-left corner of the Visual Designer.

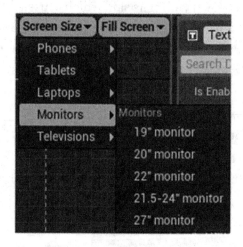

Figure 8-37. *You can preview how your layout will look on various screen sizes*

The dropdown to the right of that can be used to choose the overall size of the layout relative to the screen size (Figure 8-38). With this set to *Fill Screen*, the layout will always be the size of the screen it's on. With this set to *Custom*, you can choose a specific size for the layout to be, regardless of the screen it's on. *Custom on Screen* is the same as Custom except there is an additional outline for the screen size itself. *Desired* will cause the bounds of the layout to be just large enough to fit all of the widgets within it while still honoring the spacing set by the Anchors. With *Desired on Screen* you can also see the edges of the screen.

232

Figure 8-38. *Use this menu to adjust the size of the layout relative to the screen size*

Text Widget

The *Text Widget* can be found in the Common category of the Palette. When you first create a Text Widget, it will start out with the default text "Text Block." To change this text, go over to the Details window and edit the *Text* property in the *Content* category (Figure 8-39).

Figure 8-39. *The Content category of the Text Widget*

The next category is *Appearance* (Figure 8-40). As you saw earlier, you can set the color of the text and how transparent it is by using the Color and Opacity property. If you check Inherit, it will inherit the settings from the Foreground Color of its next highest parent.

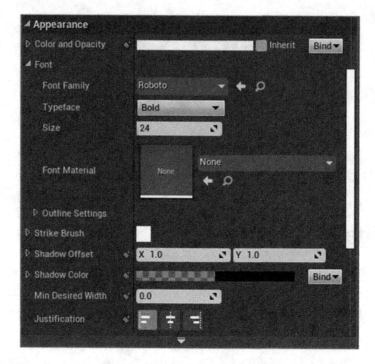

Figure 8-40. *The Appearance category of the Text Widget*

Next is the *Font* property. Unreal Engine only comes with one font – *Roboto*.

The *Font Material* property allows you to add a Material to your font. Just be aware that the Materials in the Starter Content are made for surfaces and can't be used here. You have to use a Material specially designed for fonts.

You can use the properties under *Outline Settings* to add an outline to your text.

The next property, *Strike Brush*, is used to set what brush to use when adding a strikethrough to text. Be aware that the term "brush" here is used in the more traditional graphic design sense and does not refer to a Geometry Brush. You can either set an image to use or you can use a color by setting the *Tint* property.

The next two properties, *Shadow Offset* and *Shadow Color*, enable you to add a shadow to your text, as seen in Figure 8-41. By default, the color of Shadow Color is set to black, but its opacity is set to be fully transparent, meaning it will be invisible by default. To use the shadow, you will need to increase the Alpha channel so that it will be visible. A value of 1 will make the shadow fully opaque, meaning it cannot be seen through at all.

Figure 8-41. *A shadow effect has been added to this text*

The Shadow Offset property is used to set how far in the X and Y directions the shadow should be located, relative to the base text. If you increase in the X direction, the shadow will move out to the right. At first, this has the effect of making the shadow thicker, but if you keep going, eventually the shadow will completely separate from the base text.

Next is the *Min Desired Width* property. This is used when you have a widget in a container that is competing for space with other widgets. Setting the Min Desired Width will cause the widget to be at least that wide, even if the text doesn't require it.

The *Justification* property will simply align the text to the left, center, or right, relative to its container.

Down in the *Wrapping* category, there are two properties that can be used to wrap text (Figure 8-42). The *Auto Wrap Text* property will automatically wrap text down to the next line once it reaches the edge of the widget. The *Wrap Text At* property will wrap text once it reaches the width specified.

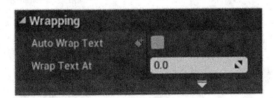

Figure 8-42. *The Wrapping category*

Button Widget

The *Button Widget* can be found in the Common category of the Palette. In the Details window, there is an *Appearance* category where you can modify how the button looks (Figure 8-43).

Figure 8-43. *The Appearance category of a Button Widget*

Starting with the two color properties, *Color and Opacity* will set the color of the button *and* its content, while *Background Color* will only set the color of the button itself. If you were to add a Text Widget as a child of the Button Widget, and then set the Color and Opacity of the button, both the button *and* the text will change color. If you were to set the Background Color, only the color of the button itself will change, and not the text.

The *Style* property is actually a collection of properties, which in turn have their own sub-properties, as seen in Figure 8-44. The first four properties, *Normal, Hovered, Pressed*, and *Disabled*, each represent a different state of the button. By expanding their menus, you will find several properties you can edit to alter that state's appearance.

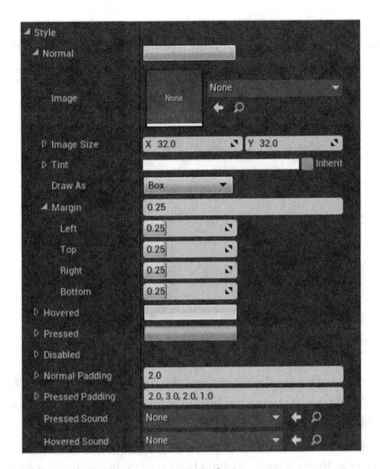

Figure 8-44. *Style properties of a Button Widget*

For example, if you expanded the Hovered property, and set its *Tint* to purple, then when the mouse cursor hovers over the button, its color will change to purple. Note that if you have set a Background Color, the Tint will combine with that color. So if the Background Color is blue, and the Tint of the Normal state is yellow, then the button will appear green when in its Normal state.

You can also use an image for the button's background by using the dropdown next to the *Image* property. If you have any colors applied to the button's background, it will use that color as a filter on top of your image.

The next property, *Image Size*, doesn't affect the button when it's in a Canvas Panel. In other Panels, the Image Size property will change the size of the button, regardless of whether or not it actually contains an image.

The *Draw As* property affects how the image is drawn onto the button. If Draw As is set to *Border*, it will use the image to create a border along the edges of the button (Figure 8-45), and you can then use the *Margin* property to set the thickness of the border on each edge.

Figure 8-45. *The Draw As property of this Button Widget has been set to Border*

Next are a couple of properties used to set the padding for the button's contents. You can set different paddings for when the button is in its Normal state and for when it is Pressed. By default, the Pressed padding has a little more padding on top and a little less on the bottom, which causes the contents of the button to shift down when the button is pressed. This creates the appearance of the button actually being pressed as if it were a 3D object.

You also have the option of having a sound play whenever the button is pressed or hovered over, by using the dropdowns of the *Pressed Sound* and *Hovered Sound* properties and selecting a sound asset.

At the very bottom of the Details window, the Button Widget has an *Events* category (Figure 8-46). Not all widgets have Events tied to them, but those that do will have an Events category.

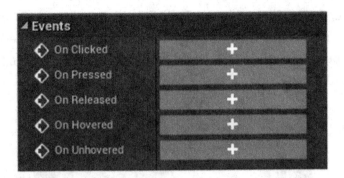

Figure 8-46. *The Events category of a Button Widget*

The Button Widget has five events. The *On Pressed* event fires when the button is pressed. The *On Clicked* and *On Released* events will fire once the button has been pressed and then released. The *On Hovered* event fires when you hover the mouse cursor over the button, and the *On Unhovered* event fires when you move the mouse cursor back off the button.

By clicking the green buttons next to their names, you can add a Node for that Event to the graph of this widget. Note that these Events work the same whether you are using the mouse or the keyboard to press the button. So the "click" of the On Clicked Event refers to the Button Widget being clicked, not the clicking of a mouse.

Border Widget and Image Widget

The *Border Widget* has two main categories, Content and Appearance.

In the *Appearance* category (Figure 8-47), you can alter the appearance of the border by giving it an image or by setting its color. So if you wanted a simple black border, you would set the *Brush Color* to black.

Figure 8-47. *The Appearance category of a Border Widget*

At first glance, the Border Widget will look more like a box than a border. But when you add a child to it, the child will be centered within it, covering up the majority of it, and whatever peeks out around the edges essentially acts as a border, as shown in Figure 8-48.

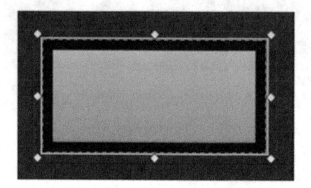

Figure 8-48. *A Button Widget inside of a Border Widget*

In the *Content* category (Figure 8-49), you can adjust the padding that is placed around the child of the widget. However thick the padding is is how thick your border will appear. You can also use this category to adjust the horizontal and vertical alignment of the widget's child or to set the child's Color and Opacity.

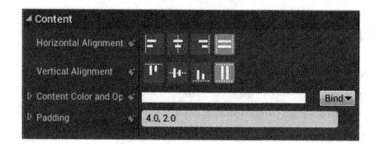

Figure 8-49. *The Content category of a Border Widget*

The only real difference between the Border Widget and the *Image Widget* is that the Border Widget has a Content category since it is especially designed to have children, and the Image Widget is not.

Progress Bar Widget

The *Progress Bar Widget* is often used to display things like the amount of health, magic, or energy a player has remaining. It will measure these values by percentage by using the *Percent* property of the *Progress* category (Figure 8-50).

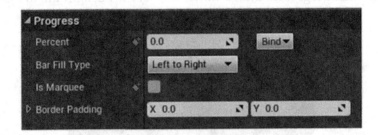

Figure 8-50. *The Progress category of the Progress Bar Widget*

With Percent at 0, the bar will be completely empty. If it was set to 0.5, the bar would be 50% filled, as shown in Figure 8-51, and if it was set to the max value of 1.0, the bar would be 100% filled. The Percent property is normally bound to the variable it is meant to represent so that it will automatically update as that variable's value changes.

Figure 8-51. *A Progress Bar Widget with its Percent set to 0.5*

The color that is used to fill the bar can be set with the *Fill Color and Opacity* property (Figure 8-52).

Figure 8-52. *The Appearance category of the Progress Bar Widget*

You also have the option of using an image to fill the Progress Bar or have an image used as its background. In the *Style* category (Figure 8-53), the *Fill Image* property is used for the image that will fill the bar, and the *Background Image* property will specify the image that will be used for its background. If you still want the background to be a solid color, just not gray, you can leave the Image property blank, but choose a color for the *Tint* property of the Background Image, and it will set the background to that color.

Figure 8-53. *The Style category of the Progress Bar Widget*

The default direction that the bar will fill is from left to right, but you have the option of having it fill in different directions, such as right to left or top to bottom, by setting the *Bar Fill Type* property.

If the *Is Marquee* property is checked, the Progress Bar will change from a genuine Progress Bar into a *Marquee*, as seen in Figure 8-54.

Figure 8-54. *A Progress Bar Widget with its Is Marquee property set to True*

A Marquee is a bar that, instead of filling up, shows continual movement. This is generally used to indicate to the user that some action is taking place, when it is unknown how long it will take to complete, and thus can't be represented by a regular Progress Bar. An example of a Marquee would be when a program crashes in Windows and it gives you the "Windows is checking for a solution" message (Figure 8-55). That green bar is a Marquee.

Figure 8-55. *This bar with the green in it is an example of a Marquee*

In the Style category, you can set an image to use for the Marquee with the *Marquee Image* property. If you change the X value of the Image Size property of the Marquee Image, it will increase or decrease the speed of the Marquee.

Horizontal Box and Vertical Box

So far, the only Panel that has been covered is the Canvas Panel, which allows for absolute layout. This is good when you want a high level of manual control over the placement of widgets, but it's not the best for aligning widgets.

There are several other Panels which are much more useful for aligning widgets, and one of those is the *Horizontal Box*. The Horizontal Box is comprised of a single row of slots of equal height. It's useful for aligning widgets side by side.

For example, if you placed three Button Widgets into a Horizontal Box, they would stack up side by side, as seen in Figure 8-56. If you wanted to change their order, you could select one of them and use the arrows that appear to move them to the slot to the left or right. If you wanted to move all of them, you could move them all as a group by moving the Horizontal Box itself, and they would all remain aligned with each other.

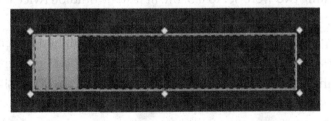

Figure 8-56. *Three Button Widgets in a Horizontal Box Panel*

If you selected one of the buttons, you would see that the properties in its Slot category are different than what we've been seeing because the button is in a *Horizontal Box Slot* as opposed to a Canvas Panel Slot (Figure 8-57).

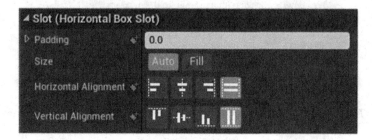

Figure 8-57. *Properties of the Horizontal Box Slot*

The *Padding* property can be used to add padding around the content of the slot.

By default, the *Size* property will be set to *Auto*. With it set to Auto, the slot will be just big enough to fit its contents. So if the width of a button inside the slot was increased, the slot would automatically widen to fit it. If Size is set to *Fill*, the slot will expand to take up the rest of the room available, as seen in Figure 8-58.

Figure 8-58. *The Size property of the third button has been set to Fill*

If other slots are set to Fill, the amount of space that each slot uses relative to each other is determined by the value to the right of the Fill button. This value can be any number between 0 and 1. For example, if there were three slots, and the first was set to 1.0 and the remaining two were set to 0.5, the first slot would be twice the size of the other two.

The next two properties determine how the content is aligned within the slot. By default, these are set to Fill. So note that the Fill settings of the Alignment properties refer to the content of the slot filling up the slot, while the Fill setting of the Size property refers to the slot filling up the Horizontal Box.

The *Vertical Box* works just like the Horizontal Box, except the widgets placed in it will stack vertically instead, as seen in Figure 8-59.

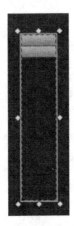

Figure 8-59. *Two Button Widgets in a Vertical Box Panel*

Summary

In this chapter, you learned how to use UMG to create user interfaces. You learned about various UMG widgets and their properties. In the next chapter, you will learn about using audio in Unreal Engine, so you can add dialogue, sound effects, and music to your game.

CHAPTER 9

Audio

This chapter will cover the use of audio within the Unreal Engine, so that you will be able to add dialogue, music, and sound effects to your game. The Audio folder in the Starter Content contains some existing audio assets you can use as you read this chapter.

Audio Overview and Sound Waves

Unreal Engine uses *.wav* files, pronounced "wave," to import audio. If you have some audio you want to use that's in a different format, such as an MP3, you will first need to convert it to a wave file, which will be covered later in the chapter.

When you import a wave file into Unreal Engine, it will be stored internally in a proprietary, compressed format and will become a *Sound Wave* asset in the Content Browser. Its icon will have a black background with the actual waveform of that sound shown in white, as seen in Figure 9-1. If the wave has more than one channel, there will be a separate waveform for each channel.

Figure 9-1. *A Sound Wave*

If you want to combine sounds and/or add effects to them, you can do so using a *Sound Cue*, which is represented by an icon with a blue background and a picture of a speaker and waveform (Figure 9-2). Note that, unlike the Sound Wave, the waveform on the Sound Cue icon is generic and doesn't represent the actual waveform that is produced by the asset.

© David Nixon 2020
D. Nixon, *Beginning Unreal Game Development*, https://doi.org/10.1007/978-1-4842-5639-8_9

Figure 9-2. *A Sound Cue*

Ambient Sound Actor

If you drag either a Sound Wave or a Sound Cue into your Level, it will create what's called an *Ambient Sound Actor* (Figure 9-3).

Figure 9-3. *An Ambient Sound Actor*

It will automatically assign whatever asset you dragged in, as the asset for that Actor's *Sound* property (Figure 9-4).

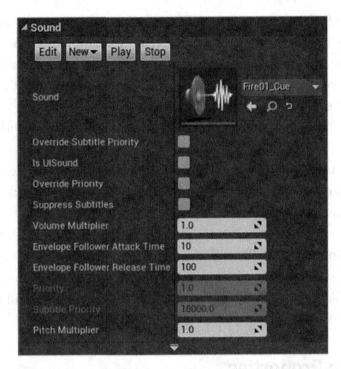

Figure 9-4. *The Sound category of an Ambient Sound Actor*

If you want to preview the sound, you can use the Play and Stop buttons, located above the Sound property. For Sound Cues, you can use the Edit button to open the Sound Cue in the *Sound Cue Editor*. If you want to create a new Sound Cue to use for the Actor, you can use the New button.

Below, you'll see four properties with "Priority" in their name. These properties are used when this Actor is playing multiple instances of its sound concurrently. The concept of concurrency will be covered later in the section.

By default, any sounds coming from an Ambient Sound Actor will be paused when the game is paused. If you want a sound to be able to play while the game is paused, you would need to set the *Is UISound* property to True.

If your Sound Cue or Sound Wave has subtitles, you can turn them off by setting the *Suppress Subtitles* property to True.

You can use the *Volume Multiplier* property to increase or decrease the volume of the sound. Note, however, that setting the volume too high could cause clipping in your waveform which will cause distortion in the audio.

The *Envelope Follower Attack Time* property will set the amount of time, in milliseconds, that it takes for the sound to reach its peak amplitude. Conversely, the *Envelope Follower Release Time* property sets how long it takes for the sound to decay back to silence. Note that these properties only apply when the Sound Cue or Sound Wave is used in the audio mixer.

The *Pitch Multiplier* property can be used to increase or decrease the pitch of the sound.

Down in the *Activation* category is the *Auto Activate* property. By default, an Ambient Sound Actor's Auto Activate property is set to True. With it set to True, the sound will play as soon as the Actor is created.

By default, the Ambient Sound Actor will only play its sound once. If you want the sound to be continuous, you will need to set it to loop. With a Sound Wave, this can be accomplished by setting its *Looping* property to True. With a Sound Cue, this is done by using a *Looping Node*. The Looping property can be found on the Sound Wave Properties page.

Sound Wave Properties

If you want to edit the properties of a Sound Wave, you simply need to double-click it in the Content Browser.

Starting at the top in the *Format* category (Figure 9-5) is the *Is Ambisonics* property. Ambisonics is a specific type of surround sound format. If your wave file is in that format, you would want to set this to True.

Next, there are two properties under the *Quality* category that can be used to balance the quality of the wave file vs. its size.

First, you can set the compression of the wave using the *Compression* property. This can have a value from 1 to 100, where lower numbers represent more compression and higher numbers represent better quality. So if you want the sound to sound as good as it can, and you're not worried about the file size, you would want to set this to a high number. If you don't care about the quality of the sound and you just need to save space somewhere, you could set this to a low number.

Figure 9-5. *The Format category of a Sound Wave*

If you need to lower the file size even more, you can use the *Sample Rate* property to lower the sample rate of the wave; otherwise you should just leave the value at Max.

In the *Sound* category (Figure 9-6), you can adjust the volume and pitch of the Sound Wave, and you can also place it into a *Group*. So you can specify if it should go in Effects, UI, Music, or Voice. Or, if it doesn't fit into any of those categories, you can just leave it in the Default group. Groups are useful for being able to apply a setting to an entire group of related Sound Waves, instead of having to apply that setting to each individual one.

Figure 9-6. *The Sound category of a Sound Wave*

The *Class* property is similar in concept to Group, except it's more robust, you can save and reuse classes, and you can create your own custom groupings.

In the *Subtitles* category (Figure 9-7), you can add subtitles to the Sound Wave and edit their properties. To add a subtitle, go to the *Subtitles* property and click the plus sign. Then you enter the text of the subtitle in the *Text* property and the time it should appear on the screen in the *Time* property. The Time property refers to the amount of time that has elapsed since the Sound Wave began playing.

Figure 9-7. *The Subtitles category of a Sound Wave*

There is also a *Spoken Text* property. The difference between the Spoken Text property and the Text property is that the Text property is for the text that should appear on the screen, while the Spoken Text property is for the dialogue that was actually spoken. For example, there might be the word "angrily" in brackets indicating that the speaker is speaking in an angry tone. Or if the subtitles are in a different language, then obviously the two texts will be different.

The *Mature* property is used to flag a piece of audio that contains mature content, such as adult language. This can be used to more easily create a "clean" version of your game later, by having the ability to filter out all mature content.

By default, the Engine will automatically wrap your subtitles to the next line if they get too long, but if you don't want the Engine to do this – for example, if you have already split the subtitles manually – you can set *Manual Word Wrap* to True to disable automatic wrapping. If you want to force all subtitles to only display on one line, you can set the *Single Line* property to True.

Next is the *Subtitle Priority* property. If two pieces of audio are playing at the same time and both have subtitles, which subtitle will appear on the screen will be determined by the Subtitle Priority, with higher numbers representing a higher priority. You will remember that there were two properties on an instance of a sound – *Override Subtitle Priority* and *Subtitle Priority*. The Subtitle Priority property on the Sound Wave Properties page will, by default, be used for *all* instances of that sound. But you can override this on an *individual* basis by setting the instance's Override Subtitle Priority to True and then entering a new value in the instance's Subtitle Priority property.

The final Subtitle property is *Comment.* If you plan on having your game translated into other languages, the Comment property can be useful for adding contextual information about the piece of dialogue that the translator can use to create a more accurate translation.

A few categories down is the *Voice Management* category (Figure 9-8). Within that, under the *Concurrency* sub-category, there are several properties used to specify what should happen when multiple instances of the Sound Wave are played at the same time. If you want to use preexisting Concurrency Settings, you will need to set the Override Concurrency property to False and then select the settings using the dropdown. If you want to specify new concurrency settings, then you need to set Override Concurrency to True, and then you will be able to expand the Concurrency Overrides property.

Figure 9-8. *The Voice Management category of a Sound Wave*

The *Max Count* property specifies how many instances of the sound are allowed to be playing at once. The *Limit to Owner* property specifies if the Max Count should only be applied per sound Actor, or if it should be applied to all instances of the Sound Wave that are being played from any sound Actor.

If the Max Count is reached and another instance of the sound tries to play, you can set how the conflict should be resolved using the *Resolution Rule* property. For example, you could set it to prevent the new instance from being played, or set it so that the oldest instance is stopped to make room for the new instance, and so on.

With the *Volume Scale* property, you can cause older instances to become quieter as new instances of this sound are played. With this set to 1.0, there will be no difference in volume. But if you set this below 1.0, older instances will become quieter and quieter as newer instances are played, and the lower the number is, the more dramatic the effect.

The *Attack Time* property determines how long it takes for an instance to become quieter once a new instance starts playing.

If the *Can Release* property is set to True, an instance that has gone quieter can get louder again if another instance stops playing. The amount of time that this takes to happen after the other instance stops playing is determined by the *Release Time* property.

If a sound instance is forced to stop completely due to another instance starting, the amount of time it takes for the older sound to fade out is determined by the *Voice Steal Release Time*. With this at 0, the sound will stop immediately.

In addition to there being a limit to the number of the same sounds that can play at once, there is also a limit to the number of sounds in general that can play at once. If this limit is met, by default, the *Priority* property, combined with the volume of the sound, will be used to determine which sound is stopped and which keeps playing. If the *Bypass Volume Scale for Priority* property is set to True, then the Priority property alone will be used to make that determination, and the volume of the sound will be ignored.

In the Details Panel of an individual instance of a sound, there is an *Override Priority* property you can use to override the priority on an individual basis, which allows you to set a new value in the instance's *Priority* property.

Play Sound Nodes

We already saw how to have a sound play immediately when the Level begins, but oftentimes, you won't want a sound to be played until certain conditions are met or a certain event is triggered. In these cases, you can use Blueprints to specify when the sound should be played.

If you go into the Level Blueprint, open the Node Menu, and type "Play Sound," you will see several Nodes available for playing a sound, as seen in Figure 9-9. For one thing, you can choose to either play a sound or spawn a sound. The difference is that when you spawn a sound, you have control over it. You can choose to stop playing the sound at any point or modify its properties. But when you play a sound, you don't have any control over it. You can't modify it or stop it. It will continue playing until it's finished, and if it's set to loop, it will continue playing repeatedly.

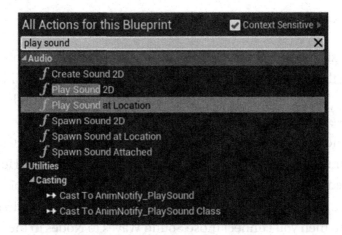

Figure 9-9. *There are various Nodes you can use to play a sound*

You can also choose to have a sound come from a certain location in the game or make it a 2D sound which will be heard at the same volume, and the same stereo position, regardless of your location in the game. If you use one of the location Nodes, such as *Play Sound at Location*, you will need to pass in the location where you want the sound to play from. If you wanted it to play from the location of a certain Actor, you could use the *GetActorLocation* Node to get that Actor's location, as shown in Figure 9-10. Or, with the *Spawn Sound Attached Node*, you can attach a sound to an Actor directly and the sound will travel with that Actor.

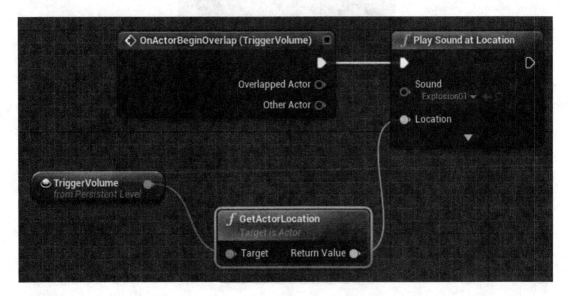

Figure 9-10. *This logic will play a sound, emanating from the location of a Trigger Volume, whenever any Actor enters the Trigger Volume*

Sound Cues

Sound Cues use existing Sound Waves to create new sounds, by combining Sound Waves and/or adjusting their properties or adding effects to them. To create a new Sound Cue, click the Add New button in the Content Browser, scroll down to Sounds, select Sound Cue, and then give it a name.

To edit a Sound Cue, simply double-click it to open it in the Sound Cue Editor. The Sound Cue Editor uses a node-based graph very similar to Blueprints. However, it uses its own specialized Nodes instead of the types of Nodes that are available in Blueprints.

The basic idea is that you start with one or more Nodes on the left that represent Sound Waves, and then you connect those Sound Waves to Nodes in the middle that will combine and modify them. Finally, whatever gets outputted to the *Output Node* on the right (Figure 9-11) is the sound that the Sound Cue will actually play.

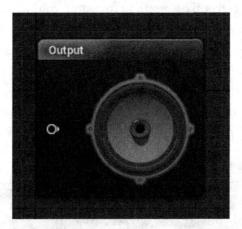

Figure 9-11. *The sound that is passed into the Output Node is the sound that the Sound Cue will play*

To hear what the output will sound like, click the *Play Cue* button in the Toolbar (Figure 9-12). To hear what an individual Node sounds like by itself, select that Node and click the *Play Node* button.

Figure 9-12. *The Play Cue and Play Node buttons*

You can add Nodes like you do in Blueprints, by right-clicking the graph and selecting from a Node Menu. Or you can drag and drop Nodes from the Palette window on the right side of the Editor (Figure 9-13).

Figure 9-13. *The Palette window in the Sound Cue Editor contains several Nodes you can use to modify sounds*

Audio Nodes

A *Wave Player Node*, shown in Figure 9-14, is used to output Sound Waves. If you select it, you can edit its properties in the Details Panel on the left. The *Sound Wave* property will specify which Sound Wave the Node should output (Figure 9-15).

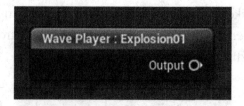

Figure 9-14. *The Wave Player Node*

Figure 9-15. *Properties of the Wave Player Node*

A *Looping Node* (Figure 9-16) will take a sound as input and output that sound as a loop. In the Details Panel, you can choose to have it loop a specific amount of times or have it loop continuously (Figure 9-17).

Figure 9-16. *The Looping Node*

Figure 9-17. *Properties of the Looping Node*

The *Delay Node* (Figure 9-18) can be used to add a delay before a sound is played. Each time the Delay Node is activated, the amount of delay will be a random value between the *Delay Min* and *Delay Max* (Figure 9-19). So if you set this to 1 and 3, for example, each time the sound is played, the delay will be between 1 and 3 seconds.

If you wanted the delay to always be the same value, you would need to enter that value for both the Min and Max properties.

Figure 9-18. *The Delay Node*

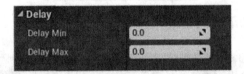

Figure 9-19. *Properties of the Delay Node*

The *Doppler Node* (Figure 9-20) can be used to add the Doppler effect to a sound. This is the effect that occurs when sounds, such as the siren of an ambulance, increase in pitch as they move toward you and decrease in pitch as they move away. The *Doppler Intensity* property (Figure 9-21) can be used to specify how pronounced this effect should be, with higher values increasing the effect.

Figure 9-20. *The Doppler Node*

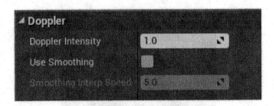

Figure 9-21. *Properties of the Doppler Node*

The *Modulator Node* (Figure 9-22) can be used to play a sound at a random pitch and volume each time it's played. This can be used to make the audio sound slightly different each time so as not to get repetitive. The range of the random values generated can be set in the Details Panel (Figure 9-23).

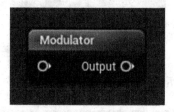

Figure 9-22. *The Modulator Node*

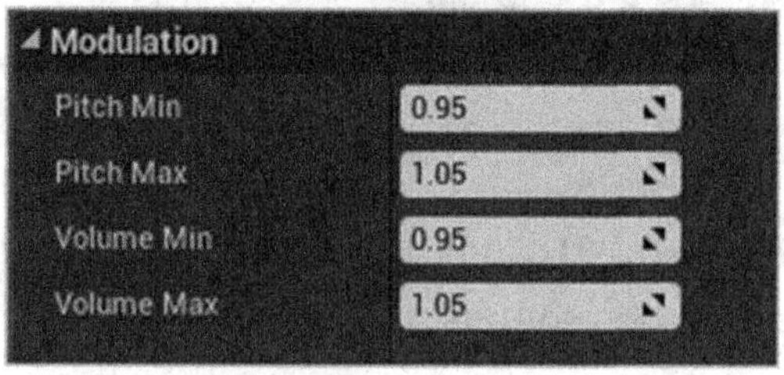

Figure 9-23. *Properties of the Modulator Node*

The *Oscillator Node* (Figure 9-24) can be used to add a continuous modulation of volume and pitch within a single instance of a sound being played. The first two properties are used to enable the modulation of the volume and/or pitch (Figure 9-25). *Amplitude* refers to the height of the Sound Wave, with larger waves producing louder volumes. *Frequency* affects the pitch of a sound, with higher frequencies resulting in higher pitches. The remaining properties deal with more advanced wave physics, with the *Offset* properties controlling the wave's phase and the *Center* properties controlling the center of oscillation.

Figure 9-24. *The Oscillator Node*

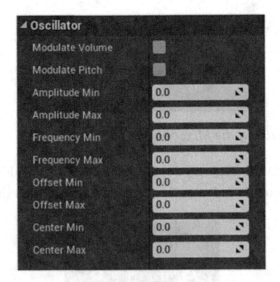

Figure 9-25. *Properties of the Oscillator Node*

In addition to Nodes that alter sounds, the Palette also contains many useful Nodes for combining sounds. A *Mixer Node*, shown in Figure 9-26, takes two or more sounds as input and outputs all of those sounds being played simultaneously. In the Details Panel, you can adjust the volumes of each input (Figure 9-27).

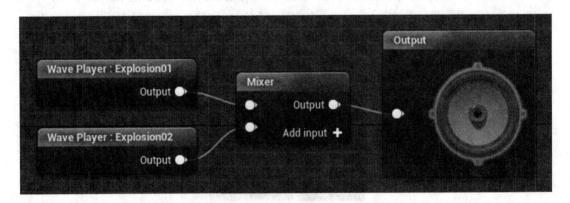

Figure 9-26. *The Mixer Node in use – this logic combines two different sounds and plays them simultaneously*

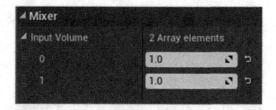

Figure 9-27. *Properties of the Mixer Node*

The *Concatenator Node* (Figure 9-28) is just like the Mixer Node, except that instead of playing its input sounds simultaneously, it plays them one after the other.

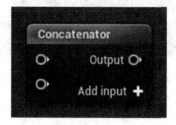

Figure 9-28. *The Concatenator Node*

A *Random Node* (Figure 9-29) will randomly output just one of its input sounds each time it's activated. By default, each sound has an equal chance of being played each time, but you can change this using the *Weights* property (Figure 9-30). For example, if you set the weight of the first sound to 2 and leave the weight of the second sound at 1, then the first sound has twice the chance of being played each time.

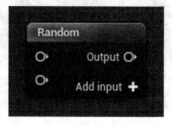

Figure 9-29. *The Random Node*

You can use the *Preselect at Level Load* property to trim down the number of possible inputs that can be selected from. For example, if the Random Node has ten inputs and Preselect at Level Load is set to 5, then as soon as the Level loaded, it would randomly select five of the inputs and then only randomly select from those five each time the Sound Cue was played. This can be used to trim down memory usage for Random Nodes that have several inputs. Note that this Node doesn't have any effect when simulating your game, it will only work when playing a build outside of the Editor.

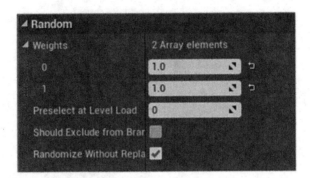

Figure 9-30. *Properties of the Random Node*

With the *Randomize Without Replacement* property checked, it will ensure that each sound gets played once before the same sound can be randomly selected again.

The *Branch Node* (Figure 9-31) will output one of its input sounds based on the value of a Boolean variable. In the Details Panel, you use the *Bool Parameter Name* property to specify the name of the Boolean variable that should be evaluated (Figure 9-32). If that Boolean has a value of True, whatever sound is connected to the *True* pin will be outputted. If the value is False, the sound connected to the *False* pin will be outputted, and if the Boolean has a value of Null, then the sound connected to the *Parameter Unset* pin will be used.

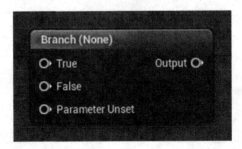

Figure 9-31. *The Branch Node*

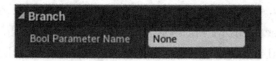

Figure 9-32. *Properties of the Branch Node*

The *Switch Node* (Figure 9-33) is just like the Branch Node, except it outputs a sound based on the value of an Integer variable instead of a Boolean variable.

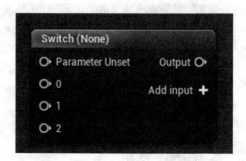

Figure 9-33. *The Switch Node*

Attenuation

Attenuation is a scientific term that refers to the reduction in strength of a signal. In the case of an audio signal, this refers to the decrease in volume that occurs due to distance. In Unreal Engine, you have the ability to edit the attenuation properties of the sounds in your game, affecting the rate at which their volumes decrease across distances.

When it's selected, the Ambient Sound Actor will have two spheres around it, an inner sphere and an outer sphere, as seen in Figure 9-34. At any point within the inner sphere, the sound will be heard at 100% volume. Going from the outer edge of the inner sphere to the outer edge of the outer sphere, the volume will decrease from 100% to zero.

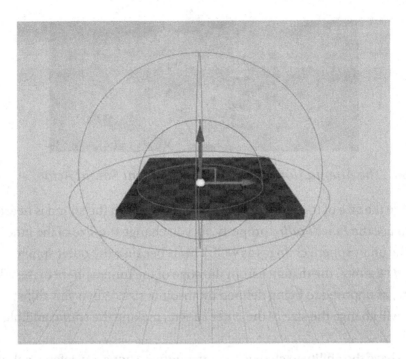

Figure 9-34. *The inner and outer attenuation spheres of an Ambient Sound Actor*

In the Details Panel, under the *Attenuation Distance* category (Figure 9-35), you can edit the sizes of these spheres. Note that the *Override Attenuation* property, in the *Attenuation* category (Figure 9-36), needs to be checked in order to edit the attenuation properties.

Figure 9-35. *The Attenuation Distance category of an Ambient Sound Actor*

Figure 9-36. *The Attenuation category of an Ambient Sound Actor*

To change the size of the inner sphere, the area in which the sound is heard at full volume, you use the *Inner Radius* property. As you change the size of the inner sphere, the size of the outer sphere changes as well. This is because the outer sphere is defined by the *Falloff Distance*, the distance from the edge of the inner sphere to the edge of the outer sphere, as opposed to being defined by absolute size. When you adjust the Falloff Distance, it will change the size of the outer sphere, making the sound audible at greater distances.

You also have the ability to change the *Attenuation Shape*. By default, spheres are used, as this is the most natural way that sound will attenuate. But if, for example, you had a sound coming from within a rectangular room, you might want to use the Box shape in order to better fit the attenuation to the shape of the room.

Attenuation Curves

As mentioned already, in the area described by the Falloff Distance, the sound will go from 100% volume to zero. But the *rate* at which this occurs can be adjusted, by setting the *Attenuation Function* that should be used to define the *Attenuation Curve*. By default, this will use a *Linear* curve, meaning the volume will decrease evenly.

Using the *Logarithmic* curve, the volume will decrease more rapidly at first, then the rate of decrease will slow as the sound approaches the bounds of the attenuation shape. The *LogReverse* curve, as its name indicates, is the reverse of that. The volume will decrease slowly at first, then more rapidly.

The *Inverse* curve is similar to the Logarithmic curve except the volume decreases extremely rapidly at first, then very slowly for the remainder of the distance. The *NaturalSound* curve is somewhere in between the Logarithmic curve and the Inverse curve and is supposed to represent the most natural attenuation curve that sounds have in the real world.

Finally, you can create your own custom attenuation curves, using the tool of the *Custom Attenuation Curve* property (Figure 9-37), which creates curves the same way the Timeline Editor did in the section on Timelines. So you hold down the *Shift* key and left-click the graph to add a new point on the curve. Then you can click and drag those points, or manually adjust their locations, to change the shape of the curve.

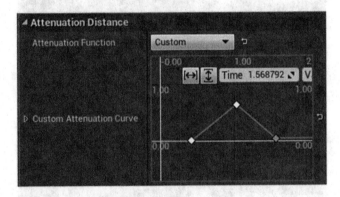

Figure 9-37. Creating a custom attenuation curve

Attenuation Hierarchy

At the highest level, you can create an Attenuation asset that can be saved and applied to multiple sound assets. To create a new *Sound Attenuation asset*, click Add New, go to Sounds, then select Sound Attenuation (Figure 9-38). You can double-click it to edit its properties, which are the standard set of attenuation properties that were just covered.

You can apply this Sound Attenuation to as many sound objects as you want, and then you only need to make changes for the entire group in one place. For example, if you open a Sound Cue, under the Attenuation Settings property, you can select the Sound Attenuation asset you created, and it will apply those attenuation properties to the Sound Cue.

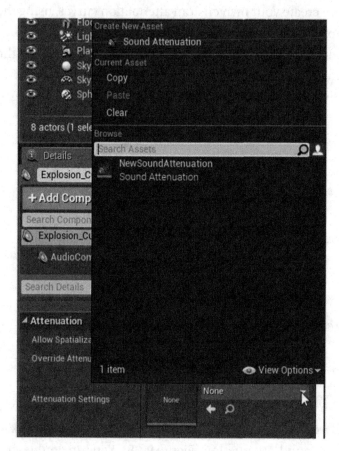

Figure 9-38. *Applying a Sound Attenuation asset to a Sound Cue*

But if you decide you want to set different settings for the Sound Cue, you can check the Override Attenuation property, and that will cause the Attenuation Settings property to be ignored and will instead use the settings defined in the Sound Cue itself.

Now let's say you drag several instances of the Sound Cue into your Level and you want to change the settings for just one of the instances, without changing the settings of the Sound Cue itself. You can select that instance and then edit its Attenuation properties directly in the Details Panel by checking the Override Attenuation property. Or you can choose an existing Sound Attenuation asset to use just for that instance.

Importing and Converting Audio

Most of the time, importing audio files into Unreal Engine will be as straightforward as importing any other type of file. You can either click the Import button in the Content Browser and browse to the file you want to import or you can simply drag and drop the file directly into the Content Browser.

If the file is a wave file, it will be converted to a Sound Wave asset which you can then use as you like. But if you have a file in a different format that you want to use, such as an MP3 file, you would need to convert it to a wave file before you can use it in Unreal.

Audacity

To get the file into the proper format so that the Engine can import it, you simply need to open the file in an application that can read it and then export it back out in the proper format. One program that can do this is Audacity, shown in Figure 9-39. It is free to download and use, can read many different types of audio files in various formats, and can export those files in a format which the Unreal Engine can read.

To download Audacity, go to `www.fosshub.com/Audacity.html`. If you have Windows, you can click the "Audacity Windows Installer" link and then run the .exe file that is downloaded. If you have a Mac, you'll need to download the .dmg file, and if you have Linux, you will have to download the source code and compile it yourself.

Once you have Audacity installed, converting your audio files into the proper formatting is pretty simple. First, go to "File ➤ Open," and open the file you want converted. Now, go back up to the File menu and choose "Export ➤ Export As WAV." Now click "Save," and when the Edit Metadata box pops up, you can simply press OK without making any changes.

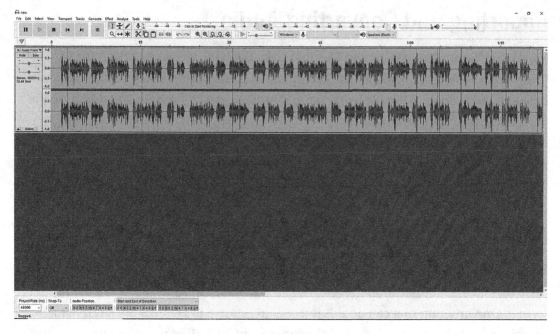

Figure 9-39. *The free software application Audacity can be used to convert sound files into a format that Unreal Engine will accept*

Summary

In this chapter, you learned about using audio in UE4 and how to add and manipulate dialogue, sound effects, and music. In the next chapter, you will learn about various topics that didn't fit neatly into one of the other chapters, such as migrating content between projects, finding existing content to use, importing 3D objects into your project, and packaging your project so it can be played outside of the editor.

CHAPTER 10

Additional Topics

This chapter will cover some additional topics that didn't fit into any of the previous chapters. You will learn how to easily pass content from one project to another, where to find content to download, how to import content, and how to package projects.

Migrating Content Between Projects

If you have assets in a project that you would like to use in another, migrating those assets is a simple process. To migrate one or more assets, select them in the Content Browser, then right-click them, go to "Asset Actions" in the menu that appears, then select "Migrate…." To migrate a folder, right-click it and select "Migrate…."

From there, a pop-up will appear allowing you to review all the assets that will be migrated. It's important to note that if an asset has any dependencies, those assets will be migrated as well, and then if those assets have any dependencies, those will be migrated, and so on. For example, if you wanted to migrate the SM_Chair mesh from the Props folder of the Starter Content, it would migrate all of the assets shown in Figure 10-1. It would migrate the Static Mesh, the Material that the Static Mesh uses, and the Textures that the Material uses.

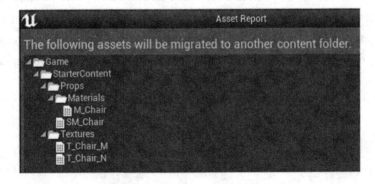

Figure 10-1. *These assets will be migrated when you migrate the SM_Chair mesh*

© David Nixon 2020
D. Nixon, *Beginning Unreal Game Development*, https://doi.org/10.1007/978-1-4842-5639-8_10

From there, a pop-up will appear allowing you to select the Content folder of the project you wish to migrate the asset(s) to. Once you click "Select Folder," the migration will begin. The next time you open the project that you migrated the assets to, they will be there, in the Content Browser, ready to use.

Downloading Content from the Epic Games Launcher

This section will show you how to use the Epic Games Launcher to download content to use in the creation of your games. On the Unreal Engine page of the Epic Games Launcher, the *Learn* tab contains content you can download for free, and the *Marketplace* tab contains content you can purchase (Figure 10-2).

Figure 10-2. *The tabs of the Unreal Engine page in the Epic Games Launcher*

Learn Tab

If you go to the Learn tab and scroll down, starting with the *Engine Feature Samples* category, you will find a lot of content you can use in your games and also sample projects that help to illustrate various concepts and features of the Engine.

For example, the *Open World Demo Collection*, shown in Figure 10-3, contains various meshes like grass, rocks, bushes, and trees that you can use to make nice-looking outdoor terrains. There are downloads for water, mountains, particle effects, Blueprints, and so on. There's also projects you can download that demonstrate certain gameplay concepts or even entire sample games. You can click any of the boxes to get more details and to actually download the content, add it to a project, or create a new project out of it (Figure 10-4).

Figure 10-3. *Click a box such as this one to learn more information about that content*

Figure 10-4. *A sample platform game you can download for free from the Learn tab*

Marketplace Tab

The Epic Games Marketplace is where you can find assets to purchase. You can get to the Marketplace either by clicking the Marketplace tab in the Epic Games Launcher or by clicking the Marketplace button in the Toolbar of the Level Editor.

The Marketplace is divided into various categories based on the assets provided. For example, you have environments, materials, audio, and so on. You can get to the various categories by hovering over the "Browse" option in the menu, as shown in Figure 10-5. Same as the Learn tab, just click the boxes to learn more about that content or to download it.

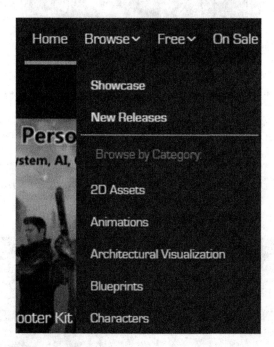

Figure 10-5. *The Marketplace is subdivided into categories*

Vault

When you download something through the Learn tab or the Marketplace, you can access it by clicking the *Library* tab and going down to the *Vault* section. If the content is a sample project, you can click the yellow button under its name to create that project (Figure 10-6). If the content is a group of assets, you can click the yellow button to add those folders to the Content Browser of an existing project that you specify.

Figure 10-6. *Access content you download through the Vault section of the Library tab*

Importing 3D Objects from the Internet

This section will show you a couple more places where you can find free 3D objects to download and how to import those objects into Unreal Engine.

www.free3d.com

One great web site to get free 3D models from is `www.free3d.com`. You can use the search box to look for something specific (Figure 10-7), or you can browse by category. Along the top, there is a strip of icons to browse models by file type. Or, along the left-hand side of the page, you can browse models by the types of objects they represent. So if you were looking for grass and tree models, for example, you could click the "Plants" link (Figure 10-8). Then down under the description of the category will be a list of subcategories you can choose from.

Figure 10-7. *The search box at `www.free3d.com`*

Plants

Models in this category are very
popular, some of them got over 100
thousand downloads. Extremely
useful for exterior scenes are our
ready to use tree models that can be
dropped in any scene easily.
Subcategories: Tree, Flowers, Plant,
Trees, Vegetation, Palm, Pine, Grass,
Indoor Plants

Figure 10-8. *Each category will have a description and a list of subcategories*

One of the great things about this site is that it is specifically devoted to free 3D objects. There is a section on the right advertising models for a price, but other than that, all the results that appear will be free to download. However, something you need to be aware of that is very important if you're planning on making games that you charge money for is that just because an asset is free to download, that doesn't necessarily mean you are free to use it in a commercial game (a game that makes money).

For example, some assets come with a *Personal Use Only* license. This means you're allowed to download it, and import it in your projects, and make a game with it; but the only thing you can do with that game is play it yourself or perhaps give it away for free to a few friends. If you started charging money for the game, the person who created the asset would be allowed to sue you for violating the terms of the license.

So if you're looking for models to use in commercial games, you'll need to find ones that come with a license for commercial use or a royalty-free license which, unfortunately, are only available on the paid models on this site.

One good thing about this site is that it doesn't require you to have an account to download. When you're ready to download an object, simply click the Download button on the objects description page, and it will bring up a list of the available files for download, as shown in Figure 10-9. Often, there will be a .zip or .rar file containing the object in all the different file formats available for that model. Note that the only 3D object type that Unreal Engine can directly import is the .fbx file type.

Available Files
1f9jtr180dxk-Tree1ByTyroSmith.zip
.3ds .obj .blend

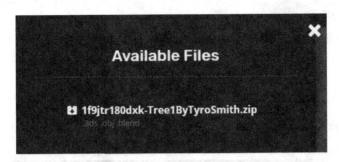

Figure 10-9. *The download button will open a pop-up containing the file formats available*

Luckily, most of the web sites you can download 3D objects from have a way for you to narrow down the results to a specific type you're looking for. For example, on this site, there will be a strip of links showing the different file types available (Figure 10-10), and clicking a type will narrow the results down to only objects that have a version of that type available. So if you click "FBX," you will only see those objects that are available as an .fbx file.

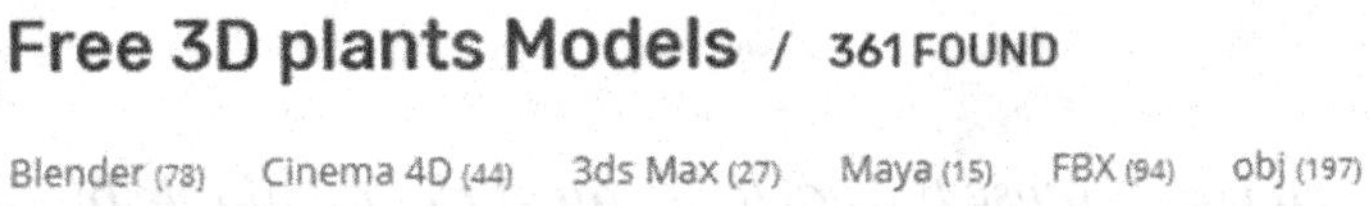

Free 3D plants Models / 361 FOUND
Blender (78) Cinema 4D (44) 3ds Max (27) Maya (15) FBX (94) obj (197)

Figure 10-10. *You can filter your results by file format*

www.cgtrader.com

Another 3D object web site you can use is `www.cgtrader.com`. You can use the search bar (Figure 10-11), or if you want to browse by category, you can go up to the top of the page, hover over "3D models," and then click the category you're interested in, as shown in Figure 10-12. From there, you can choose to either browse that category as a whole or click down into one of its subcategories.

Find the exact right 3D content for your needs, including AR/VR, gaming, advertising, entertainment and 3D printing

Figure 10-11. *The search box at* www.cgtrader.com

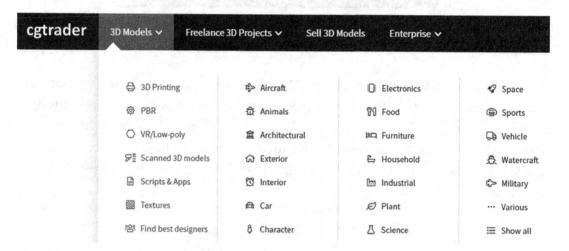

Figure 10-12. *You can browse the various categories available by clicking the 3D models menu at the top of the home page*

By default, you will mainly see listings of the objects for sale, so if you're only interested in the free objects, you will need to check the "Free" checkbox (Figure 10-13). This will still return paid content, but every other model listed will be a free model. This site has a dropdown you can use to search by file type.

Figure 10-13. *Narrow results down by price and/or file format*

Just like with the last site, or any site that you download artistic content from, make sure you check the details to see what kind of license agreement it has and what the terms of that agreement are. Unlike the last site, you will need to have an account in order to download from www.cgtrader.com.

Importing .fbx Files

Importing .fbx files into Unreal Engine works pretty much the same as importing any other file. You can either use the Import button in the Content Browser or drag and drop the files into the Content Browser directly.

One difference when importing an .fbx file, however, is that the import is heavily customizable. A pop-up menu will appear giving you a long list of options regarding how you want the object imported, as shown in Figure 10-14. For example, if you want to import the object as a skeletal mesh, you would check the *Skeletal Mesh* checkbox.

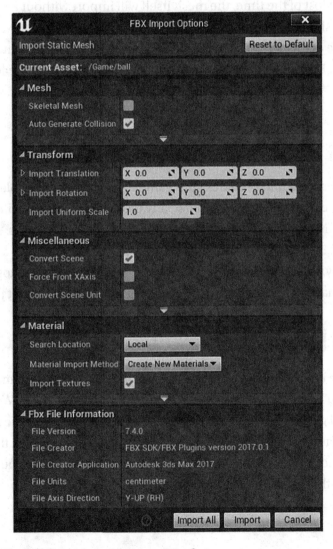

Figure 10-14. *The FBX Import Options window*

By default, the object will be added to the center of the Level, with it rotated and scaled the same as it was when it was exported, but you can change these settings if you wish. You can also choose if you want the Materials and Textures imported as well, or if you only wish to import the underlying mesh. When all the options are to your liking, you simply need to click the Import button to complete the import. You may get some warning messages if the file wasn't formatted exactly how the Engine likes it, but often, the import will still work.

One thing you need to be aware of, however, is that, even with the restriction of only being able to import .fbx files, and despite Epic Games' best efforts, the system is still far from perfect. Most of the time, the mesh itself will import without any problem, but there are still considerable technical issues regarding Materials and Textures importing properly. Because of this, Epic Games actually recommends that all Materials be applied within the Unreal Editor itself, rather than trying to import them in already applied to the mesh.

Packaging

Packaging is the process that prepares your game to run on a specific platform. There are several steps in the packaging process. First, any C++ source code specific to that project will be compiled. Next, all of the project's assets, like Meshes, Materials, Audio, and so on, are converted into a format that can be read by the target platform, a process known as *cooking*. Finally, the compiled code and cooked assets are bundled together into a package of files that can be used to run or install the game on the target platform.

Selecting a Default Map

Before your game is packaged, you need to ensure that it has a default map selected. The default map is the Level that will be loaded when the game first starts. Without a default map, nothing will get loaded and you will only see black when the game runs.

To set the default map, first go to Edit ➤ Project Settings, then click the "Maps & Modes" link on the left-hand side. Under the Default Maps category, you can set the default map with the Game Default Map property (Figure 10-15).

Figure 10-15. *Setting the default map*

Packaging the Game

When you're ready to package your game, you can do so by going to File ➤ Package
Project and then selecting the platform you want to target (Figure 10-16). You will then
be prompted to choose a folder to save the packaged project to. Once you have chosen a
folder, click "Select Folder" and the packaging will begin immediately.

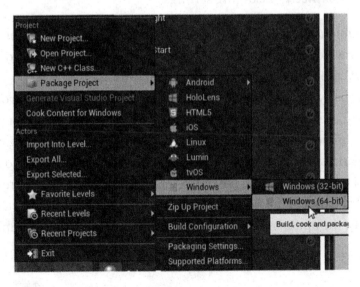

Figure 10-16. *Selecting the target platform*

The packaging will run in the background, and you will still be able to use the Editor. In the bottom-right corner of the screen will be a small window that will display the progress of the packaging. This window will also have a Cancel button to cancel the packaging process and a Show Log link to view the output log of the process.

Advanced Packaging Settings

Unreal Engine has some advanced settings you can configure for the packaging process (Figure 10-17). To get to these settings, go to either Edit ➤ Project Settings ➤ Packaging or File ➤ Package Project ➤ Packaging Settings.

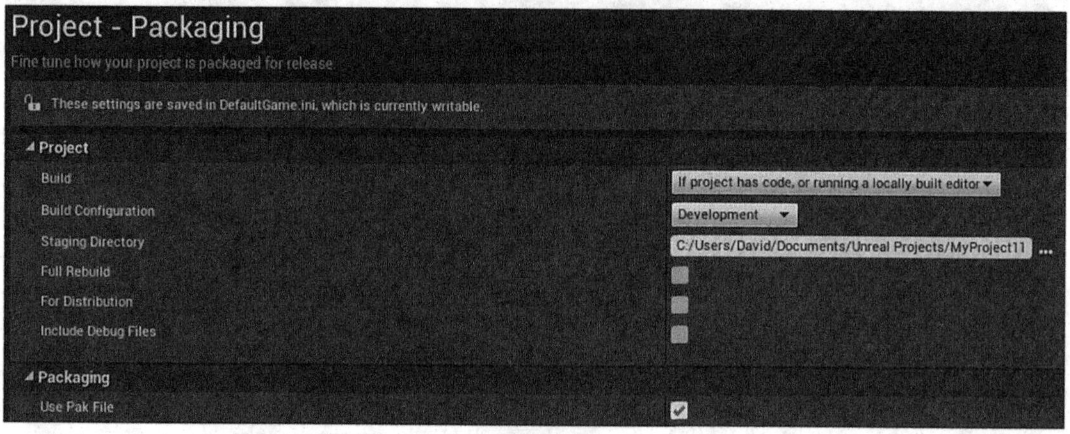

Figure 10-17. Advanced packaging settings

Under the *Project* category, the first property is *Build*. With this property, you can tell the Editor under which circumstances it should build the project as part of the packaging process. In most cases, you can just use the default setting.

The next property is *Build Configuration*. If you're wanting to debug your game, and you have a code-based project, meaning you are using C++ code, you would want to set the Build Configuration to *DebugGame*. If you're wanting to debug your game, and are only using Blueprints, and not any C++ code, you would want to set this to *Development*. Also, for both of these scenarios, you need to set *Include Debug Files* to True. If you're wanting to package your game for distribution to end users, you would want to set this to *Shipping*. Finally, the options ending in "Client" are used for online multiplayer games.

The *Staging Directory* is just the target directory where the packaged project is saved to. This is the same directory that you are asked to select when you start the packaging process.

The *Full Rebuild* property specifies whether all of the code should be compiled or just the code that has been modified since the last build. If you are doing a Shipping build, you should set this property to True.

If you are targeting the Android or iOS platform, you need to package your game for distribution. You can do this by setting the *For Distribution* property to True.

Pak Files

Down in the *Packaging* category, there is a property called *Use Pak File*. A *.pak* file is a file containing all of the assets of your game. If Use Pak File is set to False, the assets will all be individual files, but if it is True, then all assets will be combined into a single .pak file.

If you are packaging a game to be distributed to the public, and you are using a .pak file, you will want to add some security to that file. You can do this by clicking the "Crypto" link on the left-hand side of the Project Settings. Here, you can choose to encrypt and/or sign your .pak file (Figure 10-18).

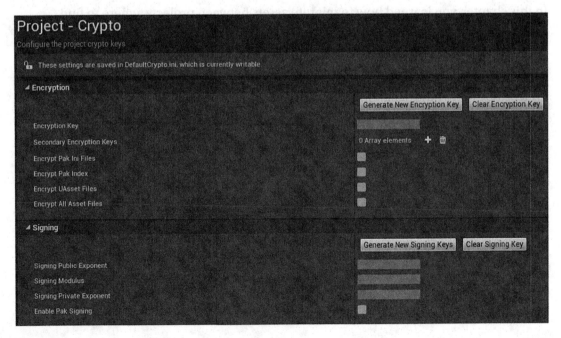

Figure 10-18. *Encryption and signing settings*

In the *Encryption* category, you can generate encryption keys and select which files you want encrypted. In the *Signing* category, you can generate signing keys and choose whether or not you want your .pak file signed.

Back on the Packaging page of Project Settings, if you expand the Packaging category to view the advanced properties, you will see a property called *Create compressed cooked packages*. If you set this property to True, it will compress your .pak file. Whether or not you should compress your .pak file is largely dependent on the target platform.

If you are targeting the Xbox One, you should always compress your .pak file as this will always improve the loading times. If you are targeting the Nintendo Switch, you need to test compression for each title, as it will result in faster load times for some games and slower load times for others. For the PS4 and Oculus platforms, you should never compress your .pak file. The PS4 already uses compression, and the Oculus cannot process a compressed .pak file. For Steam, compressed .pak files will result in less space being needed on the end user's device, but longer download times when patching, and it is thus a matter of personal preference.

Summary

In this chapter, you learned how to migrate assets between projects, where to find additional content to use in your projects, how to import that content, and how to package projects. You have now learned all the theory you need to begin creating simple games using Unreal Engine 4! This theory will also provide you with a solid foundation for learning more advanced topics. In the next chapter, you will go through a series of tutorials to apply all the theory you have learned thus far, in order to create an actual game.

CHAPTER 11

Tutorials

In this chapter, you will complete a series of tutorials in which you will create an entire sample game from scratch. When the game is complete, you will be able to control a humanoid character, using a keyboard and mouse or a joystick, from a first-person perspective. The goal of the game will be to find and collect three orbs and reach the end of the level. Along the way, you must navigate obstacles and avoid enemies. If your health reaches zero, you lose the game. Figure 11-1 shows a screenshot of the finished game.

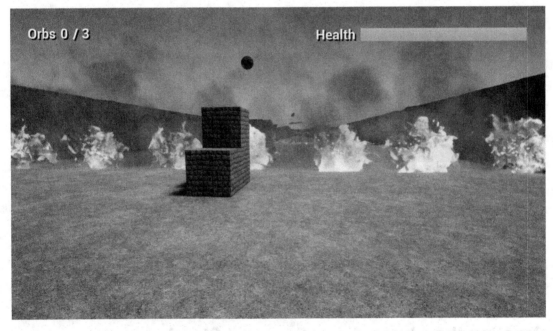

Figure 11-1. *Screenshot of the completed demo game*

© David Nixon 2020
D. Nixon, *Beginning Unreal Game Development*, https://doi.org/10.1007/978-1-4842-5639-8_11

Tutorial 1 – Creating the Sky

In this tutorial, you will be creating a new project and a new Level and will be constructing the sky for the Level. You will create the sun, a blue sky, and some clouds.

Creating a New Project and Empty Level

If you don't already have it open, start the Epic Games Launcher and then launch the Engine. Or, if you already have the Editor open, go to File ➤ New Project. Either way, you want to get to the "New Project" tab of the Unreal Project Browser.

1. Choose the "Blank" template blueprint.

2. Make sure the options "Desktop/Console," "Maximum Quality," and "With Starter Content" are set (Figure 11-2).

3. Give the project a name.

4. Click the "Create Project" button.

Figure 11-2. *Use these settings for your new project*

It usually takes a while for the Engine to create a new project, so don't worry if it looks like nothing is happening for a minute.

Now go to File ➤ New Level and select "Empty Level." This will give you a completely black, empty Level.

Creating the Atmosphere, Sun, and Clouds

1. Go to the Visual Effects tab in the Modes Panel.

2. Drag and drop an Atmospheric Fog into the Viewport. Now, instead of being all black, the Level has an atmosphere.

3. Go to the Lights tab.

4. Drag and drop a Directional Light into the Viewport.

5. Use the textbox at the top of the Details Panel to change the name of the Actor to "Sunlight." This way, if we add more Directional Lights to our Level later, we will be able to tell them apart in the World Outliner and find the one we want more quickly.

6. This Light won't move, so in the Transform category, set the Mobility of the Light to "Static." Setting it to Static will save processing power and will make builds a lot faster.

7. Click the arrow at the bottom of the Light category to expand the menu.

8. Set the Atmosphere/Fog Sun Light property to True by checking the checkbox. Now, instead of being on the horizon, the sun disc of the Atmospheric Fog will be positioned based on the rotation of the Directional Light Actor.

9. Set the Rotation of the Light to (0, -70, 0).

10. Click the Build button in the Toolbar to rebuild the lighting. This will make the sun slightly off-center in the sky, similar to what you might see around 11am or 1pm. This will give objects added to the Level a slight shadow.

11. Select the All Classes tab.

12. Scroll down to the BP_Sky_Sphere Actor, and then add one to the Level.

13. In the Details Panel, under the Default category, set the Directional Light Actor to our "Sunlight" Actor.

If you look up in the Viewport, you will see that the Sky Sphere has added some clouds to the sky (Figure 11-3). The clouds are moving, but they're moving pretty slow, so change the Cloud Speed to 4.0, so that the cloud movement is easier to see.

Figure 11-3. *Your Level should now have a sun, a blue sky, and clouds*

Now save the Project, so you don't lose any of your hard work.

1. Press either Ctrl+Shift+S or go up to File Menu and choose "Save All." This will prompt you to save your Level. First, make a proper folder to save it in.

2. On the left side of the Save Level As window, right-click and select "New Folder."

3. Name the folder "MyContent."

4. At the bottom of the window, name the Level "DemoLevel."

5. Press Enter, or click the Save button.

Setting the Game Default Map

1. Go up to the Edit menu and select "Project Settings."

2. Go to Maps and Modes.

3. Change the Editor Startup Map and the Game Default Map to the DemoLevel that we just saved.

This will make DemoLevel the default Level for this project and will cause it to load automatically every time you open the project.

So now your Level has a nice-looking sky, and in the next tutorial, you will start constructing the actual playing area.

Tutorial 2 – Creating the Playing Area

In this tutorial, you're going to construct the playing area for your game, using Brushes, Meshes, and Materials.

Creating the Ground

First, create the ground objects that the player will use to walk on.

1. Select the Geometry tab in the Modes Panel.

2. Add a Box Brush to the Level, and rename it "Ground1."

3. In the Transform category, change the Location of the Brush to (0,0,0).

4. In the Brush Settings category, use the X, Y, and Z properties to change the size of the Brush to 2700 x 5000 x 10.

5. Click the button in the top-left corner of the Viewport that currently says "Perspective" and change that to an orthographic Top view. This way, you can see the layout of your Level from a bird's eye view.

6. Scroll down on the mouse wheel to zoom out, and right-click and drag the mouse to pan the view.

7. Add another Box Brush to the Level and name it "Ground2."

8. Change its size to 2700 x 10000 x 10.

9. You want to line up Ground2 with Ground1 along the X-axis and Z-axis, so change Ground2's X location and Z location to 0.

10. Change the Y location to 8,750. This will create a 12.5 m gap between Ground1 and Ground2.

Now add a Material to your Ground objects so that they look more like actual ground.

1. First, go back to Perspective view.

2. Zoom out until you can see the top of both Ground1 and Ground2.

3. Go up to the Toolbar and click Build to rebuild the lighting so that you can see your ground objects correctly.

4. In the Content Browser, browse to Content ➤ Starter Content ➤ Materials, then locate the M_Ground_Grass Material. Drag and drop this Material onto the top surface of both Ground1 and Ground2 (Figure 11-4).

5. Press Ctrl+Shift+S, or click File ➤ Save All to save your work.

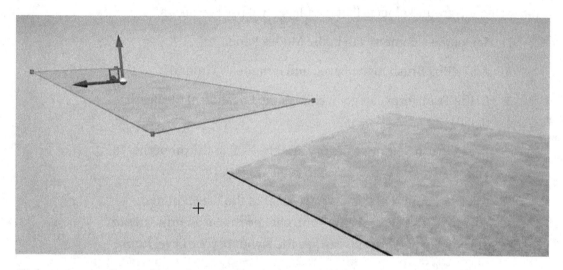

Figure 11-4. *Ground1 and Ground2 with a grass material applied*

Adding a Player Start Actor

Now add a Player Start Actor to the Level so you can define the location the player should start from when the Level begins.

1. Go to the Basic tab in the Modes Panel and drag a Player Start Actor into the Level.

2. Set its Location to (0, -2300, 100).

3. Set its Rotation to (0, 0, 90).

4. Press Play on the Toolbar to see the perspective from which the player will start the Level. They will start at one end of the 50-meter-long Ground1, then there will be a 12.5 meter gap, followed by 100 meters of Ground2.

Adding the Wall Enclosure

Now add some walls to enclose your playing area (Figure 11-5). But this time, you will select the Material first so that it will be automatically added to every surface of the Actor.

1. Go back to the Materials folder if you're not already there and select the M_Brick_Cut_Stone Material.

2. Go to the Geometry tab in the Modes Panel and drag another Box Brush into the Level. Notice that it already has the Material applied to all sides.

3. Rename the Box "Left Wall."

4. Change its size to 75 x 16250 x 400.

5. Change its Location to (1312.5, 5625, 205).

Now, to make the wall for the other side, you could go through all these steps again. However, a better solution would be to make a copy of the existing wall, which will save a lot of time.

1. With the Alt button held down, grab the red arrow of the Left Wall and drag it toward the other side of the playing area.

2. Name this copy "Right Wall."

3. Change its X location to *negative* 1312.5.

Now you will make the walls for the "top" and "bottom" of the Level.

1. Add another Box Brush and rename it "Bottom Wall."

2. Change its size to 2550 x 75 x 400 and its location to (0, -2462.5, 205).

3. Hold down the Alt button and drag the green arrow of the Bottom Wall to make a copy.

4. Name this Actor "Top Wall."

5. Change its Y location to 13712.5.

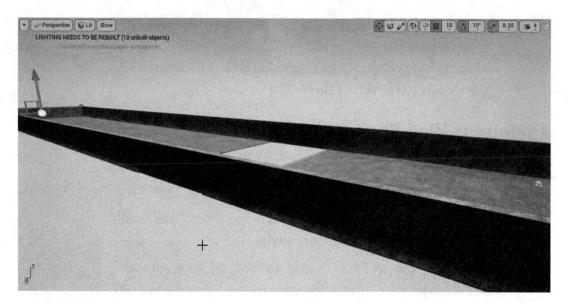

Figure 11-5. *Your Level should now be enclosed within four walls*

So now, you have defined the bounds of your Level and have a fully enclosed playing area. In the next tutorial, you will add the internal structures of your Level.

Tutorial 3 – Building the Inner Structures

In this tutorial, you will add the internal structures for your Level, including walls, platforms, and houses.

Adding the Inner Walls

First, add the inner walls.

1. Go to the Materials folder in the Content Browser and select the M_CobbleStone_Rough Material.

2. Drag a Box Brush into the Level and rename it "LowWallBottomLeft."

3. Change its size to 800 x 200 x 200.

4. Change its Location to (875, 5875, 105).

5. Hold down the Alt key and drag the red arrow of the wall to make a copy.

6. Rename it "LowWallBottomRight."

7. Change its X location to *negative* 875.

8. Hold down the Alt key and drag along the green arrow of this wall.

9. Rename the copy "LowWallTopRight."

10. Change its X size to 1150.

11. Change its X location to -700 and its Y location to 8530.

12. Hold down the Alt key and drag the red arrow to make a copy of this wall.

13. Rename it "LowWallTopLeft."

14. Change its X location to *positive* 700.

15. Press Ctrl+Shift+S to save your work.

So now your inner walls should be complete (Figure 11-6). In Tutorial 5, you will add enemies in between the gaps in the walls.

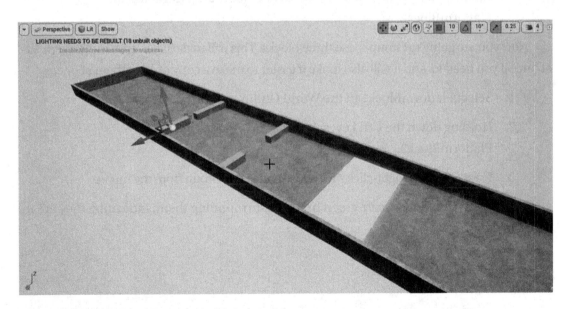

Figure 11-6. *The inner walls of the Level*

Adding a Platform of Blocks

Now make a platform of blocks that will be used to jump over a fire right at the beginning of the Level.

1. With the M_CobbleStone_Rough Material selected, add a Box Brush to the Level.

2. Rename it "PlatformBlock1."

3. Change its size to 110 x 110 x 110.

4. Change its Location to (0, -800, 60).

5. Hold down the Alt key and drag the green arrow to make a copy of the block. Notice that it is automatically renamed "PlatformBlock2."

6. Change its Y location to -690 to place it directly in front of PlatformBlock1.

7. Hold down the Alt key and drag the blue arrow of PlatformBlock2 to make a copy.

8. Change the copy's Z location to 170 to place it directly on top of PlatformBlock2.

Now you are going to Group these three blocks. This will make it easier to move them all at once if you need to, and it will also make it easier to make a copy of all of them at once.

1. Select PlatformBlock1 in the World Outliner.

2. Holding down the Ctrl key, select PlatformBlock2 and PlatformBlock3.

3. Press Ctrl+G, or right-click the mouse and select Group from the menu.

The blocks should now have green brackets surrounding them, indicating they are in a locked Group.

1. Hold down the Alt key and drag the green arrow of the group of blocks to make a copy.

2. Press the E key to switch to the Rotate Tool.

3. Manually rotate the group of blocks around the Z-axis by clicking the blue curve and dragging the mouse. A number will pop up showing you how many degrees you have rotated by so far. Rotate the blocks either 180 degrees or -180 degrees.

Note that you had to rotate manually in order to rotate the Group itself. If we had tried to set the Z rotation to 180 degrees in the Details Panel, it would have rotated each of the blocks individually around their own axes.

Now, you want to create a gap of about five meters between the two platforms (Figure 11-7).

1. Switch back to an orthographic Top view.

2. Pan the view so that the blocks are in the center of the Viewport, then zoom in until the scale in the bottom-left shows 1m and is the width of a single block of the grid.

3. To create a gap of five meters, drag blocks 4, 5, and 6 until there is a distance of five grid lines between the two Groups. Note that this Top view is showing the Level in the opposite direction than your player faces when starting the Level. So blocks 4, 5, and 6 are the Group at the bottom from this perspective. So drag that Group by the green arrow until there are five grid blocks between the two Groups.

4. Switch back to Perspective view.

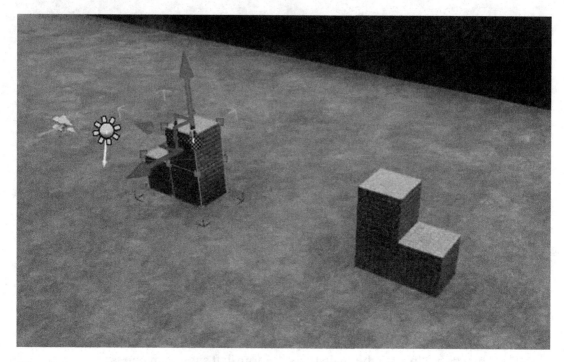

Figure 11-7. *The platforms at the beginning of the Level*

Adding a Fire Obstacle

Now, give the player a reason to need to use these platforms and add some fire in the gap between them (Figure 11-8).

1. Go to the Particles folder in the Starter Content.

2. Drag in a copy of the P_Fire particle system and place it between the two structures.

3. Increase its Scale by 4 overall.

4. Use the Alt key to drag out several copies of the Actor to create a row of fire that stretches from wall to wall.

Figure 11-8. The fire at the beginning of the Level

Adding the House Structures

Now, the last thing you will do in this tutorial is create some houses at the end of the Level. First, you will construct the stone fence for one of the houses.

1. Select the M_Brick_Cut_Stone Material.

2. Drag a Box Brush into the Level.

3. Rename it "HouseFenceWall1-1."

4. Change its size to 900 x 50 x 400.

5. Change its Location to (-825, 9100, 205).

6. Drag another Box Brush into the Level.

7. Rename it "HouseFenceWall2-1."

8. Change its size to 50 x 1300 x 400.

9. Change its Location to (-400, 9775, 205).

10. Drag another Box Brush into the Level.

297

11.   Rename it "HouseFenceWall3-1."

12.   Change its size to 550 x 50 x 400.

13.   Change its Location to (-700, 10400, 205).

Now that the fence is complete, you can start to build the house itself.

1.   Select the M_Basic_Wall Material.

2.   Drag a Box Brush into the Level.

3.   Name it "House1."

4.   Change its size to 500 x 500 x 500.

5.   Change its Location to (-850, 9750, 250).

6.   Set its Hollow property to True so that the player will be able to walk around inside it.

Now you need to add a doorway.

1.   Set the camera in the Viewport so that it's facing the wall of the house that's on the opposite side of the gap in the fence.

2.   At the bottom of the Geometry tab, change the Brush Type to "Subtract."

3.   Drag in a Box Brush.

4.   Name it "Doorway1."

5.   Change its size to 200 x 10 x 300.

6.   Change its Location to (-850, 9500, 155).

Now you can start designing the inside of the house.

1.   Find the M_Wood_Floor_Walnut_Polished Material in the Materials folder.

2.   Drag it onto the floor of the house.

3.   Go to the Props folder.

4. Drag the SM_Chair mesh into the Level.

5. Rename it "Chair1."

6. Press the End key to snap the chair to the floor.

7. Rotate the chair so that it's facing away from one of the corners and then move it into that corner.

8. Drag an SM_TableRound mesh into the Level. Rename it "Table1."

9. Position it in the center of the room.

10. Drag an SM_Lamp_Ceiling mesh into the Level.

11. Rename it "Lamp1."

12. Attach it to the middle of the ceiling.

13. Go to the Lights tab of the Modes Panel.

14. Drag a Point Light into the Level.

15. Rename it "LampLight1." Change its Mobility to Static.

16. Position it in the same place as the bulb of lamp mesh.

17. Zoom out until you can see the blue spherical radius of the light.

18. Change its Attenuation Radius property to 500, so that the sphere is only slightly larger than the house (Figure 11-9).

So now the house is complete. Click the Build button to see how everything looks with the lighting built.

Figure 11-9. *The Attenuation Radius of LampLight1 around the finished house*

Now you are going to combine the house, the fence, and the furniture into a single Group so you can make a copy of that Group.

1. In the World Outliner, select "Chair1."

2. With the Ctrl key held down, also select Doorway1, House1, HouseFenceWall1-1, HouseFenceWall2-1, HouseFenceWall3-1, Lamp1, LampLight1, and Table1.

3. Press Ctrl+G to group the Actors.

4. Switch to orthographic Top view.

5. Zoom out until you can see the entire house group and also the end of the Level.

6. Hold down the Alt key and drag the green arrow to make a copy of the Group.

7. Position it so that there is roughly an equal amount of space between it and the first group and it and the wall at the end of the Level.

8. Hold down the Alt key again and drag the red arrow to make another copy of the Group.

9. Press E to switch to the Rotate Tool.

10. Rotate the Group 180 degrees.

11. Press W to switch back to the Move Tool.

12. Use the red arrow to move the Group until the edge of the house fence is flush with the Level wall. Zoom in close and use the grid and Grid Snapping in order to get it to line up perfectly.

13. Hold down the Alt key and drag the green arrow to make the final copy of the house group.

14. Position it so that it roughly lines up with the first house group.

15. Switch back to Perspective view.

16. Press Ctrl+Shift+S to save your work.

17. Rebuild the lighting.

So now, all of the inner structures of your Level should be complete (Figure 11-10). Click the Play button to fly around the Level and take a look at your work.

Figure 11-10. *The Level with all the inner structures finished*

Tutorial 4 – Building the Elevator Platform

In this tutorial, you will use Blueprints to create your first custom Actor – a platform that will continually move up and down.

1. In the Content Browser, browse to the MyContent folder you created earlier.

2. Click the Add New button, then choose "Blueprint Class."

3. Go down to "All Classes" and search for the StaticMeshActor and select that as the Parent Class.

4. Name the class "PlatformUpDown."

5. Double-click it to open it in the Blueprint Editor.

6. In the Components window in the upper-left, select the StaticMeshComponent.

7. In the Details Panel, under the Static Mesh category, set the Static Mesh property to Shape_Cylinder.

8. Change its Scale to (3, 3, 0.2).

9. Set its Mobility to Moveable.

The physical characteristics of the platform are now set. Now you will begin to script its behavior. First, you will create a Timeline for the platform.

1. Go to the Event Graph tab.

2. Right-click the graph, scroll all the way down to the bottom of the menu, and select "Add Timeline...."

3. Name it "PlatformUpDownTimeline."

4. Double-click the Node to open the Timeline Editor.

5. Click the gray "V" button to create a Vector track for the Timeline.

6. Name the track "StartUpTrack."

7. You only want to affect the platform's up and down movement, the movement along the Z-axis, so click the lock icons next to the X and Y axes.

8. You want the animation to last a total of eight seconds, so change the Length property from 5 to 8.

9. You don't need to ignore the last keyframe in this situation in order to get a smooth animation, so go ahead and check the Use Last Keyframe property.

10. You want the animation to repeat over and over, so check the Loop property.

Now you will create the Timeline curve itself.

1. Hold down Shift and left-click inside the track to add a key.

2. Set the key's Time to 0 and its Value to 0.

3. Add another key and set its Time to 4 and its Value to 500.

4. Add a third key and set its Time to 8 and its Value to 0.

5. Click the "Zoom to Fit Horizontal" and "Zoom to Fit Vertical" buttons and then zoom out until you can see the whole Timeline curve at once (Figure 11-11).

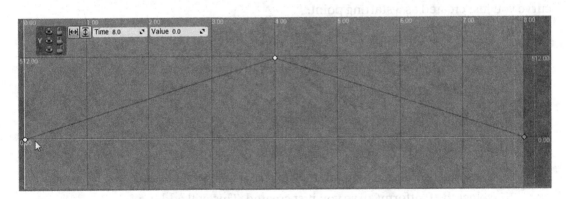

Figure 11-11. *The initial Timeline curve*

This curve will cause the platform to go from rest to full speed instantaneously and will also cause it to go from full speed to rest instantaneously. But there is a way you can edit this curve to make its movement closer mimic that of an elevator, where it gradually increases speed at first, then gradually decreases speed before stopping.

1. Right-click the first key and select "Auto" from the Key Interpolation menu.

2. Now do the same thing to the second key. This curve will give you the movement you want (Figure 11-12).

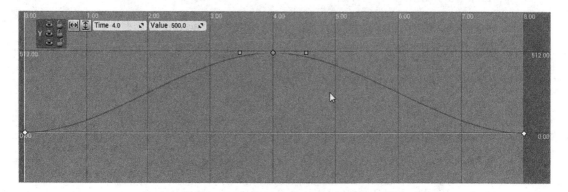

Figure 11-12. *The Timeline curve with interpolation applied*

So this track will cause the initial movement of the platform to be upward, but you also need a track for situations where you want the initial movement of the platform to be downward. Instead of redoing all these steps over again, however, you will use the curve you just created as a starting point.

1. Right-click the graph and choose "Create External Curve."

2. Choose the MyContent folder to save it in and name it "PlatformCurve."

3. Click the "V" button again to create another Vector track.

4. Name it "StartDownTrack."

5. Click the dropdown beneath the "External Curve" label and select the PlatformCurve you just created. This will add the PlatformCurve to this track.

6. Click the X icon beneath the External Curve label so that you can edit the curve.

7. Click the second key and change its Value from 500 to -500.

Now go back to the Event Graph tab. The first thing you need to do is create a couple of variables that will help you with the logic that you want to script. You need a variable to store the initial location of the platform that the Timeline can use to make its calculations. You will also create a variable to specify whether you want the platform's initial movement to be up or down.

1. In the My Blueprint window, create a new Vector variable and name it InitialPlatformLocation.

2. Create a Boolean variable named StartWithUpwardsMovement.

3. In the Details Panel, set this variable's Instance Editable property to True.

4. Compile the Blueprint.

5. Give the variable a Default Value of True.

Now you can begin to script the logic.

1. Drag the InitialPlatformLocation variable into the Event Graph and choose "Set" to create a Set Node.

2. Connect the Event BeginPlay Node to the Set Node.

3. Drag a wire out of the Set Node's input pin and add a GetActorLocation Node.

4. Leave the Target pin set to "self" so that it will return the location of the platform itself.

So this logic is saying that as soon as the Platform comes into existence, get its location and store that value in the InitialPlatformLocation variable (Figure 11-13).

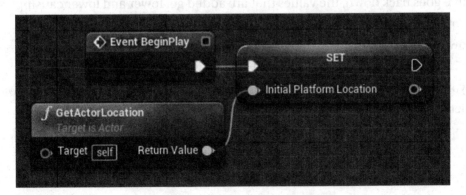

Figure 11-13. *Setting the initial location of the platform*

1.   Drag a wire out of the Set Node's output execution pin and connect that to the Play pin of the Timeline Node.

2.   Drag a wire from the Update pin to a Branch Node.

3.   Drag the StartWithUpwardsMovement variable into the graph and create a Get Node.

4.   Connect the Get Node to the Condition pin of the Branch Node.

5.   Drag a wire from the True execution pin of the Branch Node and connect it to a SetActorLocation Node.

6.   Right-click the graph to bring up the Node Menu and type "vector plus" to find the "Vector + Vector" Node and then add it to the graph.

7.   Connect the output pin of the InitialPlatformLocation Set Node to one of the input pins of the Vector + Vector Node.

8.   Connect the Start Up Track output pin of the Timeline Node to the other input pin of the Vector + Vector Node.

9.   Connect the output pin of the Vector + Vector Node to the New Location pin of the SetActorLocation Node.

This will create the movement for platforms whose StartWithUpwardsMovement variable is True. For every tick of gameplay, the location of the platform will be determined by adding the value of the Timeline at that moment to the starting position of the platform. So as the curve of the StartUpTrack rises, it will add larger and larger values to the platform's initial location, causing the platform itself to rise. Then, as the curve goes back down, the values that are added get lower and lower causing the platform to lower back down to its original position.

Now you need to create the movement for platforms whose StartWithUpwardsMovement variable is False. This will use the exact same logic, but this time, you will add the values coming from the StartDownTrack. Figure 11-14 shows the completed structure.

1. Connect the False execution pin of the Branch Node to another SetActorLocation Node.

2. Create a second Vector + Vector Node and again connect the output pin of the InitialPlatformLocation Set Node to one of the input pins of the new Vector + Vector Node.

3. This time, however, connect the Start *Down* Track output pin to the second input pin of the new Vector + Vector Node.

4. Connect the output pin of this second Vector + Vector Node to the New Location pin of the second SetActorLocation Node.

5. Compile and save the Blueprint.

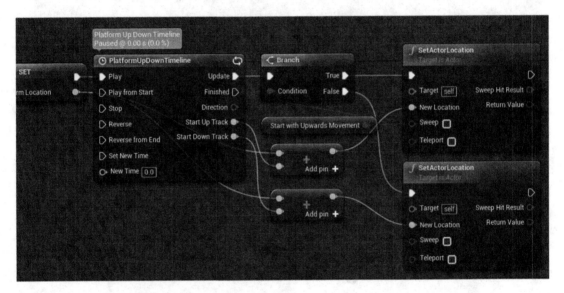

Figure 11-14.   *The Event Graph should now look like this*

The elevator blueprint is now complete. You can now use this blueprint to add as many elevators to the Level as you want (Figure 11-15).

1. Go back to the Level Editor.

2. Drag a copy of PlatformUpDown into the Level.

3. Change its Location to (0, 2850, 0).

4. Drag another copy into the Level.

5. Change its Location to (0, 3400, 500).

6. Set its Start With Upwards Movement property to False, so that it will start with a downward movement.

7. Save your work.

8. Click Play and test your Level to make sure the elevator platforms are working correctly.

Figure 11-15. *The Level with working elevator platforms added*

Tutorial 5 – Creating the Enemies

In this tutorial, you are going to create the Blueprint for the enemies in your Level, which will be very similar to how you constructed the elevator platform.

First, you will create the Blueprint file.

1. Go to the MyContent folder in the Content Browser.

2. Click the Add New button, and select Blueprint Class.

3. Choose StaticMeshActor as the Parent Class and click "Select."

4. Name the class "EnemySphere."

5. Double-click it to open it in the Blueprint Editor.

Now you will add the physical characteristics of the Blueprint.

1. In the Viewport tab, in the Components window, click the StaticMeshComponent.

2. Set its Mobility to Moveable.

3. Set its Static Mesh to Shape_Sphere.

4. Go back to the Components window and click the Add Component button.

5. Under the Common category, choose "Particle System."

6. Rename the particle system to "Fire."

7. In the Details Panel, under the Particles category, set the Template property to the P_Fire particle system.

8. Use the Move Tool to drag the fire to the center of the sphere (Figure 11-16).

Figure 11-16. *The enemy sphere that will be used for the game*

This will complete the physical structure of the Actor. Now create its Timeline curves.

1. Go to the Event Graph tab.

2. Right-click the graph, scroll to the bottom of the menu, and select "Add Timeline...."

3. Name it "EnemySphereTimeline."

4. Double-click it to open the Timeline Editor.

5. Add a new Vector track.

6. Name it "XMovementTrack."

7. Lock the Y and Z axes.

8. Change the Length to 3 seconds.

9. Set the Loop property to True.

10. Hold down Shift and left-click the graph four times to create four keys.

11. For the first key, set its Time and Value to 0.

12. For the second key, set its Time to 0.75 and its Value to 400.

13. For the third key, set its Time to 2.25 and its Value to -400.

14. For the fourth key, set its Time to 3 and its Value to 0.

15. Click the Zoom to Fit Horizontal and Zoom to Fit Vertical buttons to fit the whole curve on the screen at once.

The idea behind this curve is that you place the Actor wherever you want the center of its oscillating movement to be. It will start out moving in the positive X direction, then it will start going in the negative X direction, passing its center of movement, then going an equal distance in the negative direction, before returning to its center and starting the loop over again.

Now you're going to create the same curve, but along the Y-axis, which is why you can't simply copy and paste it (Figure 11-17).

1. Add another Vector track.

2. Name it "YMovementTrack."

3. Lock the X and Z axes.

4. Add four keys. One at (0,0), one at (0.75, 400), one at (2.25, -400), and one at (3, 0).

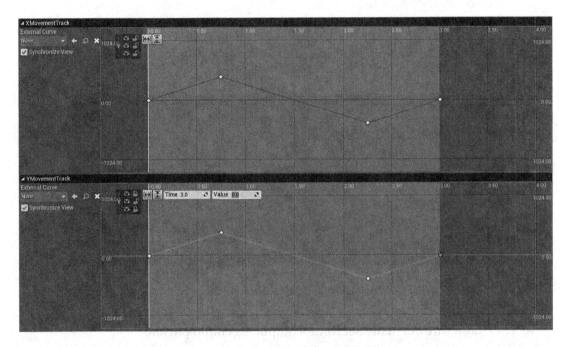

Figure 11-17. *The Timeline curves for the enemy Blueprint*

Now go back to the Event Graph. Like you did with the elevator platform, you need to make a variable for the initial location of the Actor and a variable to specify which direction it should move.

1. Create a new Vector variable.

2. Name it "InitialEnemyLocation."

3. Create a Boolean variable.

4. Name it "UseXMovement."

5. Make it Instance Editable.

6. Give it a default value of True.

311

Now you can begin to script the logic.

1. Drag the InitialEnemyLocation variable into the Event Graph and choose "Set" to create a Set Node.

2. Connect the Event BeginPlay Node to the Set Node.

3. Drag a wire out of the Set Node's input pin and add a GetActorLocation Node.

So this logic is saying that as soon as the enemy comes into existence, get its location and store that value in the InitialEnemyLocation variable (Figure 11-18).

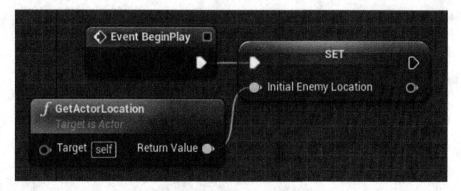

Figure 11-18. *Getting the initial location of the Actor*

1. Drag a wire out of the Set Node's output execution pin and connect that to the Play pin of the Timeline Node.

2. Drag a wire from the Update pin to a Branch Node.

3. Drag the UseXMovement variable into the graph and create a Get Node.

4. Connect the Get Node to the Condition pin of the Branch Node.

5. Drag a wire from the True execution pin of the Branch Node and connect it to a SetActorLocation Node.

6. Right-click the graph to bring up the Node Menu and type "vector+" to find the "Vector + Vector" Node and then add it to the graph.

7.   Connect the output pin of the InitialEnemyLocation Set Node to one of the input pins of the Vector + Vector Node.

8.   Connect the XMovement Track output pin of the Timeline Node to the other input pin of the Vector + Vector Node.

9.   Connect the output pin of the Vector + Vector Node to the New Location pin of the SetActorLocation Node.

10.   Connect the False execution pin of the Branch Node to another SetActorLocation Node.

11.   Create a second Vector + Vector Node.

12.   Again, connect the output pin of the InitialEnemyLocation Set Node to one of the input pins of the new Vector + Vector Node.

13.   This time, however, connect the *Y*Movement Track output pin to the second input pin of the new Vector + Vector Node.

14.   Connect the output pin of this second Vector + Vector Node to the New Location pin of the second SetActorLocation Node.

15.   Compile and save the Blueprint.

So what this is doing is using the value of the UseXMovement variable to determine if the enemy should move in the X direction, using the XMovement Track, or if it should move in the Y direction, using the YMovement Track (Figure 11-19).

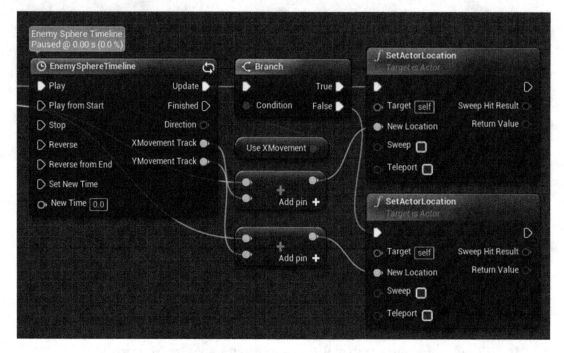

Figure 11-19. *This logic is what causes the enemy spheres to move*

Now you will add the enemies to the Level.

1. Go back to the Level Editor.

2. Drag a copy of EnemySphere into the Level.

3. Change its Location to (0, 5870, 100).

4. Drag another copy into the Level.

5. Change its Location to (0, 8530, 100).

6. Set its Use XMovement property to False, so that it will move in the Y direction.

So the first enemy sphere will move back and forth along the X-axis, and the other sphere will move back and forth along the Y-axis (Figure 11-20).

Figure 11-20. *The first two enemies of the game*

Now, add a few more enemies to your Level.

1. Place an enemy at the entrance to each of the houses.

2. For each of these, uncheck the Use XMovement property so that they will move in the Y direction.

3. Save your work.

4. In the Viewport, navigate to the location of one of the spheres.

5. Right-click the Viewport and choose Play From Here.

6. Make sure the enemy spheres move as desired (Figure 11-21).

315

Figure 11-21. *This enemy sphere is guarding this house*

Tutorial 6 – Creating a Rotating Door

In this tutorial, you're going to use a Timeline to animate the opening of a door. Unlike the previous Timelines you made, which dealt with translational movement, you will be using this Timeline to create rotational movement.

At the end of the Level, there will be a door that you can open once you've collected all the orbs. Right now, you're not going to worry about the player meeting any requirements, you're just going to script logic that will cause the door to open as soon as the Level begins.

So first, you need to create the doorway.

1. Add a new subtractive Box Brush to the Level.

2. Name it "EndOfLevelDoorway."

3. Change its size to 115 x 75 x 215.

4. Change its Location to (0, 13712.5, 112.5).

5. Add a Material to the sides of this newly created passageway so that it looks more realistic. Go to the Materials folder and use the M_Brick_Cut_Stone Material.

Now add a door frame.

1. Go to the Props folder in the Starter Content.

2. Drag the SM_DoorFrame mesh into the Level.

3. Change its Location to (0, 13687, 5).

4. Change its Rotation to (0, 0, -90).

Now add a bright light behind the doorway for visual effect (Figure 11-22).

1. Go to the Lights tab in the Modes Panel.

2. Add a Spot Light to the Level.

3. Rename it "EndOfLevelLight."

4. Change its Mobility to Static.

5. Change its Location to (0, 13790, 100).

6. Change its Rotation to (0, 0, -90).

7. Set the Intensity property as high as it can go, which is 160 candelas.

8. Set the Inner Cone Angle and the Outer Cone Angle both to 80.

9. Rebuild the lighting.

Figure 11-22. *The completed doorway*

Now that the doorway is complete, you can start building your Door Actor. First, create the Blueprint file.

1. Go to the MyContent folder.

2. Click the Add New button, and select Blueprint Class.

3. Choose StaticMeshActor as the Parent Class.

4. Name the class "EndOfLevelDoor."

5. Double-click it to open it in the Blueprint Editor.

Now construct the physical door object.

1. In the Viewport tab, in the Components window (Figure 11-23), select the StaticMeshComponent.

2. Set its Static Mesh property to SM_Door.

3. Set its Mobility to Moveable.

4. Click the Add Component button and select Static Mesh to add a Static Mesh subcomponent to the door.

5. Name the subcomponent "Glass."

6. Set its Static Mesh to SM_GlassWindow. This will prevent the Character from being able to walk through the opening in the door.

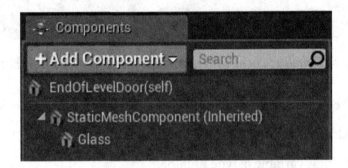

Figure 11-23. *The door's Components*

Now create the Timeline that will be used to define the rotational movement of the door when it opens (Figure 11-24).

1. Go to the Event Graph.

2. Create a new Timeline Node.

3. Name it "OpenDoorTimeline."

4. Double-click it to open it in the Timeline Editor.

5. Click the "f" button to create a new Float track and name it "OpenDoorTrack."

6. Change its Length to 1.

7. Set Use Last Keyframe to True.

8. Hold down Shift and left-click the graph to create a key.

9. Set its Time to 0 and its Value to 0.

10. Add another key.

11. Set its Time to 1 and its Value to 90.

12. Click the Zoom to Fit Vertical button to see the entire curve.

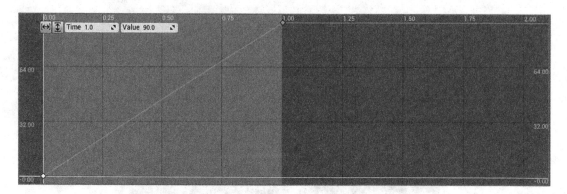

Figure 11-24. *The Timeline curve that defines the rotational movement of the door*

Now script the logic for the door.

1. Go back to the Event Graph.

2. Create a new variable of type Rotator.

3. Name it "InitialDoorRotation."

4. Drag it into the graph and create a Set Node.

5. Connect the execution pins of the Event BeginPlay Node and the Set Node.

6. Drag a wire out of the input pin of the Set Node and connect it to a GetActorRotation Node.

7. Connect the output execution pin of the Set Node to the Play pin of the Timeline Node.

8. Drag a wire out of the Update pin of the Timeline Node and connect it to a SetActorRotation Node.

9. Drag a wire out of the New Rotation pin and connect it to a Make Rotator Node.

10. Now drag a wire out of the output pin of the Set Node and connect that to a *Break* Rotator Node.

11. Between the Break Rotator Node and Make Rotator Node, add a Float - Float Node.

12. Connect the Z pin of the Break Rotator Node to the first input pin on the Float - Float Node.

13. Connect the Open Door Track pin on the Timeline Node to the second input pin of the Float - Float Node.

14. Connect the output pin of the Float - Float Node to the Z pin of the Make Rotator Node.

15. Finally, connect the X pin of the Break Rotator Node to the X pin of the Make Rotator Node and also connect the two Y pins together.

16. Compile and save the Blueprint.

This logic will cause the Timeline track to gradually change the rotation of the door around the Z-axis while keeping the rotation around the X and Y axes the same (Figure 11-25).

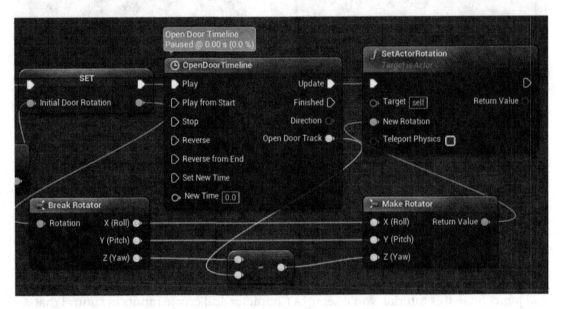

Figure 11-25. The Blueprint logic that will open the door

Now all that's left to do is add the door to the Level.

1. Go back to the Level Editor.

2. Drag a copy of the EndOfLevelDoor into the Viewport.

3. Change its Location to (45, 13677, 5).

4. Change its Rotation to (0, 0, -90).

Now, you can right-click the Viewport in front of the door and select "Play From Here" to test your work. As soon as the game starts, the door should open (Figure 11-26). If everything looks good, press Esc to exit out, then press Ctrl+Shift+S to save.

Figure 11-26. *The door should open as soon as the Level starts*

Tutorial 7 – Creating a Playable Character

Right now, your game is using the default pawn Actor which can fly around the Level, but you will want to use a character that is affected by gravity and can do things like run and jump. So in this tutorial, you'll set up a Character and create inputs to control that Character. You'll also add pause functionality to the game and the ability to open the end of Level door by pressing a button.

Creating a Game Mode

The first thing you need to do is create a Game Mode.

1. Go to the MyContent folder.

2. Click the Add New button and select Blueprint Class.

3. Select "Game Mode Base" as the parent class.

4. Rename it "MyGameMode."

Now you need to set this as the default Game Mode.

1. Go up to the Menu Bar, click Edit, and then Project Settings.

2. Select Maps & Modes from the list on the left.

3. Set the Default GameMode property to "MyGameMode" (Figure 11-27).

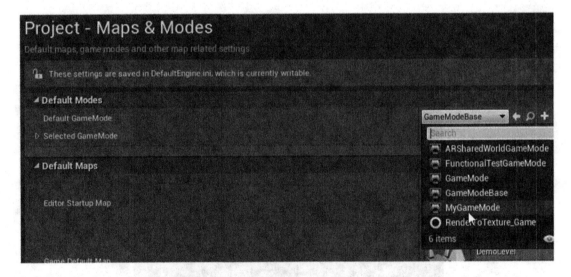

Figure 11-27. Set the Default GameMode property to "MyGameMode"

Creating the Character

Now you will create your Character. First, create the Blueprint file.

1. Go back to the Content Browser.

2. Click Add New and select Blueprint Class.

3. Select Character as the parent class.

4. Rename it "MyCharacter."

5. Double-click it to open it in the Blueprint Editor.

Now, set up the Components.

1. In the Components window, click the Add Component button and select Camera.

2. Change its Location to (20, 0, 60). This will give the Character a first-person perspective (Figure 11-28).

3. Select the CharacterMovement component.

4. In the Details Panel, under the Jumping/Falling category, change the Air Control from 0.05 to 0.5.

5. Compile, save, and close the Blueprint.

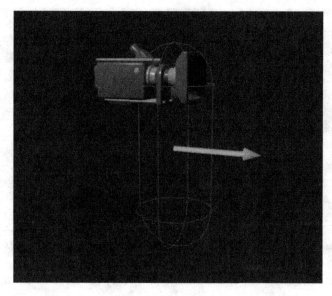

Figure 11-28.   *The Components of the Character Blueprint*

Now create the Player Controller.

1.   Click Add New and select Blueprint Class.

2.   Select Player Controller as the parent class.

3.   Rename it "MyPlayerController."

4.   Open the MyGameMode Blueprint.

5.   Set MyCharacter as the Default Pawn Class.

6.   Set MyPlayerController as the Player Controller Class.

7.   Compile, save, and close the Blueprint.

Now create the Action Mappings.

1.   Go to Edit ➤ Project Settings.

2.   Click Input from the menu on the left-hand side.

3.   Under the Bindings category, add a new Action Mapping.

4.   Name it "Jump."

5.   Map it to the Space Bar and the Gamepad Face Button Bottom.

6.   Add another Action Mapping.

7.   Name it "UseObject."

8.   Map it to the F key and the Gamepad Face Button Left.

9.   Add a third Action Mapping.

10.   Name it "Pause."

11.   Map it to the P key and the Gamepad Special Right button.

Now create the Axis Mappings.

1.   Now add an Axis Mapping.

2.   Name it "LookUpDown."

3.   Map it to Mouse Y and Gamepad Right Thumbstick Y-Axis.

4.   If you don't want the mouse to be inverted, change its Scale to -1.0.

5.   Create a second Axis Mapping.

6. Name this one "LookLeftRight."

7. Map it to Mouse *X* and the Gamepad Right Thumbstick *X-Axis*.

8. Create a third Axis Mapping.

9. Name it "MoveForwardBackward."

10. Map it to the W key, the S key, and the Gamepad Left Thumbstick Y-axis.

11. Change the Scale of the S key to -1.0.

12. Create a fourth Axis Mapping.

13. Name it "MoveLeftRight."

14. Map it to the D key, the A key, and the Gamepad Left Thumbstick X-Axis.

15. Change the Scale of the A key to -1.0.

When the input mappings are complete, they should look like Figure 11-29.

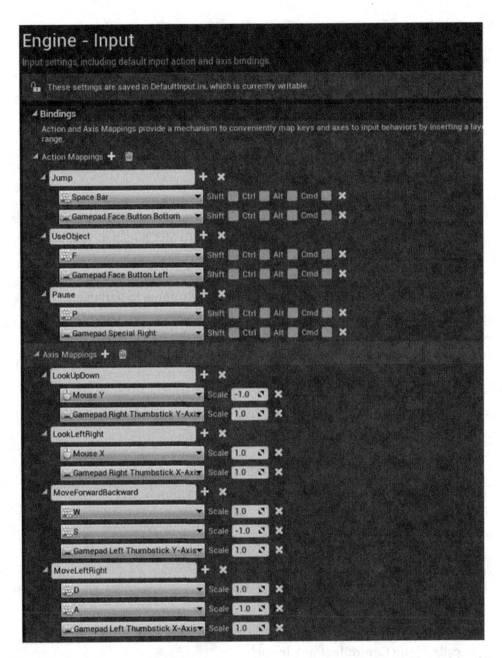

Figure 11-29. *When you're finished, your input mappings should look like this*

Now that the mappings are set up, you will script your Character's movements.

1. Double-click the MyPlayerController Blueprint to open it in the Blueprint Editor.

2. If you see a message at the top saying "This is a data only blueprint," then click the link at the end of that message that says "Open Full Blueprint Editor."

3. Go to the Event Graph.

4. Create a Get Player Character Node.

5. Drag off the Return Value pin and add a Cast To MyCharacter Node.

6. Connect the Event BeginPlay Node to the Cast Node.

7. Drag off the As My Character pin and select Promote to Variable.

8. Name the variable "MyCharacter."

Now go to an empty part of the graph to script the Character's jump functionality.

1. Right-click to open the Node Menu.

2. Type "Jump" and add the Jump Event that corresponds to the input mapping you made earlier.

3. Add a Get Node for the MyCharacter variable.

4. Drag a wire out of its pin and add a Jump Function Node.

5. Connect the Pressed pin of the Jump Event to the input execution pin of the Jump Function.

Now script the look movements.

1. Add the LookUpDown Event.

2. Drag another wire off the MyCharacter node, and add the function called "Add Controller Pitch Input."

3. Connect the execution pins between the two Nodes.

4. Connect the Axis Value pin of the LookUpDown Node to the Val pin of the Pitch Input Node.

5. Add the Node for the LookLeftRight mapping.

6. Drag another wire off the MyCharacter node, and add the function called "Add Controller *Yaw* Input."

7. Connect these Nodes the same way as the previous Nodes (Figure 11-30).

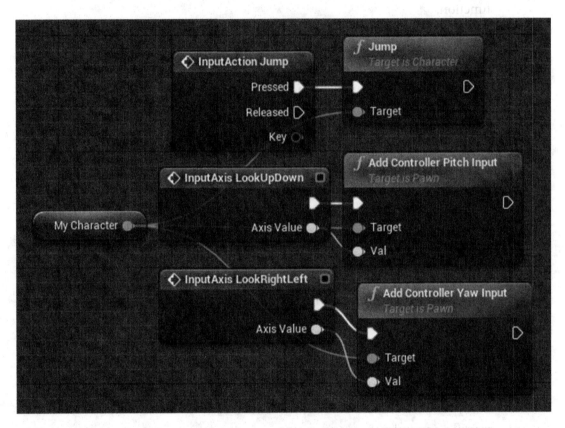

Figure 11-30. *The Character's jump and look functionality*

Now script the walking movements (Figure 11-31).

1. Move to an empty section of the graph.

2. Create another MyCharacter Get Node.

3. Add the Node for the MoveForwardBackward mapping.

4. Drag off the My Character Node and add a function called "Add Movement Input."

5. Connect the execution pins together.

6. Connect the Axis Value pin to the Scale Value pin.

7. Drag off the My Character Node again, and add the function "Get Control Rotation."

8. Drag off the Return Value pin, and add the "Get Forward Vector" function.

9. Connect the Return Value of that Node to the World Direction pin of the Add Movement Input Node.

10. Add the MoveLeftRight Node and another Add Movement Input Node and hook those two together.

11. Drag another wire from the Return Value pin of the Get Control Rotation Node and add a Get Right Vector Node.

12. Connect the Return Value of that Node to the World Direction pin of the new Add Movement Input Node.

13. Compile, save, and close the Blueprint.

14. Open the MyCharacter Blueprint.

15. In the Details Panel, under the Pawn category, check the "Use Controller Rotation Pitch" property.

16. Compile, save, and close the Blueprint.

17. Do a Save All.

18. Test your work to make sure the movement controls are working correctly.

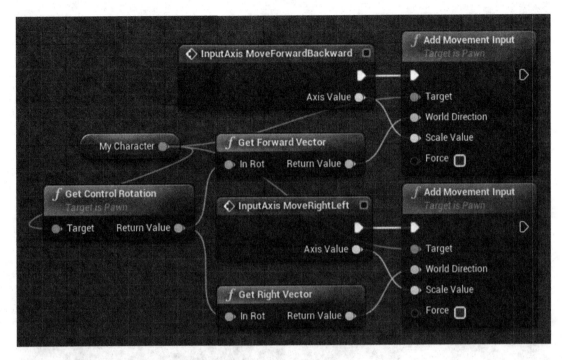

Figure 11-31. *The Character's walking functionality*

Adding Pause Functionality

Now you're going to add the pause functionality (Figure 11-32).

1. Open the MyPlayerController Blueprint.

2. Add the Pause Action Event you created.

3. Connect the Pressed pin to a Branch Node.

4. Connect the Condition pin of the Branch Node to an Is Game Paused Node.

5. Connect the True pin of the Branch Node to a Set Game Paused Node.

6. Leave the Paused pin set to False.

7. Connect the False pin of the Branch Node to another Set Game Paused Node.

331

8. Set the Paused pin of this Node to True.

9. Select the Pause Action Event Node, and in the Details Panel, set the Execute When Paused property to True. Without making this change, you would be able to pause the game but would not be able to unpause it.

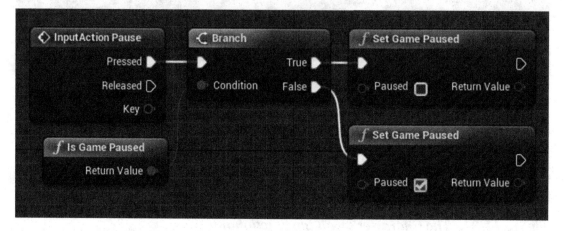

Figure 11-32. *The game's pause functionality*

Making the Door Open with a Button Press

Now you're going to change the behavior of the end of Level door so that, instead of opening automatically, it will open when the player presses a button.

1. Open the EndOfLevelDoor Blueprint.

2. In the Event Graph, disconnect the Event BeginPlay Node.

3. Replace it with the UseObject Action Event.

Right now, this still won't work because the Player Controller needs to give permission to the Door Blueprint to receive input.

1. Connect the Event BeginPlay Node to an Enable Input Node.

2. Add a Get Player Controller Node.

3. Connect its Return Value to the Player Controller pin of the Enable Input Node (Figure 11-33).

4. Compile, save, and close the Blueprint.

5. Simulate the game and test that the door will open when you press the F key.

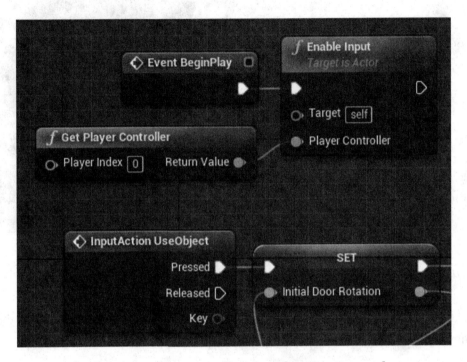

Figure 11-33. *The door should now only open after you press a key*

Tutorial 8 – Adding a Damage System

In this tutorial, you will be adding collision and damage functionality to your game.

First, surround the fire at the beginning of the Level with a Pain Causing Volume (Figure 11-34).

1. Go to the Volumes tab in the Modes Panel.

2. Drag a Pain Causing Volume into the Level.

3. Change its Location to (0, -420, 105).

4. Change its width in the X direction to 2500.

5. Under the Pain Causing Volume category, change its Damage Per Sec to 0.2.

Figure 11-34. *This Pain Causing Volume will apply Damage to Actors that overlap it*

Next, add a Trigger Volume under the Level, so that if the player falls through the gap, they will be killed instead of falling forever.

1. Go to the Basic tab.

2. Add a Box Trigger to the Level.

3. Name it "GameOverTriggerBox."

4. Change its Location to (0, 3150, -300).

5. Change its size, using the Box Extent property, to 2000 x 1000 x 50.

6. Open the MyGameMode Blueprint.

7. Right-click the Event Graph and search for Add Custom Event.

8. Name the custom event "EventGameOver."

9. Drag a wire from it and connect it to a Quit Game Node.

10. Compile, save, and close the Blueprint.

11. Go back to the Level Editor.

12. With the GameOverTriggerBox selected, open the Level Blueprint.

13. Add an OnActorBeginOverlap Node.

14. Drag a wire out of the Other Actor pin of the Overlap Node and create a Cast To MyCharacter Node.

15. Right-click the Event Graph and create a Get Game Mode Node.

16. Drag a wire out of the Return Value pin and create a Cast To MyGameMode Node.

17. Connect the Cast To MyCharacter Node to the Cast To MyGameMode Node.

18. Connect the Cast To MyGameMode Node to an EventGameOver Node that should be available now that you've created it.

19. Connect the As My Game Mode pin to the Target pin.

This EventGameOver Node (Figure 11-35) will *raise* the Game Over Event, and the Event Node in the MyGameMode Blueprint will fire whenever that event is raised.

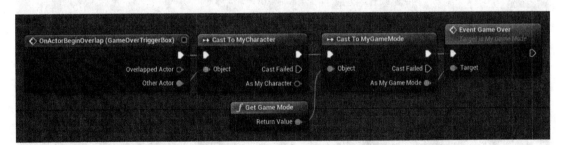

Figure 11-35. *This logic will raise the Game Over Event*

Now you will edit the EnemySpherea so that it will cause Damage to the Character if the Character collides with it (Figure 11-36).

1. Double-click the EnemySphere Blueprint to open it in the Blueprint Editor.

2. In the Components window, select the StaticMeshComponent.

3. In the Details Panel, under the Collision category, set the Generate Overlap Events property to True.

4. Set Collision Presets to OverlapAll.

5. In the Event Graph, look for the Event ActorBeginOverlap Node which should have been added by default.

6. Drag a wire out of its output execution pin and connect it to a Cast To MyCharacter Node.

7. Connect the Other Actor pin to the Object pin. This will ensure that this logic only occurs if the Actor that collided with the enemy is the player's Character and not some other Actor.

8. Drag a wire out of the first output execution pin of the Cast Node, and connect that to an Apply Damage Node.

9. Connect the "As My Character" pin to the Damaged Actor pin.

10. Set the Base Damage to 0.2.

11. Compile, save, and close the Blueprint.

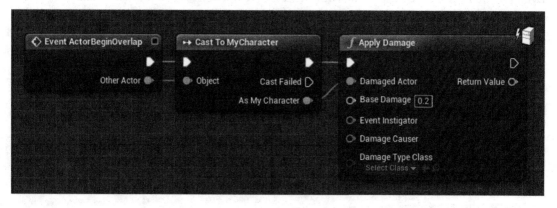

Figure 11-36. *This logic will apply Damage to the Character if it collides with an enemy sphere*

So now you have some Actors in the Level that will apply Damage to the Character, but you haven't yet defined what that means. First, you need to define a Health variable.

1. Open the MyCharacter Blueprint.

2. Create a new Float variable.

3. Name it "Health."

4. Compile the Blueprint.

5. Give the Health variable a Default Value of 1.0.

Now you can script the logic of what happens when the Character is damaged.

1. In the Event Graph, add an Event AnyDamage Node.

2. Connect that to a DoOnce Node.

3. Create a Set Node for the Health variable.

    Connect that with the DoOnce Node.

4. Create a Get Node for the Health variable.

5. Create a Float - Float Node.

6. Connect the Get Node to the first input of the Float - Float Node.

7. Connect the Damage pin of the Event AnyDamage Node to the
    second input of the Float - Float Node.

8. Connect the output of the Float - Float Node to the Set Node.

This logic receives a value representing incoming damage and subtracts that value from the current value of the Health variable and then updates the Health variable with the new value.

Now you will script the logic for what happens when the player loses all their health.

1. Connect the Set Node to a Branch Node.

2. Create a Float <= Float Node.

3. Connect the Float output pin of the Set Node to the first input of
    the Float <= Float Node.

4. Keep the second pin hardcoded to zero.

5. Connect the Boolean output of the Float <= Float Node to the
    Condition pin of the Branch Node.

6. Add a Get Game Mode Node to the graph.

7. Drag a wire out of the Return Value and create a Cast To
    MyGameMode Node.

8. Drag a wire out of the True pin of the Branch Node and connect that to the Cast To MyGameMode Node.

9. Drag a wire out of the first output execution pin of the Cast To MyGameMode Node and connect that to an Event Game Over Node.

10. Connect the As My Game Mode pin of the Cast Node to the Target pin of the Event Game Over Node.

Now, script the logic that will print the player's health to the screen.

1. Drag a wire out of the False pin of the Branch Node and connect that to a Print String Node.

2. Connect the Set Node's output pin to the In String pin of the Print String Node.

3. Connect the Print String Node to a Delay Node and set the duration to half a second.

4. Connect the Completed pin of the Delay Node to the Reset pin of the DoOnce Node.

5. Compile, save, and close the Blueprint.

6. Do a Save All.

So now, when the Character loses Health, the new Health will be printed to the screen, the Character will be invincible for a half-second after it receives Damage, and, if Health reaches zero, the Game Over Event will fire (Figure 11-37).

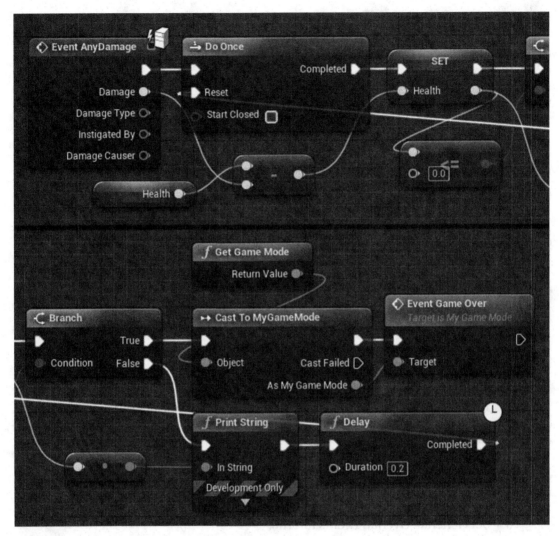

Figure 11-37. *This logic causes the Character to lose health when receiving Damage*

Tutorial 9 – Creating the Orb Item

In this tutorial, you're going to create the orbs that the player will need to collect to get through the final door. You're also going to make it so that the player will be required to be standing directly in front of the door to open it.

Creating the Orbs

First, create a variable to keep track of how many orbs the player has collected.

1. Open the MyCharacter Blueprint.

2. Create a new Byte variable.

3. Name it "OrbsCollected."

Now create the Blueprint file for the orb.

1. Go back to the Level Editor.

2. Go to the MyContent folder.

3. Click Add New and select Blueprint Class.

4. Choose StaticMeshActor as the parent class.

5. Name the new class "Orb."

6. Double-click it to open the Blueprint Editor.

Now construct the physical components of the Blueprint.

1. In the Components window, select the StaticMeshComponent.

2. In the Details Panel, assign its Static Mesh to Shape_Sphere.

3. Set its Material to M_Water_Ocean.

4. Change its Scale to 0.5 overall.

5. Set Generate Overlap Events to True.

6. Change the Collision Presets to OverlapAll.

7. Compile, save, and close the Blueprint.

Now you are going to script some behavior so that when the Character overlaps with an Orb Actor, the Orb will be destroyed and the OrbsCollected variable will be incremented by 1 (Figure 11-38).

1. Open the MyCharacter Blueprint.

2. Drag a wire off the Other Actor pin of the Event ActorBeginOverlap Node and connect it to a Cast To Orb Node.

3. Drag a wire out of the first output execution pin of the Cast To Orb Node and add a Set Orbs Collected Node.

4. Add a Byte + Byte Node to the graph.

5. Add a Get Node for the OrbsCollected variable.

6. Connect the Get Node to the first input of the Byte + Byte Node.

7. Keep the value of 1 for the second pin.

8. Connect the output of the Byte + Byte Node to the Orbs Collected pin of the Set Node.

9. Connect the Set Node to a Print String Node.

10. Connect the output of the Set Node to the In String pin.

11. Connect the Print String Node to a DestroyActor Node.

12. Drag a wire out of the As Orb pin of the Cast To Orb Node and connect it to the Target pin of the DestroyActor Node.

13. Compile, save, and close the Blueprint.

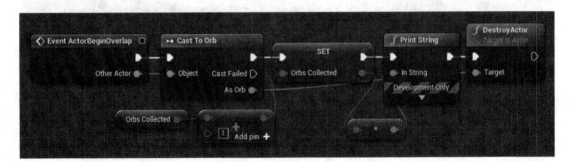

Figure 11-38. *The logic for collecting an orb*

You can now start adding Orbs to the Level.

1. Go back to the Level Editor.

2. Drag an instance of the Orb into the Level.

3. Set its Location to (0, -400, 400).

4. Drag another Orb into the Level.

341

5. Set its Location to (0, 3130, 450).

6. Add a third Orb.

7. Set its Location to (-1020, 12100, 60).

8. Rebuild the lighting.

So now, there should be an orb above the fire, between the two elevator platforms (Figure 11-39), and in the top-right house. When the player collides with an orb, it should disappear, increment the count of the orbs collected, and print that number to the screen.

Save your work and test that everything is working correctly.

Figure 11-39. *One of the orbs should be between the two elevator platforms*

Modifying the Door Behavior

Now you're going to make it so that instead of being able to open the end of Level door from anywhere, the player has to be standing directly in front of the door to open it.

First, add a Box Collision Component to the door that the Character will have to be overlapping in order to open the door (Figure 11-40).

1. Open the EndOfLevel Door Blueprint.

2. Go to the Viewport tab.

3. Select the Root Component in the Components window.

4. Click the Add Component button.

5. Add a Box Collision.

6. Name it "DoorCollision."

7. Set its Location to (50, -45, 100).

8. Change its size, using the Box Extent property, to 50 x 50 x 100.

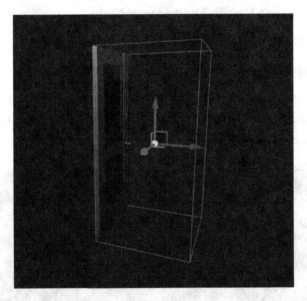

Figure 11-40. *The Box Collision Component*

Now, script the behavior that will prevent the Character from opening the door unless they are overlapping with the Box Collision (Figure 11-41).

1. Scroll down to the bottom of the Details Panel, to the Events category.

2. Click the green button next to On Component Begin Overlap to add that Event to the Event Graph.

3. Connect that Node to a Cast To MyCharacter Node.

4. Connect the Other Actor pin to the Object pin.

5. Find the section of the Event Graph where the Event BeginPlay Node is connected to an Enable Input Node.

6. Disconnect the Enable Input Node from the Event BeginPlay Node.

7. Select the Enable Input Node and the Get Player Controller Node.

8. Drag the two nodes to the right of the Cast To MyCharacter Node you created a few steps ago.

9. Connect the Cast Node to the Enable Input Node.

Now, create the same logic but with an *End*Overlap Node and a *Disable* Input Node.

1. Add an OnComponentEndOverlap Event.

2. Connect that to a Cast To MyCharacter Node.

3. Connect the Other Actor pin to the Object pin.

4. Connect the Cast Node to a Disable Input Node.

5. Drag another wire out of the Return Value of the Get Player Controller Node and connect that to the Player Controller pin of the Disable Input Node.

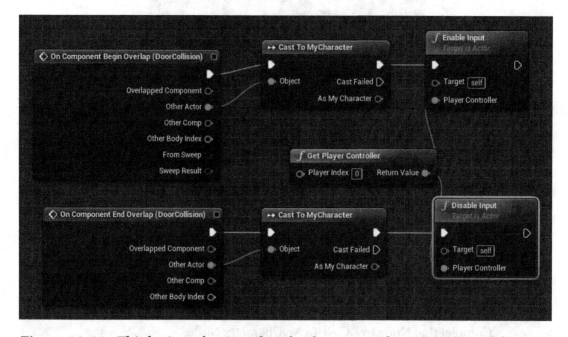

Figure 11-41. *This logic makes it so that the door can only accept input if the Character is currently overlapping with its Collision Box*

Tutorial 10 – Creating the HUD

In this tutorial, you will create a HUD for your player, so they can keep track of their health and the number of orbs they have collected.

1. Go to the MyContent folder.

2. Click the "Add New" button, scroll down to "User Interface," and select "Widget Blueprint."

3. Name the widget "MyHUD."

Before you design the layout, go ahead and attach this to the Character's display so you don't forget (Figure 11-42).

1. Open the MyCharacter Blueprint.

2. Drag a wire from the Event BeginPlay Node and add a Create Widget Node.

3. Set the Class to "MyHUD."

4. Drag a wire from the Create Widget Node and create an Add to Viewport Node.

5. Connect the Return Value pin of the Create Widget Node to the Target pin of the Add to Viewport Node.

Figure 11-42. *Adding the HUD to the Viewport*

Now, remove the Print String Nodes that are printing out the health and orbs collected variables, because you are about to improve that functionality with a proper HUD.

1. Find the Character's damage and health logic.

2. Delete the Print String Node and the conversion Node.

3. Connect the False pin of the Branch Node directly to the Delay Node.

4. Find the Character's orb collection logic.

5. Delete the Print String Node and the conversion Node.

6. Connect the Set Node directly to the DestroyActor Node.

7. Compile, save, and close the Blueprint.

Before designing the layout of the HUD, you need to get a reference to your Character so that you can access its variables (Figure 11-43).

1. Double-click the MyHUD Widget to open it in the Widget Editor.

2. In the upper-right of the Widget Editor, switch to the Graph tab.

3. Open the Node Menu.

4. Uncheck the Context Sensitive checkbox and add a Get Player Character function.

5. Drag a wire from the Return Value, and connect it to a Cast To MyCharacter Node.

6. Connect the Event Construct Node to the Cast Node.

7. Drag a wire from the As My Character pin, recheck Context Sensitive, then click "Promote to Variable."

8. Name the new variable "MyCharacterReference."

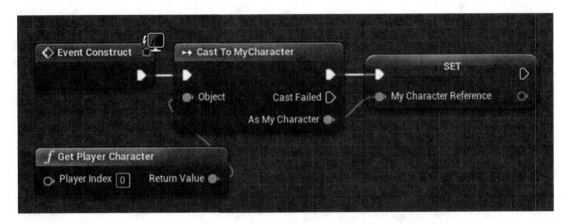

Figure 11-43. *Getting a reference to the Character*

Now you can design the layout of the HUD. First, create the display that shows the number of orbs the player has collected.

1. Go back to the Designer tab.

2. Using the Panel category of the Palette window, add a Horizontal Box as a child of the Canvas Panel.

3. Place it in the upper-left corner.

4. Set its Size to Content property to True.

5. Add a Text Widget as a child of the Horizontal Box.

6. Change its Font to size 36.

7. Change its Shadow Offset to 5 x 5.

8. Change the Alpha transparency of its Shadow Color to 1.0.

9. Copy the Text Widget and paste two copies, so that the Horizontal Box now has three Text children.

10. Change the Text of the left-most Text Widget to "Orbs " with a space after it.

11. Change the Text of the middle Text Widget to "0."

12. Change the Text of the right-most Text Widget to " / 3."

Now, script some logic that will cause the display to update when an orb is collected.

1. Select the middle Text Widget.

2. Click the Bind button next to the Text property.

Because the variable you want to bind is a Byte and this property is Text, you won't be able to bind it directly and will have to add a conversion to the Bind function (Figure 11-44).

1. Select "Create Binding" from the menu that appears.

2. Drag the MyCharacterReference into the graph and create a Get Node.

3. Drag a wire out of the Get Node and get the Orbs Collected variable by adding a Get Orbs Collected Node.

4. Connect the Orbs Collected pin to the Return Value pin of the Return Node. A conversion Node will be created automatically.

5. Compile and save the widget.

6. Go back to the Designer tab.

So now the middle Text Widget will always display whatever value is in the Orbs Collected variable at that moment.

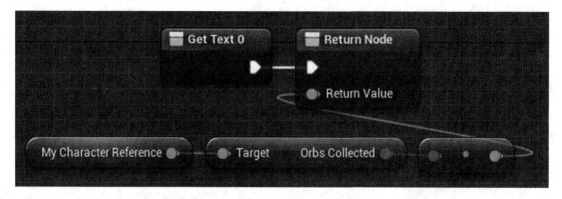

Figure 11-44. *Binding the Orbs Collected variable to a Text Widget*

Now you'll build a Progress Bar to keep track of the player's health.

1. Drag a Progress Bar from the Palette window to the upper-right corner of the Canvas Panel.

2. Anchor it to the top-right corner.

3. Change its Size to 600 x 50.

4. Change its Fill Color and Opacity to green.

5. Bind its Percent property to the Character's Health variable.

6. Drag another Text Widget into the layout as a child of the Canvas Panel.

7. Anchor it to the top-right corner.

8. Set its Size to Content property to True.

9. Change its Font to size 36.

10. Change its Shadow Offset to 5 x 5.

11. Change the Alpha transparency of its Shadow Color to 1.0.

12. Change its text to "Health."

13. Position it to the left of the Progress Bar.

14. Compile and save the widget.

The layout of the HUD widget should look similar to Figure 11-45. Now, simulate the game to test your work and make sure the HUD is working as intended.

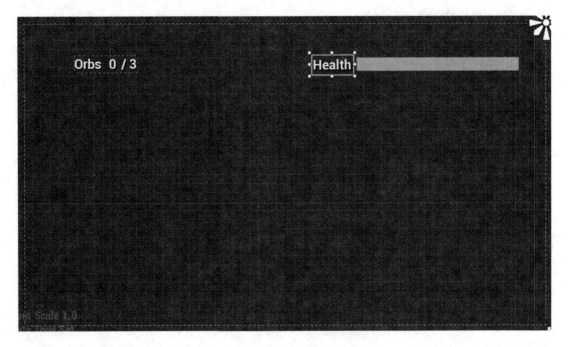

Figure 11-45. *The layout of the HUD widget*

Tutorial 11 – Damage Tint and Collect Item Tint

In this tutorial, you're going to add some functionality so that when the player receives damage, the screen will briefly flash red, and when the player collects an orb, the screen will briefly flash blue.

First, add some Boolean variables to the MyCharacter Blueprint that will be used to store whether or not that color should be active at that time.

1. Open the MyCharacter Blueprint.

2. Add a new Boolean variable.

3. Name it "ShowDamageTint."

4. Add another Boolean variable.

5. Name it "ShowOrbCollectedTint."

Now, add some logic that will set the ShowDamageTint variable to True for a fraction of a second after the Character receives Damage, and then set it back to False (Figure 11-46).

1. In the Event Graph, find the Damage logic.

2. Delete the wire connecting the False pin of the Branch Node to the Delay Node.

3. Drag the ShowDamageTint variable into the graph and create a Set Node.

4. Set the Show Damage Tint pin to True.

5. Connect the False pin of the Branch Node to the Set Node.

6. Connect the Set Node to a new Delay Node.

7. Set the duration of that Node to 0.3.

8. Connect that Delay Node to another Set Node for the ShowDamageTint variable, but this time, keep the pin set to False.

9. Connect this Set Node to the original Delay Node.

10. Change its Duration to 0.2, so that there is still an overall delay of half a second before the DoOnce Node gets reset.

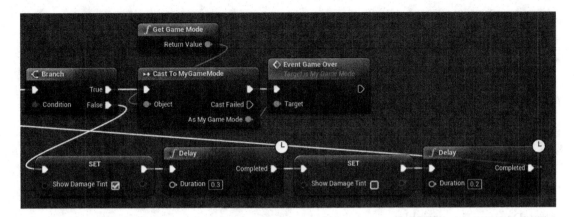

Figure 11-46. *This logic briefly sets the ShowDamageTint variable to True when the player takes Damage*

Now, add some logic that will set the ShowOrbCollectedTint variable to True for a fraction of a second after the Character collects an orb, and then set it back to False (Figure 11-47).

1. Find the orb collection logic.

2. Create a Set Show Orb Collected Tint Node.

3. Set its Boolean pin to True.

4. Break the link between the Set Orbs Collected Node and the DestroyActor Node.

5. Connect the Set Orbs Collected Node to the Set Show Orb Collected Tint Node.

6. Connect the Set Show Orb Collected Tint Node to a Delay Node.

7. Set its Duration to 0.3 seconds.

8. Create another Set Show Orb Collected Tint Node.

9. Leave this Node's Boolean pin set to False.

10. Connect the Delay Node to the Set Show Orb Node.

11. Connect the Set Show Orb Node to the DestroyActor Node.

12. Compile, save, and close the Blueprint.

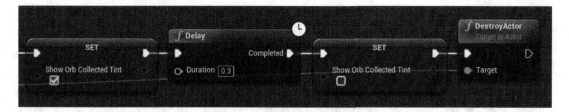

Figure 11-47. *This logic briefly sets the ShowOrbCollectedTint variable to True when the player collects an orb*

Now, add a red tint to the HUD and bind its Visibility property to the value of the ShowDamageTint variable.

1. Open the MyHUD Widget.

2. Add a Border Widget as a child of the Canvas Panel.

3. Name it "DamageTint."

4. Set the Tint of the Brush property in the Appearance category.

5. Set the color to red.

6. Set the Alpha transparency to 0.3.

7. Increase the size of the Border Widget until it covers the entire Canvas Panel.

8. Anchor it to all four corners of the screen.

9. Under the Behavior category, click the Bind button next to the Visibility property and select "Create Binding."

10. Create a Get Node for the MyCharacterReference variable.

11. Drag a wire out of it and add a Get Show Damage Tint Node.

12. Drag a wire out of that and connect it to a Branch Node.

13. Connect the Entry Node to the input execution pin of the Branch Node.

14. Connect the True pin of the Branch Node to the Return Node.

15. Use Ctrl+C and Ctrl+V to copy and paste the Return Node.

16. On the copy, change the Return Value to Collapsed.

17. Connect the False pin of the Branch Node to the second Return Node.

To summarize, the logic shown in Figure 11-48 is what is bound to the Visibility property of the red Border Panel you created. During every tick of gameplay, this logic will be run to see what value the Visibility property should be set to. For the few seconds that the ShowDamageTint variable is True, this will route the flow of execution through the True pin of the Branch Node, and this will return a value of "Visible" to the Visibility property, which causes the red Border Panel to show. The rest of the time, when ShowDamageTint is False, a value of "Collapsed" is returned to the Visibility property, which will hide the red Border Panel.

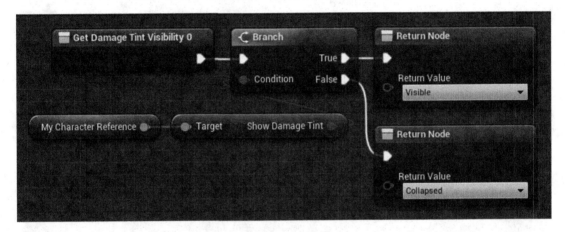

Figure 11-48. *This logic will cause the DamageTint Border Widget to be visible when the ShowDamageTint variable is True*

Now do the same thing again but for the Orb tint. Add a blue tint to the HUD and bind its Visibility property to the value of the ShowOrbCollectedTint variable (Figure 11-49).

1. Go to the Designer.

2. Add another Border Widget as a child of the Canvas Panel.

3. Name it "OrbCollectedTint."

4. Set the Tint of the Brush property in the Appearance category.

5. Set the color to blue.

6. Set the Alpha transparency to 0.3.

7. Increase its size until it covers the entire Canvas Panel.

8. Anchor it to all four corners of the screen.

9. Under the Behavior category, click the Bind button next to the Visibility property and select "Create Binding."

10. Create a Get Node for the MyCharacterReference variable.

11. Drag a wire out of it and add a Get Show Orb Collected Tint Node.

12. Drag a wire out of that and connect it to a Branch Node.

13. Connect the Entry Node to the input execution pin of the Branch Node.

14. Connect the True pin of the Branch Node to the Return Node.

15. Use Ctrl+C and Ctrl+V to copy and paste the Return Node.

16. On the copy, change the Return Value to Collapsed.

17. Connect the False pin of the Branch Node to the second Return Node.

18. Compile, save, and close the Blueprint.

19. Do a Save All.

Simulate the game and test your work, making sure that the screen flashes red when you take damage (Figure 11-50) and flashes blue when you collect an orb.

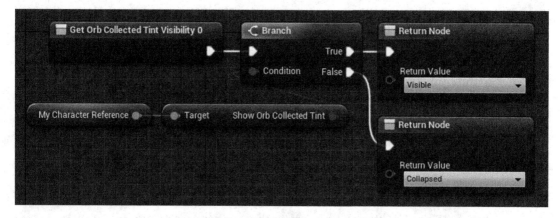

Figure 11-49. *This logic will cause the OrbCollectedTint Border Widget to be visible when the ShowOrbCollectedTint variable is True*

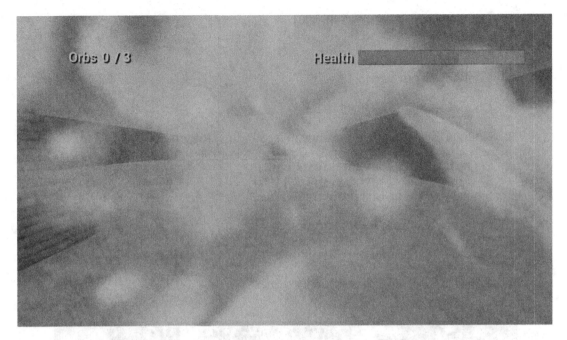

Figure 11-50. *The screen should flash red when taking Damage*

Tutorial 12 – Restricting the Opening of the Door

In this tutorial, you will modify the end of Level door logic so that the player can only open the door once they have collected all three orbs. You will also display a message in the HUD to inform the player of this rule when they get close to the door.

First, create a variable that can be used to store the text that will be displayed on the screen.

1. Open the MyCharacter Blueprint.

2. Add a new variable of type Text.

3. Name it "ScreenMessage."

4. Compile, save, and close the Blueprint.

Now, modify the HUD so that it can display messages on the screen (Figure 11-51).

1. Open the MyHUD Widget.

2. Add a Text Widget to the Canvas Panel.

3. Anchor it to the middle of the screen.

4. Change its Position to (-500, 300).

5. Change its Size to 1000 x 160.

6. Change its Font size to 48.

7. Change its Shadow Offset to 5 x 5.

8. Change the Alpha transparency of its Shadow Color to 1.0.

9. Set its Justification to Align Text Center.

10. Set its Auto Wrap Text property to True.

11. Erase the text from its Text property.

12. Bind the Text property to MyCharacter's Screen Message variable.

13. Compile, save, and close the Blueprint.

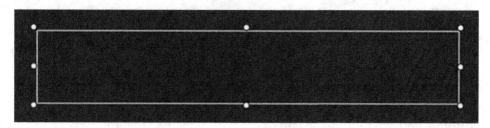

Figure 11-51. *This Text Widget will be used to display messages on the screen*

Now, change the logic of the EndOfLevelDoor so that the player must have all the orbs collected in order to open it, and add a message to the screen informing them of this (Figure 11-52).

1. Open the EndOfLevelDoor Blueprint.

2. Go to the overlap logic in the Event Graph.

3. Break the connections between the Cast Nodes and the Enable and Disable Input Nodes.

4. Move the Input Nodes and the Get Player Controller Node off to the right a bit.

5. Drag a wire from the Cast Node that is connected to the *Begin*Overlap Node.

6. Connect that to a Branch Node.

7. Drag a wire from the As My Character pin and add a Get Node for the Orbs Collected variable.

8. Drag a wire from the Get Orbs Collected Node and connect it to an Equal (Byte) Node.

9. Hardcode a value of 3 for the second pin of the Equal Node.

10. Connect the Boolean output pin of the Equal Node to the Condition pin of the Branch Node.

11. Drag another wire out of the As My Character pin of the Cast Node and add a Set Screen Message Node.

12. Do this a second time so that there are *two* Set Nodes.

13. Connect the True pin of the Branch Node to one of the Set Nodes.

14. Change the message of this Set Node to "Press F to open the door."

15. Connect the False pin of the Branch Node to the other Set Node and change its message to "You must collect all 3 orbs to unlock this door."

16. Connect the first Set Node to the Enable Input Node.

17. Go down to the Cast Node connected to the *End*Overlap Node.

18. Drag a wire out of its As My Character pin and add a Set Screen Message Node.

19. Connect the execution pins of the two Nodes.

20. Leave the Screen Message pin blank so that any message still on the screen gets erased.

21. Connect the Set Node to the Disable Input Node.

22. Compile, save, and close the Blueprint.

So now, when the Character overlaps with the DoorCollision volume, it will check to see if the player has collected all the orbs. If the player has collected the orbs, it will change the Screen Message variable to a message instructing the player how to open the door, which will then get displayed in the HUD. It will also enable input on the door which will allow the player to open the door when they press the F key. If the player has not collected all the orbs, they will see a message explaining what they need to do.

If the player backs away from the door, and thus no longer overlaps with the DoorCollision volume, the screen message is erased and input is disabled again because the player is no longer close enough to open the door.

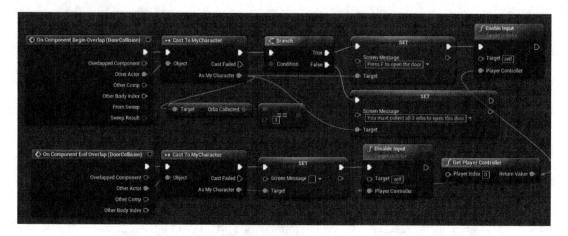

Figure 11-52. *This logic will require the player to have collected all three orbs before they will be allowed to open the door*

Simulate the game and test that everything works as expected.

Tutorial 13 – Adding a Pause Menu

In this tutorial, you will create a simple pause menu to display when the game is paused.
First, create the widget file.

1. Go to the MyContent folder.

2. Click the "Add New" button, scroll down to "User Interface," and select "Widget Blueprint."

3. Name the widget "PauseMenu."

4. Double-click it to open it in the Widget Editor.

Now, design the layout (Figure 11-53).

1. Add a Text Widget to the Canvas Panel.

2. Anchor it to the middle of the screen.

3. Set the Size to Content property to True.

4. Change its Font size to 48.

5. Change its Shadow Offset to 5 x 5.

6. Change the Alpha transparency of its Shadow Color to 1.0.

7. Change its Text to "Paused."

8. Position it in the middle of the screen.

9. Compile, save, and close the widget.

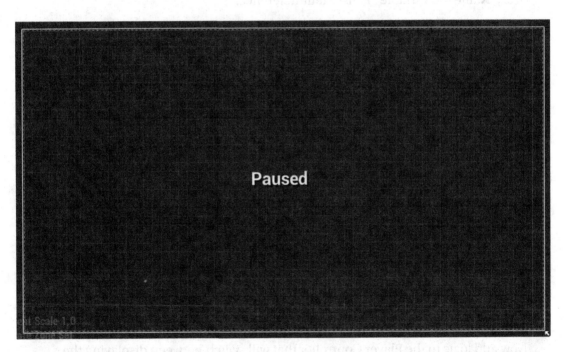

Figure 11-53. *The layout of the pause menu is simply the word "Paused" without any of the data that the HUD provides*

Now, add references to the MyHUD Widget and PauseMenu Widget to MyCharacter (Figure 11-54).

1.   Open the MyCharacter Blueprint.

2.   Find the Create My HUD Widget Node.

3.   Disconnect it from the Add to Viewport Node.

4.   Drag a wire out of the Return Value pin and select Promote to Variable.

5.   Name the variable "MyHUDReference."

6.   Connect both output pins of the Set Node to the respective input pins on the Add to Viewport Node.

7.   Connect the Add to Viewport Node to another Create Widget Node.

8.   Set its Class pin to PauseMenu.

9.   Drag a wire from the Return Value pin and select Promote to Variable.

10.   Name the variable "PauseMenuReference."

11.   Compile, save, and close the Blueprint.

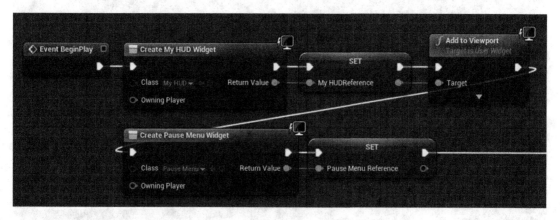

Figure 11-54. *The HUD and pause menu references*

Now add logic to the Player Controller that will switch between displaying the MyHUD Widget and the PauseMenu Widget depending upon whether or not the game is paused (Figure 11-55).

1.   Open MyPlayerController.

2.   Find the pause logic.

3. Disconnect the Branch Node from the Set Game Paused Nodes and move those two Nodes to the right.

4. Drag a copy of MyCharacter into the graph and create a Get Node.

5. Drag a wire out of the Get Node and create a Get Node for the MyHUDReference.

6. Drag another wire out of the Get My Character Node and create a Get Node for the PauseMenuReference.

7. Drag a wire from the PauseMenuReference and connect it to a Remove From Parent Node.

8. Connect the True pin of the Branch Node to the Remove From Parent Node.

9. Drag a wire from the MyHUDReference and connect it to an Add to Viewport Node.

10. Connect the Remove From Parent Node to the Add to Viewport Node.

11. Connect the Add to Viewport Node to the Set Game Paused Node where Paused is False.

12. Drag a wire from the MyHUDReference and connect it to a Remove From Parent Node.

13. Connect the False pin of the Branch Node to the Remove From Parent Node.

14. Drag a wire from the PauseMenuReference and connect it to an Add to Viewport Node.

15. Connect the Remove From Parent Node to the Add to Viewport Node.

16. Connect the Add to Viewport Node to the Set Game Paused Node where Paused is True.

17. Compile, save, and close the Blueprint.

So now, if the pause button is pressed when the game is unpaused, the HUD will be removed from the screen, the pause menu will be added to the screen, and the game will be paused. Conversely, if the player presses the pause button while the game *is* paused, the pause menu widget will be removed from the screen, the regular HUD will be added back to the screen, and the game will be unpaused.

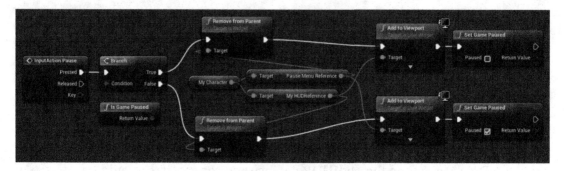

Figure 11-55. *This logic switches between the HUD and pause menu*

Simulate the game and test your work.

Tutorial 14 – Game Over and Win Screen Menus

In this tutorial, you will create a game over menu, for when the player dies, and a win screen menu for when they beat the game.

Adding a Game Over Menu

First, create the widget file for the game over menu.

1. Go to the MyContent folder.

2. Click the "Add New" button, scroll down to "User Interface," and select "Widget Blueprint."

3. Name the widget "GameOverMenu."

4. Double-click it to open it in the Widget Editor.

Now, design the layout of the game over menu (Figure 11-56). First, add a Vertical Box that will house the text and buttons of the menu.

1. Go to the Panel category of the Palette window.

2. Drag a Vertical Box onto the Canvas Panel.

3. Anchor it to the middle.

4. Set its position to (-520, -280).

5. Set its size to 1000 x 600.

Next, add the text "GAME OVER" to the screen.

1. Add a Text Widget as a child of the Vertical Box.

2. Set its Bottom Padding to 60.

3. Set its Horizontal Alignment to Horizontally Align Center.

4. Change its text to "GAME OVER" in all caps.

5. Change its Font size to 100.

6. Change its Shadow Offset to 10 x 10.

7. Change the Alpha transparency of its Shadow Color to 1.0.

Next, add a "Restart Level" button to the menu.

1. Add a Button Widget as a child of the Vertical Box and name it "ButtonRestartLevel."

2. Set its Bottom Padding to 60.

3. Change the Alpha transparency of its Background Color to 0.

4. Add a Text Widget as a child of the Button Widget.

5. Change its Text to "Restart Level."

6. Change its Color to black.

7. Change its Font size to 80.

8. Change its Shadow Offset to 2 x 2.

9. Change its Shadow Color to white.

10. Change the Alpha transparency of its Shadow Color to 1.0.

Next, add a "Quit" button to the menu.

1. Add another Button Widget as a child of the Vertical Box.

2. Name it "ButtonQuit."

3. Change the Alpha transparency of its Background Color to 0.

4. Add a Text Widget as a child of the Button Widget.

5. Change its Text to "Quit."

6. Change its Color to black.

7. Change its Font size to 80.

8. Change its Shadow Offset to 2 x 2.

9. Change its Shadow Color to white.

10. Change the Alpha transparency of its Shadow Color to 1.0.

Add a red tint to the menu.

1. Add a Border Widget as a child of the Canvas Panel.

2. Anchor it to the four corners.

3. Expand it until it fills the Canvas Panel.

4. Edit the Tint of the Brush property.

5. Change the color to red.

6. Change the Alpha transparency to 0.3.

7. Click the Vertical Box again and change its ZOrder to 1.

This last step will cause the Vertical Box to get placed on a layer above the Border Widget which still has the default ZOrder of 0. This is important because if the Border Widget gets placed above the Vertical Box that contains all the buttons, this will block input from getting through from the mouse to the Button Widgets.

Figure 11-56. *The layout of the game over menu*

Now you're going to define some logic for when these buttons are clicked (Figure 11-57).

1. Select ButtonRestartLevel.

2. In the Details Panel, scroll down to the Events category.

3. Click the green button next to OnClicked.

4. Drag a wire off the OnClicked Event Node and connect it to a Set Input Mode Game Only Node. This Node will give us control over our Character again, which we will be taking away during the Game Over Event.

5. Add a Get Player Controller Node to the graph.

6. Connect its Return Value to the Player Controller pin of the Set Input Node.

7. Drag a wire out of the Set Input Node and connect it to an Open Level Node.

8. Hardcode "DemoLevel" into the Level Name pin.

9. Go to the Designer.

10. Select ButtonQuit.

11. Click the green button next to its OnClicked property.

12. Drag a wire off that OnClicked Event Node and connect it to a Quit Game Node.

13. Compile, save, and close the Blueprint.

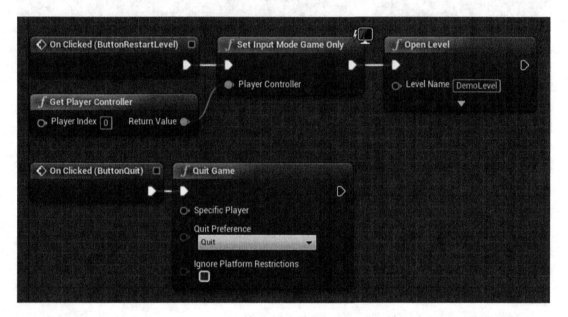

Figure 11-57. *These Nodes define what happens when the buttons of the game over menu are pressed*

Now, create a reference to the game over menu.

1. Open the MyCharacter Blueprint.

2. Find the Set Node for the Pause Menu Reference.

3. Connect that Node to a Create Widget Node.

4. Set its Class to "GameOverMenu."

5. Drag a wire out of the Return Value pin and select Promote to Variable.

6. Name the variable "GameOverMenuReference."

7. Compile, save, and close the Blueprint.

Now, add logic that will pause the game, display the game over menu, and configure the menu controls when the player dies (Figure 11-58).

1. Open the MyGameMode Blueprint.

2. Find the EventGameOver Node.

3. Delete the Quit Game Node that it's connected to.

4. Add a Get Player Character Node to the graph.

5. Drag a wire out of the Return Value pin and create a Cast To MyCharacter Node.

6. Connect the EventGameOver Node to the Cast To MyCharacter Node.

7. Drag a wire out of the As My Character Node and create a Get MyHUDReference Node.

8. Drag another wire out of the As My Character Node and create a Get GameOverMenuReference Node.

9. Drag a wire out of the MyHUDReference Node and connect it to a Remove From Parent Node.

10. Connect the Cast To MyCharacter Node to the Remove From Parent Node.

11. Drag a wire out of the Game Over Menu Reference Node and connect it to an Add to Viewport Node.

12. Connect the Remove From Parent Node to the Add to Viewport Node.

13. Drag a wire out of the Add to Viewport Node and connect it to a Set Input Mode UI Only Node. This Node will make it so that only User Interface objects can receive input, and the player will no longer be able to control the Character.

14. Connect the Game Over Menu Reference to the In Widget to Focus pin of the Set Input Node.

15. Add a Get Player Controller Node to the graph and connect its Return Value to the Player Controller pin of the Set Input Node.

16. Drag a wire out of the Set Input Node, uncheck Context Sensitive, and add a Set Show Mouse Cursor Node.

17. Set the Show Mouse Cursor pin to True.

18. Drag another wire out of the Get Player Controller Node and connect it to the Target pin of the Set Show Mouse Cursor Node.

19. Drag a wire out of the Set Show Mouse Cursor Node and connect it to a Set Game Paused Node.

20. Set the Paused pin to True.

21. Compile, save, and close the Blueprint.

22. Simulate the game to test your logic.

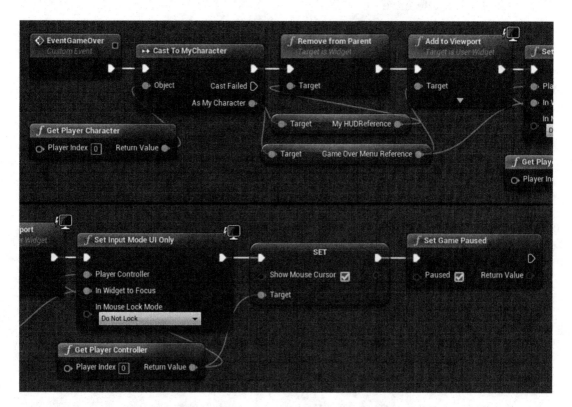

Figure 11-58. *This is the logic that occurs when the player dies*

Adding a Win Screen Menu

Now create the win screen. The win screen will be very similar to the game over menu, so you can start by copying and pasting the GameOverMenu Widget.

1. Select the GameOverMenu Widget in the Content Browser.

2. Press Ctrl+C to copy it.

3. Press Ctrl+V to paste a copy of it.

4. Rename the copy "WinScreenMenu."

5. Double-click it to open it in the Widget Editor.

Now, change the title of the menu from "GAME OVER" to "YOU WIN!"

1. Delete the Border Widget.

2. Select the "GAME OVER" text.

3. Change it to "YOU WIN!"

4. Compile, save, and close the widget.

Now, create a reference to the win screen menu (Figure 11-59).

1. Open the MyCharacter Blueprint.

2. Find the Set Game Over Menu Reference Node.

3. Drag a wire out of it and connect it to a Create Widget Node.

4. Set the Class pin to WinScreenMenu.

5. Drag a wire out of the Return Value and select "Promote to Variable."

6. Name the variable "WinScreenMenuReference."

7. Compile, save, and close the Blueprint.

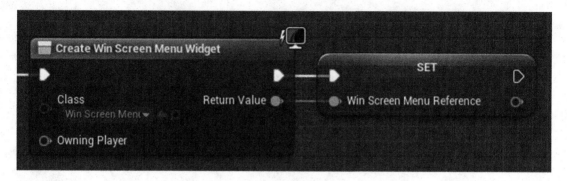

Figure 11-59. The reference to the win screen menu

Now, add the logic that will occur when the player wins the game (Figure 11-60).

1. Open the MyGameMode Blueprint.

2. Find the EventGameOver logic.

3. Zoom out until you can see all of it at once.

4. Left-click, drag the mouse, and select all of the Nodes.

5. Press Ctrl+C, then Ctrl+V to copy and paste the Nodes.

6. Select the copied Event Node and rename it "EventWinGame."

7. Replace the Game Over Menu Reference Node with a WinScreenMenuReference Node.

8. Compile, save, and close the Blueprint.

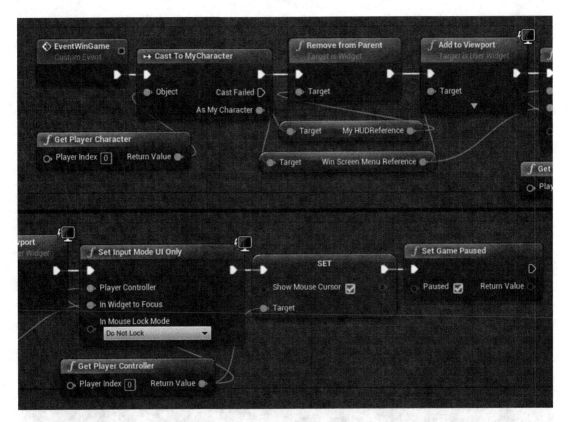

Figure 11-60. *This is the logic that occurs when the player wins the game*

Now, add a Box Trigger to the Level that will raise an event when the Character overlaps with it, indicating that the player has won the game (Figure 11-61).

1. Go to the end of the Level.

2. Add a Box Trigger behind the door.

3. Name it "WinningTriggerBox."

4. Change its Location to (0, 13800, 110).

5. Change its Size to 50 x 40 x 100.

6. With it selected, open the Level Blueprint.

7. Add an OnActorBeginOverlap Node.

8. Drag a wire out of the Other Actor pin and connect it to a Cast To MyCharacter Node.

9. Create a Get Game Mode Node.

10. Drag a wire out of the Return Value pin and create a Cast To MyGameMode Node.

11. Connect the Cast To MyCharacter Node to the Cast To MyGameMode Node.

12. Connect the Cast To MyGameMode Node to an Event Win Game Node.

13. Connect the As My Game Mode pin to the Target pin.

14. Compile and close the Blueprint.

15. Do a Save All.

16. Simulate the game and test your logic.

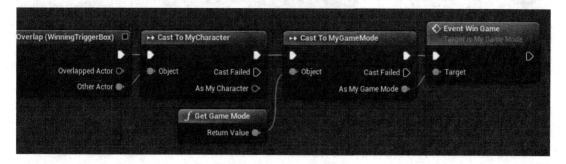

Figure 11-61. *These Nodes will raise an event when the player wins the game*

Tutorial 15 – Adding Audio to the Game

In this tutorial, you will be adding audio to your Level. You will add some outdoor noises, like wind and birds chirping, and some fire noises. You'll also add some background music that will start playing once the player reaches a certain point in the Level.

First, add the Starter_Background_Cue to the Level. This Sound Cue combines a couple of different wind sounds and one of birds and is good for creating background noise for outdoor environments (Figure 11-62).

1.   Go to the Audio folder in the Starter Content.

2.   Double-click the Starter_Background_Cue to open it in the Sound
     Cue Editor.

3.   Look in the Details Panel and notice that it doesn't have any
     Attenuation, so it will be heard at the same volume at any point
     throughout the Level.

4.   Close the Sound Cue Editor.

5.   Drag the Starter_Background_Cue into the Level. Because it doesn't
     have any Attenuation, it doesn't matter where in the Level you place it.

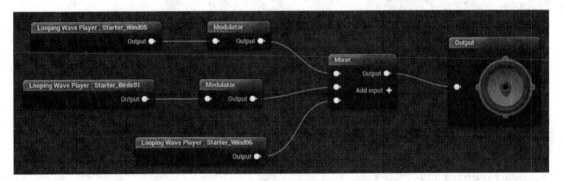

Figure 11-62. *The Starter_Background_Cue combines a few different sounds*

Now you will create some sound for the row of fire.

1.   Double-click the Fire01_Cue.

2.   Notice that, unlike the Starter_Background_Cue, this cue has
     Attenuation settings, so wherever you place it is where it will be
     heard the loudest.

3.   Close the Sound Cue Editor.

4.   Drag the Fire01_Cue into the Level and place it in the middle of
     the fire between the two platforms (Figure 11-63).

5.   Zoom out until you can see the area where the sound will be heard
     at full volume and the area where the sound will gradually fall off.

6. Hold down the Alt key.

7. Drag out two copies of the Fire Cue and place them on either side
    of the original, equidistant from the wall.

Figure 11-63. *A Fire Cue Actor inside the fire*

Now add a Box Trigger to the Level that will be triggered once the player crosses the
large gap.

1. Go to the Basic tab in the Modes Panel.

2. Add a Box Trigger to the Level.

3. Name it "MusicTriggerBox."

4. Change its Location to (0, 4750, 45).

5. Change its Size to 1250 x 1000 x 40. The reason you're making it
    so large is because you can't be sure how far the player will jump
    from the elevated platform.

Now add some background music to the game that will start playing once the player
crosses the gap in the Level and overlaps with the Box Trigger.

1. With the Box Trigger still selected, open the Level Blueprint.

2. Right-click the graph to open the Node Menu.

3. Expand the Add Event menu, expand the Collision category, and add an On Actor Begin Overlap Node.

4. Drag a wire out of the Other Actor pin of the Overlap Node.

5. Connect that to a Cast To MyCharacter Node. This will ensure that this logic only occurs if it is the *Character* that overlaps with the trigger and not another Actor such as one of the enemies.

6. Connect the Cast Node to a DoOnce Node.

7. Connect the DoOnce Node to a Play Sound 2D Node.

8. Set the Sound pin to the Starter_Music_Cue.

This logic, shown in Figure 11-64, will play the background music if the Character overlaps with the trigger and, by using a DoOnce Node, ensures that it won't try to play another copy if the Character overlaps a second time.

Figure 11-64. *This logic will play music when the player reaches a certain point in the Level*

Now add the fire sound to the enemy spheres.

1. Open the EnemySphere Blueprint.

2. Go to the Viewport tab.

3. Click the Add Component button.

4. Add an Audio Component.

5. Name it "FireSound."

6. Change its Sound property to the Fire01_Cue.

7. Compile, save, and close the Blueprint.

8. Simulate the game and test your work.

Congratulations! The tutorial game is now complete! In the final tutorial, you will package and export your game so that it can be played outside of the Editor.

Tutorial 16 – Packaging the Game

In this tutorial, you will package and export the demo game so that it can be played outside of the Editor.

Before you can export, you need to prepare the game for packaging. First, set the game's thumbnail, description, name, and title bar (Figure 11-65).

1. Go to Edit ➤ Project Settings.

2. Click the Description page in the menu on the left.

3. Set the Project Thumbnail to a 192 x 192 image or use the auto-generated one.

4. Add a short description of the game to the Description property.

5. Use the Project Name property to give the project a name such as "DemoProject."

6. In the Displayed category, use the Project Displayed Title property to set what to display in the game window's title bar.

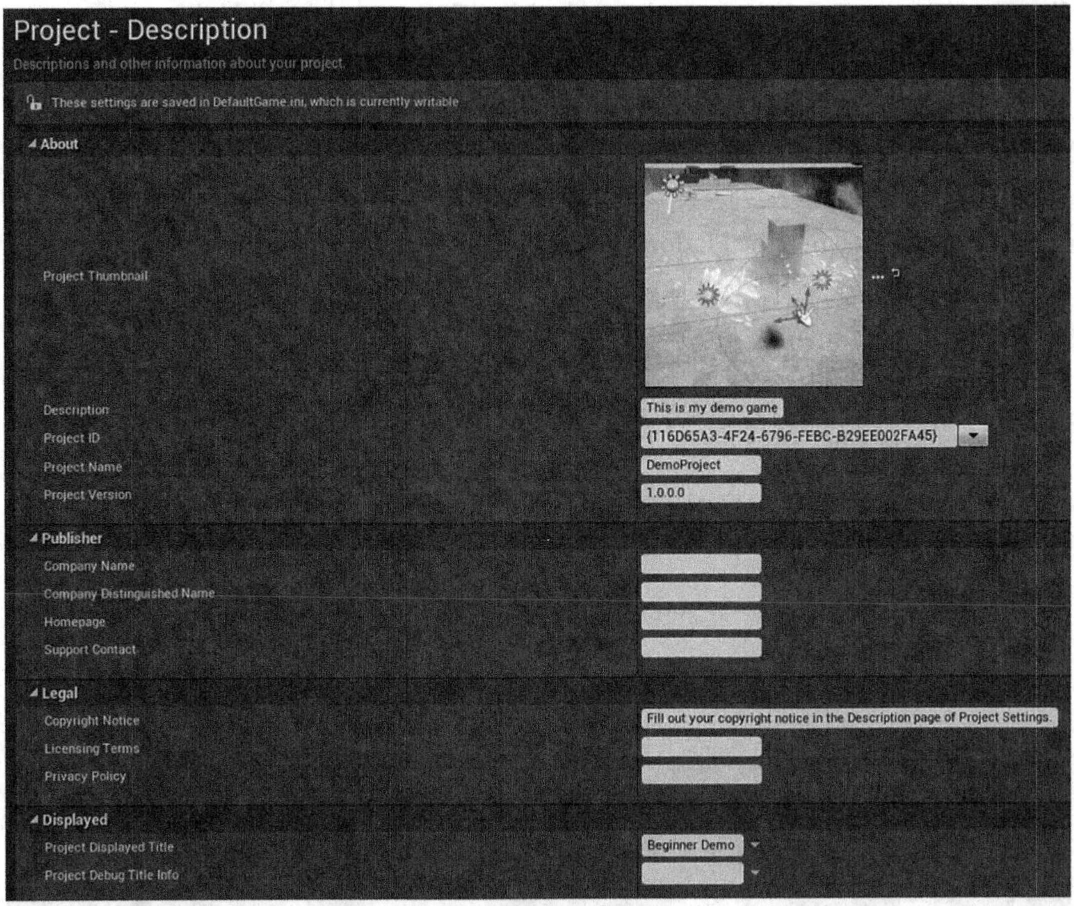

Project - Description

Descriptions and other information about your project.

These settings are saved in DefaultGame.ini, which is currently writable

▲ **About**

Project Thumbnail

Description	This is my demo game
Project ID	{116D65A3-4F24-6796-FEBC-B29EE002FA45} ▼
Project Name	DemoProject
Project Version	1.0.0.0

▲ **Publisher**

Company Name
Company Distinguished Name
Homepage
Support Contact

▲ **Legal**

Copyright Notice	Fill out your copyright notice in the Description page of Project Settings.
Licensing Terms	
Privacy Policy	

▲ **Displayed**

Project Displayed Title	Beginner Demo ▼
Project Debug Title Info	▼

Figure 11-65. *The Description page of the Project Settings*

Now set the game's default map and its build configuration.

1. Click the Maps & Modes page in the menu on the left.

2. Double-check that DemoLevel is set as the Game Default Map.

3. Go to the Packaging page.

4. Set the Build Configuration to Development.

The Build Configuration can be set to either Development or Shipping. For this tutorial, select the Development build, but if you had a game you wanted to distribute and be able to run on other computers, you would need to come here and set this to

377

Shipping. The reason why you would want to do a Development build is because you still have access to things like debugging features which aren't included in the Shipping build, such as console commands, stats, profiling tools, and logs.

Now, specify the platform you are targeting, the Rendering Hardware Interfaces to use, the load images, and the game icon (Figure 11-66).

1. Scroll down to the Platforms category in the menu on the left.

2. Select the platform that you are packaging for, such as Windows.

3. At the top, you can select the Rendering Hardware Interfaces you want to target. Just leave this targeting DirectX 11 and 12 which is the default.

4. In the Splash category, you can specify images to display while the game is loading.

5. In the Icon category, you can specify an image to use for the Game Icon.

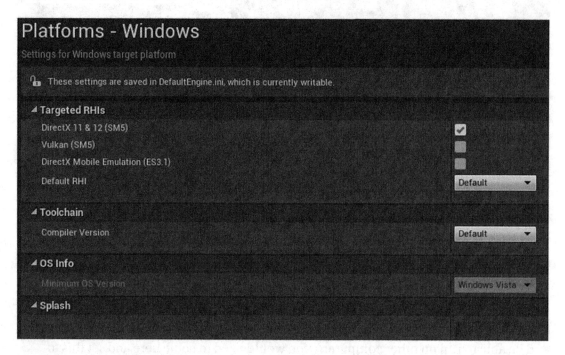

Figure 11-66. *The Platforms - Windows page of the Project Settings*

Now that the project has been prepared, you can package and export it.

1. Go back to the Level Editor.

2. Go to File ➤ Package Project and select the platform you are targeting, such as Windows 64-bit.

3. Choose the folder where you want to save the files and click "Select Folder."

This will package the game, and once it's finished you will be able to go to the folder you specified and run the game from there.

Summary

In this chapter, you applied all the knowledge you learned over the first ten chapters to create a complete game from scratch. You should now have a solid foundation for developing games on the Unreal Engine and have the tools necessary to start learning more intermediate and advanced topics.

Index

A

Access Specifier property, 138
Action Mappings, 180
Actors
  Brush
    Curved Stair, 81, 82
    definition, 76
    Hollow property, 79, 80
    Linear Stair, 80
    Sides properties, 79
    Size properties, 79
    Spiral Stair, 82, 83
    type, 78
  Brushes *vs* Meshes, 76, 77
  Component
    add button, 107
    Rotating Movement, 108
    structure, 107
  creating an event, 149, 150
  Fog, 100
  getting reference, 148, 149
  light (*see* Lights)
  Material
    elements, 86
    material scaling, 88
    surfaces, 84, 85, 87, 88
    textures, 86, 87
  Static Mesh
    Modes Panel, 73, 74

    physics, 75, 76
    replace Mesh, 74
  Volumes
    Camera Blocking, 110
    Kill ZVolume, 112
    Modes Panel, 109
    Pain Causing, 111, 112
    Physics, 112, 113
    Physics Volume, 113
    Trigger Volumes, 110, 111
Add Controller Pitch Input function, 328
Add Controller Yaw Input function, 329
Ambient Sound Actor, 248
  Pitch Multiplier property, 250
  Sound Cue Editor, 249
  sound property, 248, 249
  Volume Multiplier property, 249
Array, 128
  add node, 129
  ForEachLoop node, 128
  insert node, 130
  item node, 132, 133
  last index node, 134
  length node, 133
  remove elements, 131
  retrieving elements, 132
  set array element node, 130, 131
  zero based, 128
Atmospheric Fog Actor, 100

© David Nixon 2020
D. Nixon, *Beginning Unreal Game Development*, https://doi.org/10.1007/978-1-4842-5639-8

Attenuation
    Ambient Sound Actor
        Attenuation category, 266
        Attenuation Distance category, 265
        Falloff Distance, 266
        spheres, 264, 265
    Attenuation Curve, 266, 267
    defined, 264
    Sound Attenuation Asset, 267, 268
Audacity, 269–270
Audio
    background noise, create, 372
    Box Trigger, 374, 375
    enemy spheres, 375, 376
    Fire Cue Actor, 374
    row of fire, create, 373
Audio nodes
    Branch Node, 263
    Concatenator Node, 262
    Delay Node, 258, 259
    Doppler Node, 259
    Looping Node, 258
    Mixer Node, 261, 262
    Modulator Node, 260
    Oscillator Node, 260, 261
    Random Node, 262, 263
    Switch Node, 264
    Wave Player Node, 257, 258
Axis Mappings, 180

B

Bind function, 348
Blueprints
    actors (*see* Actors)
    classes, 116
    flow control (*see* Flow control)
    variables (*see* Variables)

Border Widget, 239–240
Breakpoints, 163, 164
Button Widget, 236–239

C

Canvas Panel
    example, 217
    properties
        Anchors, 218–220
        Size to Content, 220
        ZOrder, 221
    Widget, properties
        Behavior, 222
        Clipping, 228
        Localization, 229
        Navigation, 228, 229
        Performance, 227
        Render Transform, 223–226
Category property, 127, 138
Character movement, Input Mappings
    Add Controller Pitch Input, 186
    Add Controller Yaw Input, 186
    Axis, 183
    Blueprints, 184, 185, 187
    Blueprint, walking movements,
        188, 189
    Event Graph, 186
    JumpAction, 182
    Scale property, 183
Characters
    Components, 174
    defining, 174
    Jump function, 176
    Movement Components
        Braking Friction Factor, 176
        Crouched Half Height property, 176
        Default Land Movement Mode, 176

Default Water Movement Mode, 176

Gravity Scale property, 176

Mass property, 176

properties, 175

Collect Item Tint

OrbCollectedTint Border Widget,
354, 355

ShowOrbCollectedTint variable,
353, 354

Collision

Block

sphere falls, 196–198

sphere's WorldStatic Collision
Response, 201

Can Character Step Up On property, 195

cause damage

Apply Damage Node, 203, 204

Character temporarily
invincible, 206

Cube Mesh, 204–206

destroy character, 207

Event Hit Node, 202, 203

Enabled property, 192, 193

Object Type set, 193, 194

Overlap

Event ActorBeginOverlap, 200

PhysicsBody Collision Response, 199

Preset property, 194

Trace Responses, 194

Collisions

definition, 191

Hit Events, 191

Overlap Events, 192

Compile button, 120

Condition property, 127

D

Damage functionality, 333

EnemySphere, 335, 336

EventGameOver Node, 335

Health variable, 336

logic, script, 337–339

Pain Causing Volume, 333, 334

Trigger Volume, 334

Damage Tint

Boolean variables, 350

ShowDamageTint variable, 350,
352, 353

ShowOrbCollectedTint variable, 351

Data type

Boolean, 122

byte, 122

float, 123

integer, 122

rotator, 123

string, 123

transform, 123

vector, 123

Debugging Blueprints, 160–162

Delay Node, 120

E

Elevator Platform

blueprint, 302, 307, 308

characteristics, 302

Event Graph tab, 304, 305

initial location variable, 305, 306

StartWithUpwardsMovement
variable, 306

Timeline curve, creation, 303

Enemies
    Blueprint, create, 308, 309
    Event Graph, 311, 312
    initial location, 312, 313
    sphere, 309, 314, 316
    Timeline curves, 310
    UseXMovement variable, 313
Epic Games Launcher
    Learn tab, 272, 273
    Marketplace tab, 274
    Vault, 274
Event graph, 116
Event tick node, 117
Exponential Height Fog Actor, 103

F

FlipFlop Node, 142
Flow control
    branch node, 139, 140
    Do N node, 140
    DoOnce MultiInput node, 141
    DoOnce node, 140
    FlipFlop node, 142
    ForLoop node, 142
    ForLoopWithBreak node, 143
    gate node, 143, 144
    MultiGate node, 144, 145
    retriggerable delay node, 145
    sequence node, 145
    switches, 146, 147
    WhileLoop node, 146
Fog
    Atmospheric fog actor
        definition, 100
        properties, 101, 102
        sun disc, 100, 101
    Exponential Height

    definition, 103
    properties, 104
    Player Start Actor, 104–106
Function Node, 120
Functions
    inputs and outputs, 135, 136
    local variables, 139
    properties, 137, 138
    reusability, 137
    welcome message, 136

G

Game Mode
    Blueprint Class, 116, 166, 167
    defining, 165
    maps, 169, 170
    properties, 167, 168
    state, 165
Game over menu
    Border Widget, 364, 365
    logic, add, 367, 368
    red tint, add, 364
    reference, create, 366
    Restart Level button, add, 363
    Widget file, create, 362, 363
Gate node, 143, 144
Geometry Brush, 16–17, 29, 109, 234
Get node, 124
Grid Snapping, 41

H

HUD
    Bind function, 348
    designing layout, 345–347
    health, tracking, 345
    layout, 349

Print String Nodes, 346
Progress Bar, 348, 349
script, logic, 348
Text Widget, 348

I

Image Widget, 240
Immersive Mode, 43
Input Mapping
    Action *vs.* Axis, 179, 180
    create input, 180, 181
Instance editable property, 126
Intensity property, 157
Internal structures, building
    Fire Obstacle, add, 296, 297
    houses, add, 297–301
    inner walls, 292, 293
    platform of blocks, add, 294–296

J

Jump Function, 328

K

Keywords property, 138
Kill ZVolume, 112

L

Layout Transform, 231
Left mouse button (LMB), 30
Level Blueprint
    compiling, 120
    event graph, 116
    nodes, 117–119
    pins, 118, 119

Level Blueprint, 115
Level door logic
    DoorCollision volume, 357, 358
    HUD, modify, 355
    Text Widget, 356, 357
    variable, create, 355
Level Editor
    interface, 27
    Moving, rotating, and scaling Actors
        Move Tool, 33, 34
        Rotate Tool, 35
        Scale Tool, 35
        World Space *vs.* Local Space, 36–38
    panels
        Content Browser, 24
        Details Panel, 26
        Modes Panel, 24
        Toolbar, 23
        Viewport, 23
        World Outliner, 25
    Place Mode, 28–30
    Unreal Engine *vs.* Unreal Editor, 21
Level Editor
    Content Browser, 60, 61
        Add New button, 53, 54
        Asset Window, 51, 52
        back/forward button, 52
        breadcrumbs, 53
        Import button, 54
        Save All button, 54
        Sources Panel, 52
    Details Panel
        Property Matrix, 62
        Transform category, 64–66
        View Options, 63, 64
    Immersive Mode, 43
    orthographic views, 47, 48
    Snapping

Level Editor (*cont.*)
    End key, 38
    Grid, 41, 42
    Rotation, 42
    Scale, 43
    Surface, 38–41
  View Mode
    Detail Lighting, 46
    Game View, 50
    Lighting Only, 46
    Lit, 44
    piloting actions, 50
    Player Collision, 47
    Show Flags, 49, 50
    Unlit, 44
    Visibility Collision, 47
    Wireframe, 45
  View Options
    color-coded system, 60
    Search Asset Class Names, 59
    Search Asset Path, 59
    Search Collection Names, 59
    Show Collections, 57, 58
    Show Developers Content, 57
    Show Engine Content, 57
    Show Localized Content, 57
    Show Plugins Content, 57
    Thumbnail Edit Mode, 60
    Tiles *vs.* List *vs.* Columns, 56
  World Outliner
    data, 67
    Grouping Actors, 68–70
    organize and find Actors, 70, 71
Light Actor, 18
Lights
  build, 90
  definition, 88
  Directional
    Affects World, 94
    Cast Shadows, 94
    color, 93
    Indirect Lighting Intensity, 95
    Intensity, 92
    Point Light, 95–97
    properties, 91
    Rect Light, 98
    Sky Light, 99
    Source Soft Angle, 94
    Spot Light, 97, 98
    Temperature, 94
    Volumetric Scattering Intensity, 95
  Mobility, 90, 91
  types, 89

M, N

Maya navigation, 31
MultiGate node, 144, 145

O

Orb Item
  Box Collision, 343, 344
  components, 340
  Disable Input Node, 344
  door behavior, modify, 342, 343
  elevator platforms, 342
  EndOverlap Node, 344
  level, add, 341
  OrbsCollected variable, 340, 341
  variable, create, 340

P, Q

Packaging
  advanced settings, 282
  build configuration, 377

default map selected, 280, 281

defining, 280

export and prepare game, 376

pak file, 283

Project Settings, 378

Rendering Hardware Interfaces, 378

target platform selected, 281, 282

Pak file, 283

Pause functionality, 331

Pause menu

logic switches, 362

MyCharacter, 359, 360

MyHUD Widget, 360, 361

Widget file, create, 358, 359

Pawn

Camera Component, add, 172

definition, 170

Spring Arm Component,
   add, 172, 173

Static Mesh Component, 171

Playable Character

Action Mappings, 325

Axis Mappings, 325

Blueprint file, create, 323–325

Game Mode, create, 323

input mappings, 326, 328

jump and look functionality, 328, 329

pause functionality, 331, 332

presses a button, 332, 333

walking functionality, 329–331

Player, Controller

advantages, 178

definition, 177

input, add, 178, 179

Playing Area

ground objects, create, 289

Material, add, 290

Player Start Actor, add, 290

Wall enclose, add, 291, 292

Play sound nodes

GetActorLocation node, 255

Level Blueprint, 254

Trigger Volume, 255

Private property, 127

Progress Bar Widget, 241–243

R

Rect Light, 89, 98

Render Transform category, 223–227, 231

Replication property, 127

Retriggerable Delay Node, 145

Right mouse button (RMB), 30

Rotating Door

bright light, add, 317

Door Actor, 318

doorway, create, 316

frame, add, 317

physical object, 318

Timeline curve, 319–321

Viewport, 322

Rotation Snapping, 42

S

Scale Snapping, 43

Sky

atmosphere, sun and clouds,
   create, 286–288

default map setting, 289

Project and level, create, 286

Sky Light, 99

Slider Range property, 127

Snapping technique, 38

Sound Cue, 247, 248
  Output Node, 256
  Palette window, 257
  Play Node button, 256
  Sound Cue Editor, 256
  Sound Waves, 256
Sound Cue Editor, 22
Sound Wave properties
  Can Release property, 254
  Format category, 250, 251
  Mature property, 252
  Max Count, 253
  Sample Rate property, 251
  Sound category, 251
  Subtitle Priority property, 252
  Subtitles category, 251, 252
  Voice Management category, 253
Spoken Text property, 252
Spot Light, 97
Static Mesh Actor, 15, 73
Subtitle Priority property, 252
Surface Snapping, 38–41

T

Text Widget, 233–235
3D objects, importing
  cgtrader.com, 277, 278
  .fbx file, 279, 280
  free3d.com, 275–277
Timelines, 155
  add curve to track, 158
  curve, 157
  key, 156
  node pins, 159, 160
  options, 159
  track, 156
  types, track, 158
Tooltip property, 126

U

Unreal Editor, 21
Unreal Engine, 21
  Actors
    Brush, 16
    Components, 19
    definition, 14, 15
    Lights, 18
    Materials, 17, 18
    Particle System, 18
    Static Meshes, 15
  C++ source code, install, 5, 6
  Epic Games Launcher, 4
  Levels
    create, open and save, 12–14
    defining, 11
    Play button, 14
  licensing, 2
  Project Browser
    New Project tab, 9–11
    projects tab, 8, 9
  registration, 2, 4
  software generations, 1
Unreal Motion Graphics (UMG), 22, 209
  Editor, 22
  Widget Blueprint Editor, 210–214
User Interfaces
  Border Widget, 239, 240
  Button Widget, 236–238
  Canvas Panel, 218
  Horizontal/Vertical Box, 243, 244
  Padding property, 217
  Progress Bar Widget, 241–243
  Root Widget
    Blueprint, 215
    Color and Opacity, 215, 216
    Foreground Color property, 216
    Is Focusable, 217

Text Widget, 233–235
UMG, 210–214
Visual Designer, 230–232

V

Value Range property, 127
Variables
    data type, 121–123
    default value, 125
    delay duration, 125
    get node, 124
    properties, 126, 127
    set node, 124
View Mode, 43
Viewport, navigation
    camera speed, 32
    focusing, 31
    Maya, 31
    mouse, 30
    WASD, 30, 31

Visual Designer
    definition, 230
    device safe zones, 232
    Grid Snapping, 231
    Layout Transform, 231
    localization, 230
    Render Transform, 231
    screen size, 232, 233
    toggle dashed outlines, 230
    widget locking system, 231

W, X, Y, Z

Wave Player Node, 257, 258
Widget Blueprint Editor, 211
Win screen menu
    Box Trigger, add, 371, 372
    GameOverMenu Widget, 369
    logic, add, 370
    reference, create, 369
World Outliner, 22, 25, 31, 34, 66–68

Printed in the United States
By Bookmasters